International
Library of the
Philosophy of
Education

Authenticity and learning

International Library of the Philosophy of Education

General Editor

R.S. PETERS

Emeritus Professor of Philosophy of Education
Institute of Education
University of London

Authenticity and learning

Nietzsche's educational philosophy

David E. Cooper

Reader in Philosophy,
University of Surrey

ROUTLEDGE & KEGAN PAUL
London, Boston, Melbourne and Henley

First published in 1983
by Routledge & Kegan Paul plc
39 Store Street, London WC1E 7DD,
9 Park Street, Boston, Mass. 02108, USA,
6th Floor, 464 St. Kilda Road,
Melbourne 3004, Australia and
Broadway House, Newtown Road,
Henley-on-Thames, Oxon RG9 1EN
Printed in Great Britain by
St. Edmundsbury Press
© David E. Cooper 1983

Library of Congress Cataloging in Publication Data

Cooper, David Edward.
Authenticity and learning.
(International library of the philosophy of education)
Bibliography: p.
Includes index.
1. Nietzsche, Friedrich Wilhelm, 1844–1900. 2. Education –
Philosophy. I. Title. II. Series.
LB775.N547C66 1983   370".1   83-9522

ISBN 0-7100-9552-X

Contents

v

Preface

In 1921, as a seventy-fifth birthday gift, the person who had done most to distort Nietzsche's thought for posterity, his sister Elizabeth, was presented with a volume of essays on her brother. This strange collection, in which Thomas Mann stands side by side with the budding Nazi ideologue Richard Oehler, is a generally uninspiring one; but it does contain a rare and early attempt, by the acolyte Martin Havenstein, to present Nietzsche's ideas on education. He begins: 'It must be a cause of wonder to those familiar with Nietzsche that German educational theory has up until now concerned itself so little with Friedrich Nietzsche, the greatest educator of the Germans in the last century.'(1) Had these words been written sixty years later, with whatever you wish substituted for 'German', they would be scarcely less true. It is indeed a cause for some wonder that, despite the intense interest in a philosopher which has scarcely waned since his silent, lonely death in 1900, there should be this one area of his thought that has remained a backwater. The more general interest, especially in France and Germany, has grown in recent years to almost epidemic proportions. There is hardly a major philosophical figure in these countries who does not acknowledge a debt to Nietzsche and who does not feel obliged to define his own position relative to Nietzsche's. Habermas, Gadamer, Foucault, and Derrida would be obvious examples. It is an interest, moreover, which percolates down to the general reading public, and suffuses discussions on the most diverse matters. During a month's stay in Germany last year, I never failed to encounter at least one reference each day to Nietzsche in my newspaper: Nietzsche and Islam, Nietzsche and Goethe, Nietzsche on women - and so on. But I encountered nothing on Nietzsche on education. In Karl Schlechta's comprehensive Nietzsche bibliography, there is only a handful of references to papers on Nietzsche's educational thinking, and of this handful only the tiniest clutch are by English-speaking authors.

In the English-speaking world, of course, neglect of Nietzsche's educational philosophy harmonizes with a general, if less exaggerated, neglect of his philosophy at large. (A contributing factor in the case of the educational views is that the only translations of some of the relevant writings are both awful and hard to obtain.) As a student of philosophy at Oxford during the 1960s, I was never once referred to anything by Nietzsche, and more than once I encountered the judgment that,

like Kierkegaard and Sartre, he was not 'really a philosopher'.
The judgment reflected, in part, a particular predilection for a
certain kind of philosophizing; but even relative to this, it was
an absurd judgment. The proof of its absurdity is as follows:
if Nietzsche is not a philosopher, nor is the Wittgenstein of the
'later' period, for it is difficult to find themes, associated with
Wittgenstein by most commentators, which are not sounded and
developed, often in an uncannily similar voice, by Nietzsche.
In part, also, the judgment reflected sheer ignorance; or perhaps an acquaintance with only those writings of Nietzsche,
like *Thus Spake Zarathustra*, which were most removed from
the concerns, and even more the style, of the philosophizing
then in favour.

The times, to be sure, are changing. Nietzsche's moral
philosophy, in particular, is increasingly recognized to have the
importance it does. 'It is certain', wrote Bernard Williams recently,
'even if not everyone has yet come to see it, that Nietzsche was
the greatest moral philosopher of the past century.'(2) We still
await the recognition due to Nietzsche's writings on language and
truth, and on knowledge and mind; but this, I suspect, will
emerge – and before any similar recognition of his educational
philosophy, in so far as this can be isolated.

Measured by the number of tasks attempted, my book is an
ambitious one. It attempts, first, to provide an account and
interpretation of Nietzsche's obscurely known views on education.
It aims, second, to be an introduction, again interpretative, to
Nietzsche's philosophy at large. That an understanding of
Nietzsche's philosophy of education should demand an understanding of the wider philosophy which informs it is, of course,
hardly surprising – but the traffic is two-way. Important
aspects of his political, moral, and epistemological theories are
only to be explained in terms of his unwavering focus on the
'breeding' of a certain type of person, on his educational ideal.
(The expression 'educational philosophy' in the sub-title of
this book is intended to be ambiguous: to refer both to a
philosophy of education and to the gearing of a whole philosophy
to an educative enterprise.) Third, I have unashamedly *used*
Nietzsche in conducting a critique, at several places, against
ideas which have dominated educational practice and theory in
recent years – against, for example, the technological and
vocational obsessions of those who manage our school system,
and against the influential conception of education as 'initiation'
into the disciplines or 'forms of knowledge'. 'The only valid
tribute to thought such as Nietzsche's', writes Michel Foucault,
'is precisely to use it' – even, perhaps, 'to deform it, make it
groan and protest'.(3) Finally, I identify early on what I take
to be the central concern which runs through Nietzsche's writings, and give it the name 'authenticity'; and much of the book
can be read as the dual attempt to tease out what is enveloped
in this notion and to see what an education which revolves
around it would look like.

As these latter remarks suggest, the book is more than one
about Nietzsche - but, at the same time, it is less. To begin
with, it is not a scholar's book: I do relatively little to defend
my interpretations of Nietzsche, preferring to add to the
catalogue of interpretations through which people may sift
rather than engage in such sifting. Nor, except rarely, do I
pause to do battle with other commentators on Nietzsche. This
is partly for reasons of space, partly so that the book may be
digestible by non-specialists, and partly out of agreement with
Foucault that Nietzsche is more important to use than to dissect.
Havenstein, having noted the neglect of Nietzsche's educational
thought, speculates that this might be to the good; and certainly
one might sympathize with the spirit, if not the prose, of the
remark that otherwise 'the golden corn of his living thoughts
would have been transformed, upon the mills of alexandrine
science, into scholarly flour'.(4) Nor do I engage in much
criticism of Nietzsche in the book. It would have been easy, of
course, to end sections or chapters with lists of the 'problems'
contained in what has gone before; but on the whole these are
'problems' which will suggest themselves quickly enough to the
reader. A fitting, and therefore substantial critical account
would have required a much larger book. This does not mean
that criticism has not gone into its writing; but it has issued
at the levels of selection and interpretation. There are doctrines
of Nietzsche's - that of 'eternal recurrence', for example, or the
vitriolic account of women - which I find it hard to do much
with. Such doctrines do not find their way into the book. My
interpretations reflect critical appraisal, to the extent that I
have followed a 'principle of charity', a policy of rendering
Nietzsche's views so that they emerge as powerful and plausible
as, in my view, they can. The present imperative, given the
neglect of Nietzsche, is to present his philosophical and educational challenge: there is plenty of time, later on, to take up
that challenge in a more critical spirit than I do here.
   It is a common fate for an author, having prepared a manu-
script for publication, to then encounter books which he wishes
he had read before embarking on his own. In the present
instance, I wish I had been able to read John White's *The Aims
of Education Restated,* and Richard Rorty's *Philosophy and the
Mirror of Nature.* White and I are poles apart on some educational
issues, but we are close in our dissatisfaction with current
conceptions of education and its aims; and I would have
benefited from reading his critique. Rorty's exciting book -
especially the final sections on Hermeneutics and Edifying
Philosophy - skilfully expresses much towards which I am
groping in Chapters 4, 5, and 8. I would have groped a little
closer if his book had been published earlier.
   I wish to thank Anthony O'Hear, J.P. Stern, and Nigel
Reeves for helpful comments on various chapters. I am especially
grateful to the comments of Ray Elliott, one of the few philosophers of education with a deep appreciation of Nietzsche. I am

grateful, too, to Mrs Lindsey Carew for her excellent and speedy typing.

Translations, unless otherwise specified, are my own.

1   Authenticity

The issue posed by Nietzsche is how the individual shall live
in the era of history following 'the death of God'. God's death
is his metaphor not only for the dissolution of religious faith,
but for 'the devaluation of our hitherto highest values' - those
of the Enlightenment and Romanticism as much as of Christianity.(1) Not only God, but Progress, the Perfectibility of Man,
Historical Destiny, and Universal Morality, are dead or dying.
God is dead because we killed Him, or rather abetted His suicide.
That is: our hitherto highest values have destroyed themselves
by being taken to their logical conclusion. In particular, the
religious and moral value of honesty, together with the Enlightenment spirit of enquiry and objectivity, have conspired to display the 'shabby origins' of our beliefs and values - including
those of religion, morality, and the Enlightenment themselves.
The result is that 'the universe seems to have lost value, seems
"meaningless"'.(2) The outcome is *nihilism*: the sense that 'the
highest values have devalued themselves. There is no goal.
There is no answer to the question "Why?"'.(3)

Few would deny that our century has witnessed catastrophic
events bearing the mark of nihilistic rage against traditional
beliefs and values, or that each decade has spawned movements,
among the young especially, which are distinguished more by
their iconoclasm than their constructive programmes - Flappers,
Dadaists, Futurists, Angry Young Men, Absurdists, Punks,
and so on. But the young become old, and the dominant image
today is not supplied by bomb-throwing Nekrasovs or abuse-
hurling skinheads. The dominant impression is less one of
aggressive, iconoclastic intellectual ferment than of comfortable
acceptance of many traditional values or an equally comfortable
turning aside from reflection on matters of value, an immersion
in 'the business of life'. The end of ideology, rather than of
God, seems the more manifest event of recent times.

Nietzsche would not see this as contradicting his prediction
of 'the advent of nihilism', for what he meant by that was not
at all confined to aggressive intellectual and physical iconoclasm,
to nihilism 'on the St. Petersburg model'. Nihilism, he urged,
can be manifested in many ways. To be sure, there is the
apocalyptic St Petersburg version, with men 'constantly plung-
ing, wandering through an endless night', rushing
'restlessly, violently headlong, like a river which wants to
reach its end'.(4) But there is the Buddhistic version, too: a
quiet rejection of this world and its values, in favour of an

1

immaterial state wherein self-identity is dissolved. More important, nihilism is also manifested in those attitudes which, a
moment ago, seemed to contrast with it – comfortable acceptance
of tradition, or 'the practical man's' equally comfortable
indifference to questions of value. For Nietzsche, unreflective
acceptance of established beliefs and values belongs to 'passive'
nihilism, when people 'tired and exhausted' welcome a condition
in which 'everything that refreshes, heals, calms, stuns, comes
into the foreground under various disguises; religious or moral
or political or aesthetic'.(5) As for the 'restlessness, haste,
[and] hustling', and 'the reduction of problems to ones of
pleasure and displeasure', of those who pride themselves on
getting on with the real business of life, these are but symptoms
of a deep pessimism about the reality of values, which is itself
a form of nihilism.(6) Such people, of course, have their *pursuits* – after wealth, say: but this is no longer the *purpose* it
once was in an age when belief in Progress put a value upon
wealth. Today 'the true purpose of all wealth is forgotten'.(7)

Among the various manifestations of nihilism, says Nietzsche,
it is the St Petersburg version which is to be least feared. Not
only does it reveal, in full nakedness, just what has happened
– the devaluation of values – but its suicidal ferocity ensures
that it would only be a transitional phase, to be followed by a
better age when men would return, purged, to the creation of
new values: 'an age which will carry heroism into the field of
knowledge and wage wars for the sake of principles'.(8) Far
more depressing and insidious are the muted, masked, 'self-
narcoticizing' versions which would let nihilism become 'the
normal condition'.(9) Moreover, at least nihilists of the St
Petersburg brand retain a *will*, however negative its direction;
and 'better that a man wills *nothing*, than that he does *not*
will'.(10)

There are at least two reasons why Nietzsche thinks that
comfortable acceptance and comfortable evasion are, in an age
which has seen the death of God, forms of nihilism. First:
once the massive challenge to our hitherto highest values has
been made, then the failure to grapple with it constitutes an
admission, *au fond*, that it cannot be answered. It can only be
because people suspect 'there is no answer to the question
"Why?"' that they desperately and unreflectingly hang on to
established answers or avert their gaze from the whole matter.
After all, if there *are* values and beliefs that should guide
one's life, how could it be a matter of blithe, unreflective
indifference which these were? Second, the failure to grapple
with the challenge is a denial, a negation, of one's human nature,
of the uniquely human capacity for self-conscious concern with
beliefs, values, and purposes. No doubt it has always been that
most people, for the most part, have failed to exercise this capacity,
but it is only with the death of God, with the uncovering of the
'shabby origins' of established beliefs and values, that this failure
becomes an evasion, a refusal to face what is before one's eyes.

It is only then that a challenge has been issued, to which the response may be affirmation or denial of one's human nature. This is why the death of God is an event of unparalleled significance.

Nietzsche's assimilation to nihilism, in the familiar sense, of attitudes usually thought to contrast with it, is illuminating: but it runs so strongly against our familiar talk that it is best, perhaps, to pose Nietzsche's question, 'How to overcome nihilism?', in different terms. In doing so, we introduce a theme, dimly portended in the previous paragraph, which in its various twists and turns, will occupy us throughout the book. There is a term Nietzsche himself rarely employs, but which is the most suitable label for a constant object of his philosophical concern – 'authenticity'. There are countless passages, at any rate, where he affirms the paramount value of what several later writers have intended by that term. Clearly it will not be an *in*appropriate label for what is expressed in passages like these:

> 'Better to remain in debt than to pay with a coin that does not bear our own image' – so our sovereignty wills.(11)

> The individual is something totally new and creating anew, something absolute, all his actions entirely his own. In the last resort, the individual derives the values of his actions from himself alone.(12)

Nietzsche's question could now be posed as follows: 'How to live authentically without collapsing into nihilism of the familiar, iconoclastic, negative kind?' It is not, of course, difficult to avoid that collapse: comfortable acceptance of inherited values, or comfortable evasion of questions of value, will both do the trick. But these are not authentic alternatives, for we should hardly describe those who sidestep nihilism in these ways as 'creating anew', or 'deriving values from themselves alone'. The coins in which they have bought themselves off scarcely 'bear their own image'.

When the question is posed in these terms, it is clear that Nietzsche's main focus is upon 'how to live authentically', rather than upon how to avoid nihilism (*à la* St Petersburg). It is not the latter, but inauthentic living, which threatens to become 'the normal condition', and Nietzsche's effort is devoted to struggling against that threat. In this chapter, I try to lend more precision to the question Nietzsche asks and to produce a rough picture of what our label, 'authenticity', is to express. Each subsequent chapter serves, in its way, to fill out that picture.

During his years as a university professor, Nietzsche often raised the question of authenticity as one which faces the teacher. When the teacher enters an institution, he not only encounters buildings, classrooms, and playgrounds, but policies, beliefs, purposes, and values that permeate its activities. Some of these settle what is to be taught, and how; some the manner in which the curriculum is divided; others shape the disciplinary rules in force – and so on. They are not ones of his own making, nor is he likely to have much impact upon them. A familiar disturbance felt by a teacher arises when some of these policies, values, or whatever, are not ones to which he can subscribe. He cannot, say, agree to the assumptions on which the history lessons he is to teach are based; or to the moral basis, perhaps, for some of the school's rules; or to the general aim – winning scholarships, say – which percolates through the school's activities. The disturbance produces a problem of authenticity, for unless the teacher resigns or is willing to invite considerable friction at work, he must simulate agreement to views that are not his.

A different disturbance is felt when a teacher resents the position he is placed in *vis-à-vis* his pupils: the way, perhaps, he is set up as a sure judge in front of them on matters that seem to him to be problematic, matters that do not permit the distinction between teacher and pupil which the style of the school imposes. This is the problem felt by Rickie Elliot in E.M. Forster's *The Longest Journey*, when he regrets having taken a post, at his wife's bidding, to teach classics at a boarding school:

> I feel myself a learner, not a teacher. It's different if I was really a scholar. But I can't pose as one, can I? I know much more than the boys, but I know very little. Surely the honest thing is to be myself to them. Let them accept me or refuse me as that.(13)

But the headmaster will not allow Rickie 'to be himself', so that until he resigns he does, after all, have to be a *poseur*.

Neither of these disturbances, however, induces the critical problem of authenticity that a third does. The thought which may strike the teacher is not that he cannot subscribe to, or authoritatively transmit, various beliefs and values, but that he has slipped into, fallen into, unreflective acceptance of them. They have become part of the school's furniture; they go with the job like the free stationery. The Pascalian thought might set in that, were he teaching 'on the other side of the Pyrenees' or in a different age, then it would have been a very different set of beliefs and values into which he would have slipped. He may not be able to think of reasons against what he has come to accept: what disturbs is that he has simply taken so many things on board, not worked them out for himself. Even if he does have a basis from which to criticize the beliefs and values he has accrued, this basis will itself consist of presuppositions and conceptions that can fall victim to the same worry. The subject he teaches, for example, will have its own presuppositions:

and are they not ones he simply found himself sharing as a
result of his training and the climate in which it took place?
Would he not have accepted very different ones, had he been
trained the other side of the mountains? – and, if so, what has
been *his* responsibility for his outlook?

This disturbance, once set in, has no obvious terminus: for
it is the case with all beliefs and values that they, or ones from
which they derive, have been acquired through inheritance,
hearsay, training, received opinion, everyday chatter, and so
on. Because the problem becomes global, embracing all beliefs
and values, it is not one that teachers alone confront. But
although tinkers and tailors can feel it as well, it was appropriate to introduce it in connection with teachers for, in a
peculiarly important way, they are transmitters, as well as
recipients and inheritors of beliefs and values. The teacher
confronts not only his relation to his beliefs and values, but
his pupils' relation to theirs, since he is instrumental in shaping
it. It is this latter relation, indeed, which is often the more
vivid one for teachers, and which they discuss under a heading
like 'indoctrination'. But it is bizarre if a genuine concern for
the authenticity of one's pupils' views remains accompanied by a
sanguine indifference towards the ways in which one's own
views have come about.

There is, naturally, no short answer to the question of how
the teacher, for whom this disturbance has arisen, should
proceed. At this stage, indeed, there can hardly be a long one
either, given the vagueness of notions like 'deriving values from
oneself' or 'making beliefs one's own'. But it is worth stating
at once that one response, which many might feel to be natural,
would be overhasty. I mean the response that it could only be
through 'child-centred' or 'discovery method' teaching that
pupils could be put in an authentic relation to the views they
will emerge with. This is too quick, since it could be that
thoroughly traditional methods are prerequisites for developing
that discipline without which the forging of views for oneself
would be a charade. Nietzsche, who has harsh things to say
about 'mechanical' teaching, also writes:

> The most desirable thing remains, under all circumstances,
> a hard discipline *at the right time*; namely, at that age when
> it still makes one proud to see a lot demanded of one . . .
> there are no good scholars who do not have the instincts of a
> capable soldier. . . . What does one learn in a hard school?
> *Obeying* and *commanding*. (14)

It would also be premature to judge the impact which teaching
can have in promoting authentic beliefs and values. For some,
authenticity is too private a state to be produced by the
relatively public enterprise of teaching; while, for others, it is
too much a function of wider social factors for the relatively
insulated activity of teaching to be fundamental. The first view

runs through many of Hermann Hesse's books: *Siddartha,* for example, whose hero, a young Indian noble, dedicates his life to the attempt to be 'true to himself'. No teaching, he decides can help him; not because it is false, but because it is teaching. Despite his admiration for the Buddha, he refuses to join Gautama's disciples, for this would be to succumb to the views of another, expressed in another's words. On the other hand, a main theme of Theodor Adorno's book *The Jargon of Authenticity* is that inauthentic existence is a direct result of social and economic evils which the 'superstructural' enterprise of education can hardly touch. Indeed, to encourage men to seek authenticity through personal or educational endeavour is to abdicate the real responsibility of changing the class structure which is at the root of inauthentic life.

We need not deny that no teacher can substitute for personal endeavour, that there is necessarily something lonely about the quest to forge values and beliefs for oneself. Nor need we deny that certain social conditions may be less favourable than others to this quest. But it remains that the course of this quest can surely not be unaffected by what a person hears, learns, and experiences from his teachers. The spirit, if not the letter, of the following remark of Nietzsche's will therefore serve us as a premise: 'I cannot see at all how a person can put things right again who failed to go to a good school at the right time. Such a person will not know himself.'(15)

Do many people encounter the problem of authenticity felt by our teacher? Both less and more than might appear. At times and in places during this century, concern for authenticity seems to have attained epidemic proportions – among German students of the 1920s, 'café existentialists' of post-war Paris, or the California 'hippies' of the 1960s. But one says 'appears' and 'seems' since not in all cases, presumably, was invocation of the jargon of authenticity matched by seriousness of concern. On the other hand, there are many who, without invoking the jargon, express concerns to which it would not be inappropriate; those teachers, for example, who are properly worried about indoctrination. Moreover, facing an issue is not the only response to encountering it: evasion is another, and it is tempting to construe a number of ubiquitous attitudes as evasions of the question of authenticity that others self-consciously face. Both pre-emptive dismissal of questions of belief and value, and wholesale immersion in a viewpoint which does not allow such questions to arise, might be so construed. Let us call them the attitudes of flippancy and fanaticism. (They are connected, of course, with two of Nietzsche's manifestations of 'passive' nihilism.) Flippancy need not be comic, nor fanaticism grim-faced. The flippant man may be in deadly earnest over many matters – his promotion, say, or the fortunes of a football team; while the nature of the fanatic's viewpoint may require him to be the ironic lampooner of others' beliefs. Flippancy and fanatic-

ism are opposed, but it is not always easy to tell their repre-
sentatives apart: to distinguish, for instance, between the man
who scoffs at moral debate because it is 'a waste of time' or 'up
in the clouds', and the person who dismisses it out of dogged
attachment to a brand of positivism by whose lights it is 'senseless'.

The mark of both attitudes is pre-emptiveness. On the one
hand, an unfounded cynicism and insouciance which is not the
result of a serious assessment of what gets rejected, but the
cause of the rejection. On the other hand, a desperate enthusiasm
for a position which renders otiose the need to consider its, or
any other's, merits. (Ideally, a position which allows one to dis-
miss its critics as basely motivated or as insane.) Just as
instances of flippancy and fanaticism may be hard to tell apart,
so both may be difficult to distinguish from superficially similar
ones which *do* result from actually facing the question of
authenticity: from, in the one case, a serious nihilism which is
the outcome of an unsuccessful search for value and purpose,
and in the other case, from a commitment to a position that is the
outcome of a successful search for these.

But what is this authenticity which some people seem so anxious
to attain or to evade? Shortly, I look at two inadequate, one-
sided models on the way to a better one; but first a question of
logical grammar. Of what is 'authentic' predicable? People, lives,
beliefs, attitudes, values, selves, behaviour, feelings, and much
else. But should any of these predications count as the primitive
one from which the others are derived? Could we, for instance,
think of authentic beliefs as the central notion, with feelings,
say, or behaviour only counting as authentic through their
relation to authentic beliefs? My preference will be for authentic
lives as the primitive notion, and some of the reasons for this
will emerge in this chapter. Talk of authentic beliefs, for
example, is too narrow to account for all our talk about authenticity. It is not, of course, wrong to speak of authentic beliefs,
attitudes, and the like, and I shall often do so. The point is
that such talk needs to be taken in connection with the more
primitive notion. Put crudely, a person's beliefs are authentic
when they occupy a suitable position within an authentic life.

'Authentic' is a term in everyday use, as well as a term of
art employed by several philosophers. Although the everyday
use suggests the philosophical employment, it by no means
dictates it. For one thing, the term does not, in its everyday
use, primarily refer to people, their lives, beliefs, and so on -
but to impersonal, and especially representational, entities. We
hear, for example, of (in)authentic portraits, signatures,
documents, and reproductions. Even when persons are described
as (in)authentic, there is usually a connection with a broadly
representational role. Someone is not an authentic delegate,
only an observer: someone is not an authentic Keynesian or
Freudian, since he does not represent the undiluted essence

of the master's thoughts.

Everyday use, supported by the OED and Fowler, suggests two distinguishable senses of the term. In the one case, it has to do with correspondence; in the other, with genesis. For church historians, a text is authentic when it corresponds with the events it purports to describe; whereas John's signature is authentic when it has the right genesis - John himself. An expression like 'authentic portrait' is ambiguous between its being a portrait *of* and *by* the right person. One hears a lot these days about authentic performances of old music on original instruments or their copies. But what makes the performances authentic? Is it their similarity, correspondence, to performances of centuries ago, or their being produced by the same instruments? Suppose an electronic synthesizer could accurately reproduce the ancient sounds, while the instruments, due to chemical changes in the wood, no longer sound as they did. Which should we use to produce authentic performances? It depends on whether we have the correspondence or genesis notion in mind.

A proper account of authenticity in relation to lives, beliefs, or values should have a place for both of the notions suggested by the everyday use. And there are inadequate philosophical accounts which, perhaps, are generated by one-sided attachment to one or other of these notions. Two of these inadequate models, I dub the 'Polonian' and 'Dadaist' respectively.

Polonius said to his son, 'To thine own self be true.' Others, in like vein, have said: 'Be yourself', 'Don't lose sight of who you really are', 'Find your real self', 'Know thyself', 'I want to be me', or 'Get into yourself.' Such declamations can be salutary, but they can easily encourage an unfortunate model of authenticity which distorts how people are or should be. I call it the Polonian model. It represents the person as a multiplicity of selves, only one of which is the 'true' or 'real' one. The search for authenticity is alternatively portrayed as a quest for illumination - the true self must be allowed to shine through, and the attempt made to harmonize one's life with its dictates: or as a journey, through a jungle of distracting, false selves, towards the real one. 'Each man's life is a way towards himself', writes Hesse in *Demian*, 'The trying-out of a way, the intimation of a path'.(16) Each person, on this model, has his individual essence; and to live in accord with it is to live authentically. There is an intelligible, if loose, connection between this model and the correspondence sense of 'authenticity', which presumably explains the Polonians' choice of the term.

No one should deny the sincerity, even anguish, that Polonian talk can display. Some of the most powerful testaments of personal struggle - Van Gogh's letters to his brother, for example - are strung through with it. Nevertheless, the model generated is unfortunate. For one thing, if taken literally, it is a metaphysically uncomfortable one, which raises questions that sound senseless. Does the 'true self' change? Do we discover or construct it? How do we count the number of a person's selves? Perhaps such questions can be made sense of, but it would be depressing if the intelligibility of the notion of authenticity had to depend on that possibility.

Second, the model surely starts off the search for authenticity in the wrong direction, that of obsessive introspectionism. It is no accident that many who talk in Polonian vein think that it is through drugs or meditation that the authentic self is revealed; the idea being that these will unlock the gates which bar the way to a proper inner vision.(17) Since authenticity has to do with the relation between oneself (not 'one's self') and one's beliefs and values, then concern for it will involve examining what one is like, one's motives, character, and so on. But turning on an inner searchlight is no substitute for examining the beliefs and values themselves. It would be a mistake, moreover, to think that solitary introspection is the only or best way to further self-understanding. In some ways, at least, others can understand me better than I do. Further, as Nietzsche puts it, the person is the limit to the world, and like any limit can only be identified along with what it limits. It would be wrong, that is, to suppose that self-understanding has no traffic with understanding of the world in which, however specially, one is placed. 'We laugh when we find "man *and* the world" juxtaposed, separated through the sublime presumption of the little word "and".'(18)

The worst aspect of the model, though, is that it can encourage evasion of the very issue it purports to address. The Polonian is in danger of joining the flippant and the fanatical in a pre-emptive dismissal of questions of belief and value. 'I'm a hard-headed practical man: that's how I am, so don't ask me to . . .', or 'I'm soft and sensitive: that's me, so you can't expect me to . . .'. These are ways in which people preface refusals even to consider uncomfortable questions and possibilities. But the progression to such petrified stances from the model of a true self to which one's views must conform is a smooth one.

The phenomenon is brilliantly depicted in Sartre's account of 'bad faith', where he argues that an attitude – he calls it 'sincerity' – which seems to contrast with bad faith is really a neighbour of it. 'The essential structure of sincerity', as he puts it, 'does not differ from that of bad faith.'(19) Bad faith is at work when a person pretends to himself that his situation is different from what he really knows it to be: as when the girl, in Sartre's café, succeeds in ignoring the fact that what will happen between her and the man whose attentions she is attracting depends on her choices and responses, and is not a natural phenomenon that will take its own course. 'Sincerity', the attempt in good faith to see the nature of oneself and one's situation, would seem to be the reverse. In Sartre's example, a friend is exhorting a man to admit what he is, a homosexual, instead of pretending that his behaviour is mere dilettantism or sexual experimentation. The man may be convinced and 'come out', proclaiming that, yes, that is indeed what he *is*, a homosexual. But it is unclear, says Sartre, that the outcome is different from a case of bad faith; in both instances, the person 'puts himself out of reach: it is an escape'.(20) In both cases, someone is treating himself as something object-like, fixed, without responsibility for the future. The homosexual, as much as the girl, is ignoring or foreclosing on various possible futures that are in fact open. Both exhibit a failure to distance themselves from their present characteristics or positions; and this is the failure of people who, disingenuously or not, see their nature or position as fixing what will happen.

Sartre's 'sincerity', of course, is close to the petrified stance that the Polonian notion threatens to encourage; a stance which is an evasion, or an 'escape'. The comforting evasion it permits is nicely brought out by Rilke in a passage from his novella *Ewald Tragy*. Ewald is listening to the dashing and fashionable Kranz, who has just resigned his military commission:

> 'Yes', said [Kranz], uncommonly satisfied with himself and with Tragy's astonishment, 'that's something, isn't it? I've resigned my commission. To belong to an institution whose laws one can't comply with is to be untrue to oneself!' 'Untrue to oneself', it suddenly came to Tragy during the night: how ready-made, how clear, how worn-out!(21)

Of course, what is 'ready-made' and 'worn-out' in the mouth of a Kranz can, in one like Van Gogh, reflect a truly anguished search for integrity. Nor is there any doubting an element of truth that Polonian talk can be interpreted to possess. But before we consider that, let us turn to the contrasting 'Dadaist' model.

The famous movement of that name aimed at the total overthrow of previous conventions and standards in the arts. In the 'songs' of Kurt Schwitters, for example, not only are harmony and melody abolished, but words are replaced by nonsense noises. Rejection and spontaneity were the orders of the day; even the name 'Dada' had to be chosen by whim. No work by one member of the movement was to serve as a model for another; only what issued from the mood of the moment, unfettered by rules or previous achievements, had any authenticity. Something of this idea, taken beyond the arts, provides our second, one-sided model. It is one suggested, perhaps, by the 'genesis' sense of the everyday use of 'authentic'. Just as the only requirement for the authenticity of a person's signature is that it was he, at the time, who wrote it, so the only requirement for the authenticity of a person's actions and commitments is that these issue from his spontaneous choices, unconstrained by convention, opinion, or his own past.

Sartre comes close to this idea. If sincerity is not to collapse into a variant of bad faith, it must be confined to an honest assessment of how one *has been*. Yesterday's self, however, is not to constrain, but merely to serve as one datum among others to be made note of when taking today's decisions and adopting tomorrow's projects. Authenticity, says Sartre, is 'a self-recovery of being which was previously corrupted' through bad faith or 'sincerity':(22) a recovery, that is, of the idea that nothing constrains the power to reject and choose anew. One's homosexuality, say, is like a mood: something it is up to one to take a stance towards, modify, or submit to. The freedom to choose anew is total, constrained neither by one's past nor by prevailing standards of logic, evidence, or common sense. In the case of values in particular, '*nothing*, absolutely nothing justifies me in adopting this or that value, or particular scale of values'.(23)

Ironically, the same main criticism levelled against the Polonian model - that it allows one to escape the very issue it was designed to deal with - surely applies to the Dadaist. If self-understanding is simply taking note of how one has been, of how one has been placed, how can it play any significant role in settling which beliefs and values to adopt? Indeed, nothing is supposed to settle this: information about oneself, like any other, provides no more than a springboard for taking totally free, ungrounded 'leaps'. To suppose that it could do more, that it could restrict the options available, is to fall into that 'sincerity' which is akin to bad faith. Let me elaborate.

The primary difficulty with the Dadaist view is not the psy-chological implausibility of supposing people could treat facts about their own natures and situations as mere data for free choices, but that many such facts deprive various options of intelligibility. It is not a matter of mere psychology, for example, that no one in our society can seriously announce his conver-sion to Samurai ethics; for there is no way, now, that such a code could genuinely guide the conduct of one's life. Attacking someone on Hampstead Heath cannot produce the duel of honour that Samurai encounters were. One may feel nostalgia for that age, but to behave as a Samurai requires that others do too. In our society even the sense of a declared commitment to the ethics of communism is unclear. Communism is not something a person can practise alone; nor, at present, is it a live political option which someone could sanely see his behaviour helping to bring about. I may yearn for a communist society, but values should not be identified with yearnings. I might give away my factory, but this would be a symbolic gesture, not a communist enactment. Given our situation in our society, the declaration of commitment to communism can sound as hollow as the insist-ence that one believes in primitive agrarianism.

A paramount, and constraining, feature of oneself and one's society is the language spoken - the language in which beliefs and values one may want to entertain must be expressed. It cannot do to treat this as a mere datum which a person may note and then employ in his unconstrained choice of commitments.

It restricts the degree to which, and the speed with which, people can shed beliefs or select new values. Philosophers from Nietzsche to Donald Davidson have rightly stressed how the possibility of meaning requires agreement in judgment, in what is held true, among speakers. Terms have sense only where there is some agreement on their application, so that to challenge certain judgments is to risk divesting terms of their sense - terms which, as likely as not, will be needed in any attempt to state new beliefs. Someone wants to challenge the belief that X is Y, to hold that X is not Y, only to find that in challenging it he removes sense from the terms, so that he is unable to state what he wanted to. It is unclear, for example, that people can believe - though it is sometimes fashionable to say it - that men are selfish all of the time, always acting for pleasure or out of self-interest. We speak a language in which terms like 'selfish' or 'for pleasure' are applied discriminatingly to some actions and not others; and their sense is not to be divorced from the judgments we make about the differences between actions. The person who proclaims that all action is selfish may find he has merely changed the subject; that, given his idiosyncratic usage, he is not denying what he thought he was. This is not to rule out that someone might convince us to alter our talk and judgments, for perhaps he can show us that seemingly unselfish behaviour has its seamy side, or that we accept inconsistent theories about pleasure. But this is the kind of thing he must undertake if his rejection of our usual talk and judgments is not to be self-vitiating.

The point carries over to values. It is not easy to state, let alone defend, that radical utilitarianism which denies there are special obligations to friends, neighbours, colleagues, and so on; which treats these as at best convenient myths which it is useful, for the sake of maximum utility, that the ignorant accept. It is not easy because such obligations seem written into the terminology of 'friends', 'colleagues', and other words. My friends are people who can make claims upon me and expect a response. 'Friend' is not a word that could survive, unscathed in meaning, among radical utilitarians.

The nature of social and linguistic being, then, casts doubt upon the intelligibility of Dadaist authenticity, of total absence of constraint upon the commitments one chooses to make. If a person's actions and words are to be intelligible, even to himself, constraints must be faced which, if not finally insurmountable, are not to be hurdled over by Dadaist 'leaps'. Rilke, who scented the superficiality of Polonian jargon, also furnishes a nice *reductio ad absurdum* of Dadaism in his short novel *Malte Laurids Brigge,* whose hero is much given to thoughts of spontaneous commitment, and of remaking himself anew each day, to the extent of deciding:

I won't write any more letters. Why tell anyone that I've changed? If I change, I am no longer what I was and am some-

thing different, so it is clear I can have no acquaintances.
And to strangers, to people who don't know me, I can't
possibly write.(24)

But, of course, like anyone else, he must have acquaintances:
people, that is, who can understand his actions and words -
or can, provided he can.

The Dadaist model also distorts the relation between a person's
more personal make-up and the options available to him. It may
be, as Sartre urges, that people often abdicate a serious concern for what to regard as worthwhile in their lives by retreat-
ing to an ossified image of what they are like. But it would be
as much an abdication to treat one's personality as a mere piece
of history which one may choose, or refuse, to carry with one
into the future. Honest assessment of personality, moreover,
does not only yield historical data about how one has been, but
traits and predispositions whose permanence only wishful thinking could spirit away. No one seriously considering the value
that marriage and a family have for him, and the place these
shall have in his life, can treat his record of several dismal
failed marriages as mere history, which should exert no pressure
on his judgment. 'Taking the plunge', in such a case, is no
display of authenticity.

Shortly I want to see what can be salvaged from the two
inadequate models discussed: for the moment I look at how
Nietzsche stands in relation to them.

There are passages in Nietzsche's writings with a Polonian ring:

Be yourself: you are not at all what you now do, think, and
desire.(25)

What does your conscience say? - You should become who you
are.(26)

[a man] is a dark and concealed thing; and if the hare has
seven skins, a man can peel off seven times seventy and still
not be able to say: 'Now, that's really you, and no longer a
shell'.(27)

Not only, though, are there persistent themes in Nietzsche
which militate against a Polonian interpretation of such remarks,
but these are typically followed by further remarks which
explicitly reject that interpretation. Nietzsche is, first, consistently hostile to the metaphysics of the self encouraged by
Polonian talk: to the idea of a self which persists, unchanged
in its essence, through the vicissitudes of life, and hidden
perhaps from view. Such a self is as mythical for Nietzsche
as it had been for Hume; hence his references to the 'false sub-
stantializing of the "I"', and to the wrong-headed view that
the self is the source of thought when, on the contrary, it is

'through thought that the "I" is posited'.(28) Second, as we saw, he rejects the way of introspection that the Polonian model places a premium upon. Self-understanding must come through understanding of the world in which one is placed. Philosophically it is a mistake to contrast 'man *and* the world'; and heuristically, people do better to focus, first, on what is well outside of them. 'It [is] almost senseless to want to take the non-distant [Nicht-Fremde] as an object.'(29)

How then is one to take demands to 'Be yourself' or 'Become what we are'? The first is followed by this illuminating remark: 'Your true being [*Wesen*] does not lie deeply hidden within you, but immeasurably high above you, or, at least, above that which you usually take as yourself.'(30) And the 'we' who are to 'become what we are' are the 'new, unique, incomparable, self-legislating, self-creating ones'.(31) The 'true self', 'what we are', is not something silted up by false selves, but a goal to be aimed at, the person we should strive to become. 'What we are' is not a present state, but what those who try to be 'self-legislating' and 'self-creating' are trying to be. I return later (p.16) to Nietzsche's reasons for expressing himself in (misleadingly) Polonian jargon.

There are also passages, where Nietzsche plays the gleeful iconoclast ready to sweep away everything conventional and historical, which could be from a Dadaist tract: 'I am the first to hold in my hand the measure of "truths": I am the first who is *able* to decide. . . . I contradict as has never been contradicted before. . . . I am the first immoralist: that makes me the annihilator *par excellence*.'(32) These remarks are from the frenziedly autobiographical *Ecce Homo*, written shortly before Nietzsche's mental collapse. Interpretation of them will only emerge gradually during the present book, but it can be said at once that several of Nietzsche's most persistent ideas make it impossible to read him as a Dadaist. Indeed, the points I raised against that model are Nietzsche's own. No one was more insistent than he that beliefs and values, to be intelligible, must be set against the right background or 'form of life'. His complaint against the 'Piety' advocated in Wagner's *Parsifal* was that it could not serve as a sensible guide or goal in a society that has witnessed Voltaire and Darwin, and which has been transformed by a scientific and social revolution. As a corollary, he emphasizes the difficulty of applying our own concepts upon behaviour set against alien, remote backgrounds: the difficulty, for example, of referring to justice and injustice in a society where it is not civil, but divine, retribution which awaits the wrongdoer.(33) Nor has any writer been more insistent that one's language is a repository of beliefs and values whose sudden overthrow would divest that language of sense. He is only too aware that some of his own criticisms run this risk; for example, that his attack on 'inner mental states' goes against a view blessed by a grammar, a view which 'under the seduction of language . . . understands . . . all action as conditioned by an agent,

through a "subject"'.(34) He is not being entirely frivolous
when he says that his own radical revaluations should be
danced rather than *said*, for words are so enmeshed with the
very values to be replaced. It is this awareness of the power of
language which explains his massive recourse to metaphor; for
it is only through this that the intimate ties between words and
concepts can be loosened so as to free words for new employ-
ments. It helps explain, too, why Nietzsche describes himself
as an 'annihilator', or even as a 'thorough-going nihilist'.
Ways of living and talking must first be thoroughly shaken-up
before the attempt to arrive at new beliefs or values is feasible.
This is not, primarily, because the old ways impose such powerful psychological constraints on revaluation, but because otherwise neither the actions nor the words of the revaluer could be
intelligible. Zarathustra recognized he had 'come too soon' to
effect a revaluation on the grand scale. The Dadaists' problem
is that they have come too soon without recognizing it.

What, then, is authenticity? An answer of a sort is now sketched,
but it is not in the rubrics and glosses offered that I expect
great interest to lie. The real work goes less into the sketch
than into the examination of what, given the sketch, is required
for people to live authentically. What does this require by way
of moral attitudes, or of response to the technological tendencies
of our age, or in relation to current educational goals? These
are among the interesting questions. Hence, it is the book as a
whole, rather than the rubric in this chapter, which offers an
account, if anything does, of authenticity.
  I have discussed two one-sided and inadequate models, but
in each of them there is a similar insight, which is the key to
the notion of authenticity. Indeed, we might regard them as
responses to rather different elements in this insight, emphases
upon one at the expense of the other. The insight is simple –
trite, even, for those who have never felt called to deny it –
but fundamental. Human beings are essentially distinguished by
their capacity for self-concern. This is not a unitary capacity,
but devolves into many powers: for example, to reflect upon
one's personality, to assess the situations in which one is placed,
to examine the language one speaks, to reflect on the goals to
pursue in one's life, to consider the value to be put on one's
activities, to examine how one came by one's beliefs, to assess
one's emotional responses, to think on how to widen the projects
and possibilities open to one. These are powers of self-concern,
since they are not exercised out of mere intellectual curiosity,
but in order to affect how one is or will be. And to influence
one's beliefs, values, and feelings, which are not features like
those of a physical object, since they are neither fixed nor subject to change only through external agency, maturational
development, or structural alteration.
  It is around this capacity for self-concern that the jargon of
authenticity revolves. Certainly, it is not difficult to see how

this distinction between humans and all else in nature prompts
Dadaist talk of 'existence preceding essence' or 'choosing
oneself'; for the idea is that those who do not exert themselves
in matters of commitment and choice of a future are failing to
exercise this capacity. It is less easy to see how it prompts
Polonian talk of 'true selves' or 'becoming what one *is*'. Did
we not follow Sartre in criticizing such talk for its tendency to
'reify' people - in direct conflict with the insight that drives a
wedge between men and things? But there is a way of interpreting such talk so that it expresses, rather than rejects, the
insight. A slogan like 'Be what you are!' is ambiguous. When
the pronoun is stressed, the suggestion is of a personal
essence, a fixity of self, or an individual law of self-development
to which one must tailor one's life. But if the stress is placed
on the verb, the different idea is suggested that we (you, I,
everyone) should live as the *kind* of beings we really are -
ones distinguished, that is, by the capacity for self-concern.
This is how Nietzsche construed his Polonian-sounding remarks,
which were not references to 'true selves' but to how people
should live self-creating lives. So construed, such talk is
about human essence. 'Become what you are!' means 'Live in the
way that accords with your essential nature as human beings.'
And Dadaist talk is about the same. Their insistence that 'existence precedes essence' is not a denial of *human* essence, but
of individual essences, of fixed selves unamenable to being
changed through self-concern. Consistent with this denial, the
Dadaist can say: what is essential to all persons is what distinguishes each person - his concern for *his* values, beliefs, and
the like. There is no paradox here: what is essential to all
original paintings is what distinguishes each - its originality.

  The Polonian and Dadaist models, thus doctored, are no longer
incompatible, for the essence to which the former appeals is
not what the latter rejects. In a dismissal of personal essences,
and a common embrace of a conception of human nature, they
can join hands. It remains that their emphases are different.
There is a coarse distinction, within self-concern, between what
I shall call 'situational' and 'projective' concern. A glance at
the list of powers into which the capacity for self-concern
devolves shows that some have mainly to do with taking stock -
of one's emotional make-up, say, or one's social situation; while
others have mainly to do with how one shall be - with, for
example, the purposes to set oneself. In the one case, it is my
'situation', in a very broad sense, that I am concerned to assess;
in the other, it is my 'projects', also in a broad sense, that I
am concerned to determine. The Polonian emphasis is upon the
former, the Dadaist upon the latter. Where the one fears that
enthusiasm for new commitments or 'leaps' may betray a failure
to take proper stock of one's 'situation', the other fears that a
fascinated absorption in a view of oneself can stultify one's
'projective' possibilities. Such fears may be apposite in different
types of case. Someone may be in a state of some dissolution,

grabbing greedily at this or that new belief, hurling himself into this, then that, project – tragically, like a Dostoievsky hero, or comically like a Bouvard and Pécuchet. Or a person may be in a state of some rigidity, paralysed by a picture of how he must be, insensate to possibilities of choice and re-appraisal that are in fact open to him. Neither person's life is an authentic one: the first, because his projects have no grounding in a genuine assessment of himself; the second, because his actions are not guided by genuine reflection on what he might do. Polonian and Dadaist fears are in place in these respective cases.

The distinction between 'situational' and 'projective' concern is a useful one that will run through the following chapters, even when not expressed in just these terms. Nevertheless, it is one whose coarseness of grain must be kept in mind. For a start, each form of concern is a very mixed bag. 'Situational' concern, for example, involves such disparate elements as attention to one's emotional make-up and reflection on the language one speaks. Second, their objects can coincide: thus, the very beliefs and purposes which permeate our teacher's school, and thereby figure importantly in the 'situation' of which he must take stock, are among those he is most concerned to decide about, to take a stance towards. Third, 'projective' decisions cannot always leave untouched a person's estimate of how things are. Someone with socialist commitments will see, while others do not, certain features of the social situation as *obstacles* to progress or reform. Conversely, it is in the nature of some 'situational' assessments to have a direct impact on the value a person can place on some of his 'projects'. The value he places upon, say, the books he is engaged in writing, cannot survive unscathed the realization, which may emerge as he reflects on his past, that it was one *foisted* on him at a peculiarly passive and impressionable time. Finally – and this is what makes Polonianism and Dadaism, in their extreme forms, incoherent – the two concerns are internally related: there cannot be the one without the other. A concern with what it would be worthwhile to aim at in life cannot be a serious, authentic one unless grounded in an assessment of how one is and of one's 'situation'. 'Situational' concern, conversely, would reduce to onanistic curiosity were it not a prelude to concern for what one should do and value. *Concern* for one's language is not the linguist's *interest* in it; for it is geared to consider-ing what I can – and can sensibly think that I can – undertake. This internal connection between 'situational' and 'projective' concerns is almost built into the term 'situation', for this refers not to mere states of affairs, but to what calls for attitudes to be taken, decisions made, and plans adopted.

Provided these remarks are not neglected, the distinction between the two forms of self-concern will be convenient. We can use it, even, to provide a quick gloss on 'authenticity' for those who feel the need for one. A person lives authentically just when he fully exercises his capacities for 'situational' and 'projective' self-concern. (I fear that this is less helpful than quotable.)

The everyday use of 'authenticity' suggested, but has not dictated, its employment by a number of philosophers. Unless my use of the term is to be purely stipulative, therefore, it must accord in some degree with a certain philosophical tradition. Fortunately it does accord reasonably well with the views of the most important writer in that tradition – Martin Heidegger. Here I can only sketch his rich, if obscure, views and their relation to the foregoing (which they will help to elaborate).

The fundamental features of *Dasein* – with qualifications, Heidegger's term for human existence – are that it is 'an issue for itself' and has the character of 'mineness' *(Jemeinigkeit)*.(35) A person, that is, is distinguished from any other creature by the capacity for a concern for the nature and direction of his life; moreover, each of his actions, beliefs, and values is one he can own to, call 'mine', and bear responsibility for. It is these features which make authentic *(eigentlich)* and inauthentic existence possibilities; for a creature incapable of self-concern and self-ascription can live in neither way. Although people cannot rid themselves of self-concern and responsibility, they can certainly live in ways that are a refusal to face up to what they imply. Someone may, for example, scarcely ever reflect on his existence; so that self-concern atrophies into concern with immediate objects of desire, or day-to-day plans, which he has given no place within a consistently thought-out set of purposes for himself. Or he may simply drift into this or that course of action, absorb this or that belief, just go along with some current moral viewpoint or other – thereby failing to come to terms with his responsibility for the actions, beliefs, and values of which he is, after all, the owner. It is as if someone with an inalienable title to some property let its control slip into other hands.

The general form of inauthenticity is 'fallenness' *(Verfallenheit)*; especially 'fallenness' into what Heidegger calls *Das Man*. (The German *'man'* is the French *'on'* , our 'one' as in 'one thinks that . . .'. Heidegger's translators render his expression as 'The They' or 'Them'. The impersonal 'We' or 'Us' might sometimes be better; the 'We' favoured by journalists, for example, when they refer to 'What we all agree upon' or 'What we British won't stand for'.) Heidegger describes 'fallenness' as 'absorption' into the everyday world – the immediate, the passing, the labile, the busy – so as to leave no time for the reflective self-concern which belongs to authentic living. In particular, people 'fall' into received opinion, hearsay, what is 'chattered' about. They go along with 'what we all know', 'what men think', or 'what we have all learned': in short, with *Das Man*. This becomes, thinks Heidegger, the normal state for most people; in part because it is so 'tempting' and 'tranquillizing'. People absolve themselves from that painstaking concern, inevitably accompanied by *Angst*, which facing the issue of one's life as a whole, striving to determine how it should be, demands.

The distinguishing mark of the authentic person is described by Heidegger as 'resoluteness' *(Entschlossenheit)*, which is in turn spelt out as 'concernful solicitude' and 'disclosive projection'.(36) What these indigestible terms mean, roughly, is that the authentic person will live in full awareness of the possibilities of action, belief, and purpose that are in fact open to him, and which anyone concerned with his existence as an 'issue' must consider. But at the same time, he insists, these must be the possibilities of a 'factical *Dasein* at a particular time'. Resoluteness requires 'determination of what is factically possible'. 'Resoluteness, as authentic Being-one's-self, does not detach *Dasein* from its world, does not isolate it as a free-floating "I".'(37) Or, as he also puts it, a person is 'thrown' *(geworfen)* into a particular world and time, and his various actions - like becoming a school-teacher in a given educational system - 'throw' him into situations with their own definite inheritance. Nothing about the situations into which one is 'thrown' is to be ignored if the 'resolute' facing of one's possibilities is to have any authenticity.

There is no need to labour the points of contact between Heidegger's account and my own remarks. His characterization of *Dasein* expresses in other terms the 'insight' into the fundamental difference between human and all other existence. His emphases upon 'thrownness' and 'facticity' parallel those of the (doctored) Polonian model; while the stress upon 'resoluteness' and 'projection' recalls the (doctored) Dadaist model. And 'fallenness into *Das Man*' could be a dramatic label for the position our teacher feared himself to be slipping into, and which gave rise to his crisis of authenticity.

My sketch of authenticity also accords reasonably well with Lionel Trilling's account, in his polished lectures *Sincerity and Authenticity*, of the tradition in which these notions loom large. He traces the concern with authenticity back to the fears felt by Rousseau and Wordsworth for that 'sentiment of being' which they saw threatened and corrupted in modern society; for the tendency of that society is to breed men who 'live only in the opinions of others'. The attempt to resalvage 'the sentiment of being' effected a profound aesthetic reassessment - Trilling's major interest: for the mark of great art ceased to be its beauty or power to please, but its genuineness as an expression of the artist's uncontaminated sense of himself and of what was fitting for *him* to produce. Trilling also describes the very different directions, already met with in my account, in which the search for authenticity may push men: towards spontaneous, ungrounded, 'existential' expression, or towards living in accordance with an image of a 'true self' (identified in the case of some writers with a collective unit, such as a social class or *Volk*). Like Rilke, Trilling has a good ear for the cant that talk about authenticity can degenerate into; for a 'moral slang' which

generates a 'cult' of authenticity whose very orthodoxy renders
authentic living by its devotees nugatory.

Nietzsche's name, unsurprisingly, crops up frequently in
Trilling's book, which contains at least two misleading remarks
about him. Trilling says 'Nietzsche's hostility to nihilism is
settled and explicit.'(38) But Nietzsche referred to many diverse
attitudes by the term 'nihilism', and to some of these he was
scarcely hostile at all. He welcomes, for example, that nihilistic
rejection of old values that would be a transition to new ones.(39)
And when nihilism takes the form of denying the 'true world' -
that is, the transcendental world of Plato and Christianity - it
is a 'divine way of thinking'.(40) Trilling also credits Nietzsche
with 'a principled antagonism to sincerity . . . [for he] spoke
in praise of what [he] called the mask'.(41) In support, he
quotes Nietzsche's remark that 'every profound spirit needs a
mask' - 'spirits' like 'dogmatic philosophy', 'Vedanta doctrine',
and 'European Platonism'. But aside from ignoring such statements of Nietzsche as 'nothing is today more precious and rare
to me than honesty',(42) it is strange to interpret the above
remark as praising masks; for the examples of 'spirits' given
are among the perennial targets of Nietzsche's attacks. He
thinks, it is true, that given the way men now are, there are
ideas which could not take effect unless presented in masked
forms such as myth. Even Zarathustra has to resort to this:
but it is a matter for regret, not jubilation. One reason
Zarathustra concludes, regretfully, that he has come among men
'too soon' is that he cannot convey his thoughts without com-
promise, without masking.

Several philosophers of education, in recent years, have
defended an educational goal which, on some of their descriptions, sounds not unlike the goal of authenticity. Richard
Peters, for example, defends that brand of liberal education
premised on 'the belief that it is of crucial importance that the
individual should choose what he is to become'.(43) And R.F.
Dearden argues for 'a new aim in education', which requires
that what a person 'thinks and does in important areas of his
life cannot be explained without reference to his own activity of
mind'.(44) But both writers refer to the aim in question as
autonomy, not authenticity. Why do they speak of autonomy,
and I of authenticity, when, on the surface, a similar aim is
being discussed?

The main part of the answer is that the similarity is indeed
superficial, and that the difference in terminology reflects one
of substance. Both writers, in fact, do make some mention of
authenticity. Peters says that his 'emphasis is on autonomy as
well as on authenticity',(45) making it sound as if there are two
distinguishable goals here. But what he goes on to argue is
that either talk of authenticity is of autonomy or it is scarcely
intelligible. Such slogans of authenticity as 'Do your own thing',
'self-origination', or 'construction of one's own reality' must be

interpreted into the 'less extreme and more intelligible' notion
of autonomy.(46) Dearden, too, thinks that unless 'moral
authenticity' belongs to the 'more pervasive' idea of autonomy,
it 'is the absurd enthusiasm for criterionless 'existential' commitments and 'choices of self'.(47) It is clear from these remarks
that both writers construe the jargon of authenticity along
either extreme Polonian or extreme Dadaist lines, in which case
their desire to reject it or sober it up is in order. One's only
criticism could be that had they concentrated on, say,
Heidegger's account, they would not have been so quick to
associate the jargon with these extreme models. However, their
unease with the notion of authenticity goes deeper, and would
remain even if it were Heidegger's, or my own, account they
were considering. There is something they place sovereign
importance upon, and which they find contained in the notion of
autonomy, but either missing or insufficiently prominent in that
of authenticity. This is the role of reason and criticism. Their
preference for the term 'autonomy' bears witness to the central
place they allocate to rational criticism in the mental development
of someone who is to 'choose what he is to become', and whose
attitudes are not to be 'explained without reference to his own
activity of mind'. My preference for 'authenticity' bears equal
witness to the less central place I see this occupying.

We are left in no doubt that, as for Kant, reason is the
primary ingredient in autonomy. 'What is crucial', says Peters,
'is the encouragement of criticism in the individual so that he
can eventually accept and reject what he hears, or is told, on
the basis of reasons'.(48) Dearden claims that whatever is
'constitutive of autonomy [is] essentially linked to the idea of
reason, or rather to the idea of having reasons for what one
thinks and does'. Choice, he adds, is not intelligible unless
there are 'criteria by reference to which the choice is made'.(49)
Because of this emphasis upon rational criticism, it is with
indoctrination and conditioning that an education for autonomy
is pre-eminently contrasted. Both writers offer a similar account
of such an education's nature: it will consist, first and foremost,
of 'initiating' pupils into the established disciplines and 'forms
of knowledge' which provide the forums in which rational thought
and criticism do their business. I discuss this conception in
Chapters 4 and 5; for the present, I concentrate on the
exaggerated stress upon rational criticism which, it seems to me,
is encapsulated in this talk of autonomy.

There are, to begin with, efforts and attitudes of mind which
should surely be encouraged, but which have little to do with
the seeking or giving of reasons. Among these are ones which
figured in the sketch of the authentic individual. A person will
want, for example, to obtain a clear assessment of his own
motives; of the extent, say, to which he is ambitious for
honours and position. Only in unusual circumstances would we
expect him to give reasons for regarding himself as ambitious
for these things - beyond, trivially, the reason that this is

what he is. This is not to say that such assessment is an easy
task, performed in a flash. One may need to learn, and be
taught, to see through the blandishments of those who would
encourage a rosier picture of one's motives than they deserve.
Again, it belongs to 'projective' concerns to remain open to new
possibilities of emotional response and fulfilment, in matters of
music, say, or in one's sexual life. Reasons, no doubt, can be
given why a person should do this: perhaps he will be happier,
or less bored. But reasons of this kind can also be given
against. How, as the song asks, will we keep him down on the
farm now that he's seen Paree? It is not on the basis of such
rational calculations that a person should be open to new
emotional possibilities, but because otherwise he is a limited
human being. Again, *pace* Dearden, it is neither senseless or
undesirable that people make 'criterionless' choices. Someone
deciding to devote time and energy to hearing and studying
Beethoven's music need not provide criteria for why he does
this. His behaviour is odd if he has no initial affinity to the
music, or no initial sense that it is worth studying, but this
does not mean he is able to produce criteria for why his decision
is a good one - unless, trivially, this initial affinity and sense
are deemed criteria.

There is, second, a stance people often take towards beliefs
that are of great importance to them, which could not be
regarded as an 'autonomous' stance in the sense being discussed,
because it is precisely the refusal to give up a belief despite
the judgment that, on balance, the evidence, the reasons, go
against it. A person will not always be tempted to surrender
a religious conviction by his judgment that, of the arguments
he has encountered, those which militate against his belief
are the stronger. Now it seems to me that we do not do right to
try to shake him out of this conviction. To do so successfully
could induce a feeling of self-betrayal, of being bullied by
people cleverer than himself, a lack of confidence in his right
to 'stick to his guns', even a loss of dignity and sense of
individuality.(50) It could be argued that, in a sense, rationality is on the side of someone who does remain with his conviction. He may argue, after all, that views which go against
the weight of evidence at a given time often turn out to be right;
or that, had he listened to other people or read different books,
his judgment about the weight of evidence would have been very
different; or that the reasons which go against his belief count
as good ones only from a certain perspective, which may be a
matter of fashion even if he himself is unable to form a credible
alternative. In short, he may offer reasons, meta-reasons, for
why the reasons which go against his conviction should not
clinch matters for him. But this is far from agreeing with
Peters's and Dearden's emphasis on basing beliefs upon reasons.
The fact that it is through reason that a case is made against
settling all beliefs through reasons alone does not alter the fact
that the case is made. Hesse's conclusion that the age was one

in which 'our admirable rationality has become madness, our gold is paper'(51) was the result of rational reflection, not intuitive spark or mystical insight: but this cannot show that his conclusion was wrong.

My final point is related. In our tradition, a natural response when worries about one's beliefs or values set in is to search for evidence and reasons in support. This is precisely the response of the autonomous man described by Peters and Dearden, who go on, however, to point out the limits such a search runs up against: limits of logic, rather than of time, intellectual capacity, and energy. Someone tries to justify a belief, then to justify the justification, and so on; but, perhaps rather soon, a point is reached where further justification is impossible, where one can only say 'This is how we take it that things are!' Peters and Dearden treat this situation sanguinely. Would it not be neurotic or worse to kick against the limits of logic? The sane man bows to the inevitable.

But is this sanguinity in order? What disturbs many people, surely, is not that justifications, a chain of reasons, must come to an end, but that *they* hardly travel more than a few links upon it. Others may have gone further, but then the rest of us must rely on hearsay and authority, neither of which are we able to validate for ourselves. This worry is then compounded by fear about the possible parochialism of the chains of reasons offered and the final stands taken at their ends. The point is not whether there really are good reasons, and further reasons for regarding the former as good ones; nor is it whether the final stands really are ones for which it would be inappropriate to seek further grounding. The concern, rather, is that one's own acceptance of reasons as good ones, or of certain final stands as appropriate, seems so much a function of upbringing, fashion, social conditions and trends which can and do vary in other times and climes. It is the kind of concern Nietzsche expresses in this passage: 'It is so provincial to be bound to views which a few hundred miles away are no longer binding. East and West are chalk-marks which someone draws before our eyes to make a fool of our timidity.'(52) The claim, to repeat, is not - or does not have to be - the relativist's one that there can be no objective criteria for adjudicating conflicting beliefs or forms of reason-giving. Rather it is one about the individual's power to recognize these if there are any. How can he claim to have done so when, on the other side of the Pyrenees or over the chalk-line, his judgment would have been so different?

Sanguinity, or resignation, would perhaps be in order if the only way of examining beliefs were the search for reasons pro or con. But there is another extremely important, and neglected, mode of examination: so that bowing to the inevitable - that justifications come to an end with final stands - is not equivalent to abdicating further examination. It is Descartes who provides the clue with his demon hypothesis. It would be pointless, he saw, to try to assuage doubts by gathering evidence for our beliefs, since the demon would have furnished us with our notions of evidence and reasons. What is required is to get rid of the demon, and show that we do not come by our beliefs and standards of rationality through his agency. We must, that is, 'clear' and prove the innocence of the processes whereby we come to our beliefs and modes of justification. It is not Descartes' particular strategy which matters here, but the kind it illustrates: the move from examining beliefs by gathering evidence and seeking reasons to examining the ways in which we come by them and maintain them. Nietzsche gives the term 'genealogy' to this kind of examination. It is investigation into the myriad causes, influences, props, fashions, interests, desires, and social conditions that enter into explanations of why people hold the values and beliefs they do. We encounter it in some detail in later chapters; for the moment I make a few remarks relating it to the discussion of autonomy.

The main point is that it would be quite wrong to assimilate genealogical enquiry - at least, in general - to the kind of critical enquiry Peters and Dearden associate with autonomy. Indeed, they would be as quick as most philosophers to reject this assimilation, treating it as a commission of the so-called 'genetic fallacy'. This is the alleged fallacy of supposing that questions of truth can be settled, or even touched, by considerations of the causes, interests, or whatever which may generate or maintain beliefs. Such a rejection may be *too* quick: perhaps genealogical considerations of a certain sort do pertain to truth.(53) But it can be agreed that there is no obvious inference from such considerations to conclusions about truth and falsity. When Descartes got rid of the demon, he was not showing that our mathematical beliefs, say, are true, nor offering reasons for their truth in the way he would be if deriving them from axioms. He was simply giving 'clearance' to the ways in which we conduct our mathematical thinking. Nietzsche, incidentally, is not guilty of any 'genetic fallacy' (at least in any crude form):

> The question of the origin of our evaluations and tables of the good is not at all equivalent to their *critique,* as is so often believed: however certain it is that the insight into some *pudenda origo* brings with it the feeling of a lessening of value in what originated in such a way, and prepares the way for a critical mood and attitude towards it.(54)

As the second part of this passage suggests, however, genealogical enquiry is of the first importance in affecting people's attitudes towards their values and beliefs; not by offering confirmations or disconfirmations, but by 'clearing' or 'indicting' how they are arrived at. If a person, after psycho-analysis, say, or 'denazification', comes to see that his coming by some belief had a 'shameful origin' - indoctrination, perhaps -

he can scarcely remain contentedly accepting it. According to Nietzsche, loss of religious faith has been due to the uncovering of its shabby origins, not to the logical objections of atheists. This uncovering cannot show the faith to be mistaken, but it does commit the faithful to re-examination, for they are forced to concede that the strength of their faith is explicable without reference to its truth (if it has any).

It would be a mistake, parenthetically, to now equate genealogy with some branch of the social sciences – the sociology of knowledge, say. There is no reason to limit attention to those factors which, in any useful sense, are 'sociological' – to the exclusion, say, of psychological, sexual, and quirkishly individual ones. Moreover, the sociology of knowledge has itself become a loose collection of doctrines that is fair game for genealogical enquiry. The processes whereby a remarkable number of sociologists have become convinced of some scarcely self-evident claims about the relation between society and ideas would, in fact, furnish a rather fascinating subject for such an enquiry.(55) As Foucault nicely puts it, genealogy is not a theory, but a *tactic*: a readiness to look at any factor that does its bit in influencing people's beliefs and values, without advance commitment to the import of this influence.(56)

The business of working out what is involved, with any concreteness, in the notion of authenticity, of 'situational' and 'projective' concern, is a long one. The discussion of autonomy, as conceived by some recent writers,(57) has been a beginning, for it was prompted by the question 'why authenticity rather than autonomy as an educational, indeed human, goal?'. The answer has been that the current concept of autonomy leaves out too much that men should concern themselves with. When yoked to critical rationality, the concept has no place for those concerns where the giving and criticizing of reasons is only modestly engaged, or for the importance, in the case of some individual convictions, of not being bowled over by judgments on the weight of evidence. Most worrying of all, perhaps, it has no place for that dimension of examination Nietzsche called 'genealogical'. For the concern with how one came by one's beliefs and values – and, in the case of teachers, with the role played in how others will come by theirs – is a main stroke in any portrait of authenticity.

We shall return to this business in Chapter 3, with the help of some thoughts of Nietzsche. To appreciate these, it will be helpful to know what he found wrong with the educational system of his own times.

2   'Breadwinners' and 'old maids'

During the productive years, 1872-4, Nietzsche's main writings
were a concentrated attack upon the cultural, and especially
educational, trends which the founding of the new German Reich
after the victory over France, in 1871, had accelerated. These
were trends which stretched far back, but Nietzsche was right
to think that in the new, unified, militaristic Germany they
would be given new impetus. The relevant writings are the
second and third of the *Untimely Meditations*, and the five
public lectures given before the Akademische Gesellschaft in
Basel during 1872, entitled *Über die Zukunft unserer
Bildungsanstalten* ('On the future of our educational institutions'). Already, in a letter to his friend Gersdorff in 1870,
Nietzsche had announced his intention to 'lay bare in public . . .
the culturally very dangerous power' of the Prussian education
system, which was now to spread over Germany as a whole.(1)
And sixteen years later, when reflecting on these early writings,
he wrote:

> Fundamentally, I wanted in those writings to do something
> quite distinct from Psychology: an unparalleled problem of
> education, a new creed of self-discipline, self-defense to the
> point of hardness, a way to greatness and to world-historical,
> tasks, were demanding their first expression.(2)

The emphasis, in these early years, upon education was not
unrelated to Nietzsche's personal life. In 1869, he had accepted,
at an unusually young age - and with considerable misgivings -
a Chair in Classical Philology at the University of Basel; only
to find, as predicted, that academic teaching was stifling for
him. Like many letters of the time, his five lectures on education
reveal a man struggling to decide whether he can, with
integrity, remain a teacher within the public system. A main
reason behind his choice of Schopenhauer as the hero of his
third 'Meditation' was that philosopher's renunciation of
university teaching. (Actually Nietzsche's portrait of Schopenhauer's motives and character was a strangely rose-tinted one.)
It was the advice and pressure of Richard Wagner which largely
explains why Nietzsche remained at his post. He had fallen under
the spell of the composer in 1869, when Wagner was living at
Tribschen near Basel, and was to remain under it until the
first Bayreuth Festspiel of 1876. In the five lectures, a 'Master'
convinces a 'Disciple' to remain a teacher, in order to provide a

base within academia for the dissemination of the 'Master's'
ideas. Clearly, it is 'Meister' Wagner convincing the wavering
young Nietzsche, who found it a scandal that 'official' culture,
especially within the universities, was blind, indeed hostile,
to the new Wagnerian forces. His writings at the time - *The
Birth of Tragedy* and those just mentioned - may be seen, in
part, as the attempt to impress this scandal upon those among
whom it was most marked - his fellow-scholars and teachers.(3)

After the break with Wagner, and his resignation from the
Basel Chair, Nietzsche was not again to write a book on education. In fact, he was hardly again to write *books* in the usual
sense, as against loosely connected essays, aphorisms, and
notes. Certainly his interest in 'the future of our educational
institutions' declined, mainly because he despaired that these
could become the vehicles of true education; but with the nature
of education, his concern never waned. Comments upon it,
often lengthy, are scattered throughout the writings of his last
active years up to 1889. There is a good sense, too, in which
Nietzsche's whole philosophical enterprise was educational: for
at the centre there is always the concern with a new kind of
man, who will create new kinds of value, and who can be produced only through education or 'breeding', not through social,
political, or economic reform and progress. Nor, I think, do his
last thoughts on education fundamentally conflict with his first.
There are, it is true, metaphysical themes which inform the
earlier critique and which, on the surface, do not figure later
on - but even here, we have transposition, not silencing, of the
themes. If he no longer speaks of 'the genius and the saint'
as the goals of an education that accords with 'Nature's purpose',
he does speak of the 'overman' that must be bred as the highest
expression of 'the will to power' which permeates all nature.

It is necessary, if those whose acquaintance with Nietzsche
is slight are not to go astray at this early stage, to point out
that by 'breeding' Nietzsche does not have in mind anything
like genetic engineering; by 'overman' he does not mean anything
like an S.S. Sturmbahnführer; and by 'the will to power' he
does not intend what Hitler embodied and Leni Riefenstahl filmed.
I do not agree with Walter Kaufmann's impassioned plea that there
are no significant points of contact between Nietzsche's philosophy
and Nazi ideology; but we should surely have learned from him -
and from Karl Jaspers - that there is nothing like the tight fit
pretended by both Nazi ideologists and ideologists of the 'Left',
such as Georg Lukács. It is worth stating yet again that
Nietzsche was a dedicated opponent of Racism - in an age,
incidentally, when this was very much a received idea. (Wagner's
vitriolic anti-Semitism was a major cause of Nietzsche's break
with the composer.)

In this chapter, I want to look at certain themes in Nietzsche's
early educational writings; the connection between these and
the matters discussed in the first chapter will emerge later.
Most of what Nietzsche has to say is of perennial, and certainly

contemporary, significance – but his critique was directed
against a particular education system, and some remarks on
nineteenth-century German education will set the scene for
his polemic.

One word selects itself to describe the mood in which that
system was given shape at the beginning of that century –
'idealist', in a full variety of senses. In the first place, the
prime movers of the reforms – including von Humboldt,
Schleiermacher, and their mentor, Fichte – were 'idealists' in
the philosophical sense of thinking that ultimately only mind
or spirit truly exists: the material world is, in some way, a
posit of mind. The reforming spirit was idealist, too, in the
loftiness, indeed sublimity, of the goals towards which education
was to aspire. In the words of one reformer, Altenstein, the
educational 'revolution' would be one 'in the good sense,
leading directly towards the supreme goal of the ennoblement
of humanity'.(4) Finally, the curricular emphasis was to be
almost exclusively upon *ideal* rather than *real* questions (here
it is the two German words, orthographically identical to the
English, which are being used): upon, that is, questions about
man's spiritual, artistic, and cultural nature, and not upon
matters of utilitarian, economic, or scientific concern. Hence
the remarkable focus, in the newly founded *Gymnasien* and
universities, on the study of Ancient Greece. For von Humboldt,
such a focus was essential in an unfortunate age 'when . . .
attention is directed more towards things than men, more to
men in the mass than to men as individuals, and more towards
external value than to inner beauty and enjoyment'.(5)

The nineteenth century was to see the erosion of this idealism
in two seemingly opposed ways. First, and most obviously, there
was the accelerating growth of *Realismus*. By Nietzsche's day,
the Realschulen, with their greater emphasis upon the natural
sciences and upon German studies, were coming to compete with
the *Gymnasien*, which themselves had to adapt to meet the
challenge. Boys from the *Realschulen* were soon to gain admit-
tance to the old universities, and in the meantime new technical
universities were being set up to receive them. At the end of
the century, a leading pedagogue could proclaim in words that
von Humboldt could scarcely have understood that 'knowledge
has value only through its usefulness, through making its
possessors . . . more capable of fulfilling their life-callings'.(6)

Three related factors best explain this development. The
growth of rampant, militaristic nationalism; the near-total control
of education by the state (first the Prussian, then the imperial);
and the industrial revolution which set in around the middle of
the century. One man, who virtually embodied these three in
his person, was especially keen that education should focus upon
'the practical needs of life . . . [and] bring up young *Germans*,
not young Greco-Romans'.(7) This was the young Emperor
Wilhelm II, whose pedagogic views were in full accord with those
of his great-grandfather, Frederick William III of Prussia, who

had condemned those 'abstract sciences that touch only the academic world . . . [and] are of course without any value to the welfare of the state'.(8)

The state's control of the educational system was due not only to the laws which gave it legal and financial sovereignty but to its position as the main employer of educated Germans – as soldiers, teachers, or civil servants. The aphorism, popular after 1866, that it was the Prussian schoolmaster who had defeated the Austrians at Sadowa had its element of truth; and a similar aphorism after the battle of Tannenburg fifty years later would have contained a still greater element. The growing needs of army, state, and the industrial economy transformed the system at every level: the curriculum became more 'relevant'; teachers were appointed and dismissed according to political complexion; there was a growth in 'specialisms', especially in the natural sciences; and an examination system, for filtering the future servants of the state, developed massive proportions. Treitschke could look back with nostalgia to the days when 'the disease of the universities of today, the dread of examinations, was almost entirely unknown'.(9)

The erosion of the original idealist spirit was compounded by the form that the reaction to *Realismus* took: a retreat, among traditional teachers and scholars, to the ivory tower, to its platform of 'knowledge for its own sake'. The pedantry of German scholars became, of course, a favourite butt of humour in many of the best German novels of the latter half of the century; those of Raabe and Fontane, for example. In an age when men's destinies were becoming increasingly ordered by the power of state and army, it was difficult for scholarship to be fired any longer by the zeal of a von Humboldt or a Schleiermacher. There could be little faith in a spiritual revolution, 'in the good sense', to be wrought by a study of the classics, when men were coming increasingly into the grip of an industrial revolution. In the eyes of their critics, and perhaps in their own, the message of the traditionalists had become a purely negative one: '*No* vocational education, *no* utilitarian education, *no* education for practical ends!'(10) The study of ancient Greece was, for von Humboldt, to take us away from things to men, and from 'external value' to 'inner beauty and enjoyment'. For a later educationist, the modest aim of such a study is simply 'to open the door . . . to ancient times'.(11)

These processes of erosion – the growth of *Realismus* and the pedants' response to it – were to accelerate after 1870. It was not long before the teacher was to be seen as 'half-sergeant, half-bookworm'. Ironically, it was as much the perceived failures of 1870-1 as its successes that were responsible for this. After all, it had been *Prussia,* not Germany as a whole, which had defeated Napoleon III; a fact which niggled, and thereby spurred on, the advocates of militant *grossdeutsch* nationalism. Education, as can be seen by looking at the various revisions made to the material contained in German 'readers' at school,

took on increasingly nationalistic hues. Again, it was a king -
the admittedly unwilling Ludwig II of Bavaria - and not repre-
sentatives of 'The People', who had put the imperial crown on
William I's head; an event which sparked off a wave of aggrieved
democratic sentiment, among whose results was an increasing
democratization of education, a reaction against the traditional
Gymnasien and universities in favour of *Realismus*. Finally, the
failure (in some eyes) totally to destroy France - Wagner wanted
Paris burned - meant the military occupation of Alsace-Lorraine:
Germany therefore was to remain for the foreseeable future a
permanently armed state - greedy for the appropriate fodder
which schools and universities could provide for the army and
the civil service required to administrate it.

It was against this background that Nietzsche presented his
educational critique. Put simply, his was a voice - perhaps the
loudest, and certainly the most eloquent - against the double
erosion of the spirit in which German education had been born
at the beginning of the century. Without sharing many of the
main tenets of philosophical 'Idealism', he did share with von
Humboldt and Schleiermacher a lofty conception of education's
goals: goals which were totally incompatible with the 'bread-
winning' aims of the 'Realists' and the aim of 'knowledge for its
own sake' espoused by those 'old maids', the traditionalist
scholars.

For Nietzsche, teaching which aims towards 'real' goals, such
as economic ones, cannot belong to 'true' education; nor can
teaching whose aim is the acquisition of 'knowledge for its own
sake'. His comments upon teachers or institutions which do
embrace such aims are among the most barbed in his armoury.
Gelehrten - scholars, 'men of learning' - are, besides being
'old maids', 'drudges', 'dry', 'players on only two strings',
'weak', 'flatheads', 'bent', 'humpbacked', 'decadent', 'idiots',
'mirrors', 'enemies of culture', 'maggots', 'beavers', 'ants',
'housepets', 'chatterers', 'herd-animals', 'indifferent', and
'culture-philistines'. Throughout, there is a contrast drawn
between the educated man and the merely learned or knowledge-
able. As Nietzsche saw it, the *Gymnasien* had betrayed their
original calling, and now had as their 'goal . . . not the free,
educated person, but the learned person, the man knowledge-
able in the sciences. . . . The result . . . the historical/
aesthetic cultural philistine who chatters about state, church,
and art.'(12) As for so-called education which 'sets as its goal
a position of employment or bread-winning, [that] is not
education for culture'; and there is a total contrast between
'*educational* institutions and institutions for the sake of the
necessities of everyday life *(Lebensnot)*'.(13) Since, in his
view, the *Realschulen* were dominated by such utilitarian
goals, it followed that in the whole school system - *Gymnasien*
and *Realschulen* - 'there are no educational institutions'.(14)

It would be natural to conclude, from these remarks, that
Nietzsche is implacably hostile to both vocational, practical

studies and to 'pure', scholarly studies. Natural, but mistaken.
He is, first, fully aware of the need for practical studies: 'Do
not think, my friends, that I shrink from praising our
Realschulen.'(15) And he frequently stresses the value that
dry, painstaking scholarship can have. In one passage, he
compares the educated person to a mother and the scholar to
an old maid acting as midwife: the latter, while barren, can aid
what is fertile.(16) His point is that teaching such studies –
'*real*' and 'pure' – cannot constitute *education*. It will be little
more than coincidence if the educated person is also learned, or
equipped in addition to play some particular role in the economy
or the state. The point, naturally, is not a verbal one. Whatever value may reside in *Realstudien* or in scholarship, much
greater value resides, for those who are capable of it, in education. To withhold the label 'education' from these other kinds
of teaching is, without flatly condemning them, to contrast them
with a kind of teaching that has much higher goals before it.
What he does flatly condemn is the pretence that these other
kinds of teaching *do* constitute education.

These claims about what education is not imply that Nietzsche
must have some positive conception of what it is – that he must
have 'a concept of education'. We shall be disappointed, though,
if we look for some crisp definition. True, we shall find many
sentences of the form 'Education is . . .', but usually these are
either ironical definitions ('Education [is] essentially the means
for ruining the exceptions for the sake of the rule'),(17) or
statements of particular goals which, at particular times,
appealed to Nietzsche ('Education is the production of genius').
This is less disappointing than some might think. Crisp definitions of 'education' are never, in themselves, satisfying: the
interesting work remains to be done in explicating the terms that
figure in the definition. A definition like 'Education is initiation
into worthwhile activities' may *point* in a certain direction, but
expresses something substantial only when 'initiation' and
'worthwhileness' are explicated. What we do find in Nietzsche
is the drawing of various connections and contrasts with the
notion of education. Unlike what masquerades under its name,
education has to do with 'Life', and must, in some way, accord
with 'Nature'; it is essentially related to 'understanding' and to
'wisdom'. And it is to be contrasted with what is essentially concerned with the economic, the everyday, or the conventional,
and with learning (i.e. what learned people have), knowledge,
and scholarship. To grasp Nietzsche's 'concept of education' is
to understand the connections and contrasts being drawn.
This is a task which will occupy us in future chapters.

It is worth mentioning, at this stage, a translational problem
which is encountered when trying to identify Nietzsche's, or
any German writer's, 'concept of education'. German has no
single word whose use is the same as that of our word 'education'.
'*Erziehung*' can usually be translated as 'education', though
often 'rearing' or 'bringing up' would be better; but '*Erziehung*'

is not the only word German uses where we use 'education'. In particular, there is *'Bildung'*, which is especially favoured in compound expressions, such as *'Bildungsanstalten'* (educational institutions or establishments) or *'allgemeine Bildung'* (general or liberal education). Unfortunately, *'Bildung'* bears several other senses as well: for example, 'formation', 'structure', 'culture', and 'civilization'. This does not mean that, in a given context, *'Bildung'* must bear just one of these senses: typically it will conjure up several connotations – those of our words 'education', 'culture', and 'civilization', say. Certainly, it is more difficult for a German speaker to dissociate the value of *Bildung* from those of culture and civilization than it apparently is for English speakers to dissociate education from these, and to think of education purely in terms of an institutional process. The claim that technical or vocational schools are not 'educational institutions' has a somewhat paradoxical sound to it; less so, the claim that Nietzsche makes that such schools are not *'Bildungsanstalten'*. (The behaviour of the word *'Bildung'* gives some support to those who argue that certain types of cultural value belong to the very concept of education.) Clearly this presents a problem in identifying what a German author is saying about education. What he says about *'Erziehung'* may be insufficient for us to look at; and what he says about *'Bildung'* may go beyond what is relevant (he may be talking about the Arts, say). Wherever the problem threatens to be serious, I shall mention which German word I am translating as 'education' in the relevant passages.

In the rest of this chapter, I want to draw attention to Nietzsche's important thoughts on the relation between the two kinds of schooling and teaching from which he withholds the label 'education'. His central thought is that *Realismus* and 'knowledge for its own sake' are not the clear polar opposites they at first appear; that, indeed, the differences between them are outweighed by what they share, including the enemies they have in common. No doubt the philistine advocate of education as a training for 'breadwinning' is a straw-man; as – in our day, at least – is the 'old maidish' advocate of absolutely 'pure, resultless scholarship' (*'reine folgenlose Gelehrtsamkeit'*). But while, for polemical purposes, Nietzsche's diatribes are usually directed against these extreme figures, it is clear that he intends his critique to apply to their more modest, breathing, colleagues.

Those who advocate a practical, utilitarian direction for schooling do not, typically, advocate a narrow vocationalism, a training within school for a specific role or job. This is less a nod in the direction of culture than the realization that, in an age of rapid social and technical transformation, such narrow training at too early an age might produce young people ill-equipped to adapt to the new tasks that might be thrust upon them. Equally, those who speak approvingly of 'knowledge for its own sake' are rarely advocating the acquisition of knowledge that really will pay *no* dividends at all - personal, cultural, or social. That slogan, indeed, is best construed negatively - as a response to some particular opponent's view of where the value of knowledge lies. It might be invoked, for example, in response to some technocrat's dismissal of the study of Greek history or Hegel's logic as a waste of time. In a different context, most probably, the person who invoked the slogan could be found giving reasons why such studies are valuable, beyond the mere engaging in them. To be sure, he will not appeal to the side-benefits or 'perks' - like getting a better job, or impressing people at dinner-parties - which such studies might carry. He will appeal, rather, to considerations like these: such knowledge sharpens the critical sense; it helps one appreciate culture; it widens one's vision of how men are, so that one is in a better position to select a way of life for oneself rationally; it is relevant to the understanding of the 'human condition' with which one will have to cope, it provides mental abilities relevant to becoming a more responsible citizen.(18) The slogan 'knowledge for its own sake' does not exclude, and typically incorporates, such reasons in favour of pursuing knowledge that is of no immediate, transparent, utilitarian value. Of course, it is not only 'vocationalism' and 'utilitarianism' which those who invoke the slogan mean to combat: for it is also opposed to a variety of views which would relegate the claims of *both* knowledge and utility in favour of quite different educational emphases: views, for example, which see emotional development, or the child's freedom to do as he wishes, as the main educational imperatives.

Once the utilitarian breaks away from his narrow 'bread-winning' moorings, and once the slogan of 'knowledge for its own sake' is seen, despite its wording, to be compatible with valuing knowledge beyond the mere acquisition of it, the initial contrast between the two views becomes much less striking. What we now have is, first, an approach which places at the centre of educational policy an emphasis upon the economic and professional tasks pupils will one day take on; and, second, an approach which places at the centre an emphasis upon the acquisition of theoretical knowledge in various fields - so as, in part, to enable pupils to 'cope' better with the social world, the 'human condition', into which they are to be flung. In practice, indeed, policies advocated on the two approaches might emerge as very similar, or even as the reverse of what might initially have been predicted. We might find, for example, the utilitarian recommending theoretical studies over a wide field, in the belief that only these will promote those general skills and flexibility which a developing technological society most urgently needs. Or we might find an advocate of 'knowledge for its own sake' recommending, like Ortega y Gasset, concentrated attention upon some technical, vocationally relevant subject, in the belief that this is the best way to spark off an interest in the wider theoretical and philosophical questions it can illustrate.(19)

Nietzsche himself stresses three ways in which the 'breadwinners' and the 'old maids' - or rather, their more moderate
colleagues just described - tend to converge. First, he sees
both of them as aiming to make men *current* - in the way coins
are current. The metaphor is a rich one, that vibrates more
today perhaps than in Nietzsche's time. Coins are objects
people acquire and are acquisitive towards: so to describe a
way of teaching as aiming to make men current is to highlight
its acquisitive connections. There is the practical man that
utilitarian schooling aims to produce, ready to take his acquisitive place in an acquisitive society. And there is 'the man of
knowledge', judged by how much he has acquired how quickly;
whose intelligence gets mathematically measured like his capital;
whose mind becomes a learning-bank, from which to draw when
occasions, like examinations, demand. The pursuit of knowledge,
in as much volume and haste as possible, bears witness, says
Nietzsche, to 'the union of intelligence and property'.(20) To
be current, coins must, of course, function in the *present*
monetary system: to train for currency, in the schools or
colleges, will then be to train people who will smoothly take
their place in contemporary society. It will be training for, not
against, the times. The meaning of this is clear enough in
connection with schooling whose aims are essentially practical
and utilitarian: pupils will be trained to fill those roles which
the economy of the day (or the day after) requires. But, for
Nietzsche, the same is true of schooling with more scholarly
aims: the tendency is inevitably to furnish people with the
theories and ideologies that presently prevail. Advocates of
education as initiation into knowledge may protest that a main
aim is the development of *critical* reason; but these protests
will not destroy the impression that the main effect is, in the
words of a recent author, to constrain 'the learner . . . to adopt
contemporary attitudes or concern himself with *fashionable*
problems'.(21) Coins, finally, are typically used to purchase
what people will, or think they will be, happy to possess: and
Nietzsche sees any teaching which aims to make men current as
informed by a hedonistic or eudaemonian perspective. Teaching
which emphasizes the practical aims to make men more productive,
in the belief that the more productive, the more happy. And
the aim of knowledge is informed by the idea that the way to
'get the greatest possible amount of happiness and profit' is
from one's 'cognition and knowledge'.(22) In their concerns,
then, with acquisition, with training people *for* their times, and
with happiness - in short with making people current - the two
approaches converge.

Next, Nietzsche suggests that both approaches tend to foster
institutions that can be markedly similar in form, practice, and
organization. In particular, there will be a tendency, on both '
approaches towards *specialization* - and all that implies. In a
society of such technological sophistication as our own - one

which, moreover, has witnessed an extraordinary mushrooming
of knowledge - it is inevitable that training for economic roles,
as well as initiation into disciplined systems of knowledge, must
impose specialization. True, the emphasis may be upon a number
of roles and upon a number of disciplines: but a group of
specialisms does not add up to that holistic education, that
'unity in variety', so admired by Goethe. For Nietzsche,
specialization bears many evils in its train - at any rate, it
does so when pursued at school. For one thing, specialized
knowledge and skills must be monitored: hence the growth of
an awesome examination system. It is in the nature of specialized studies, moreover, to put a premium upon both memory and
speed of learning: for not only is there a 'lot to know', but it
is required that by a certain date one emerges equipped with
one's specialized knowledge or skills. An emphasis upon memory
and speed is, for Nietzsche, incompatible with the development
of that state of mind which characterizes the educated spirit.
Specialization is responsible, finally, for the emergence of one
of Nietzsche's great *bêtes noires;* the journalist - or, today,
the media 'pundit' - as the sketchily informed synthesizer of
all that is happening in the hived-off compartments of knowledge;
the new pale imitation of 'the universal man', the unworthy heir
of the mantle left by a Goethe or a Schiller.

The two approaches are also in league on what they gang up
against. In particular, both have an interest in suppressing the
'solitary' and the 'inner' man. 'All education is (now) hated
which would make a man solitary'; and the person whose primary
concern is with his 'inner' life is accused of 'elevated egoism'
and of 'immoral epicureanism.'(23) Schooling that aims exclusively
at producing people who will be 'current' in the economy can
indeed have little time for the person who wishes to remain outside. And schooling which exclusively emphasizes initiation into
disciplines governed by public criteria of correctness and
importance can have no place, it would seem, for the person's
inner, perhaps emotional, development.

As we shall see in the following chapters, Nietzsche's main
charge against both approaches - emerging already in the
remarks of the last paragraph - returns us to the theme of
authenticity discussed in the first chapter: for the charge is
that neither approach can constitute 'true education', since
neither can foster - indeed, each can only hinder - the authentic
life.

3   Nature and technicism

Training 'breadwinners' and producing 'scholars' may not be polar opposites, for they have aims and enemies in common. There may be as much which unites as divides an education with utilitarian goals and one with the aim of initiation into 'forms of knowledge'. Nevertheless, there is a divide, and if some criticisms apply to both, others will be applicable only to one or the other. In this chapter I focus on the 'breadwinning' approach. I refer to the form it has assumed in modern times as the 'technicist' approach.

By 'technicism' I mean the broad, but identifiable, idea that the technological power at men's disposal is the fundamental feature of our times, and that their energies should primarily be directed towards utilizing this power for the sake of increased material welfare.(1) In its political incarnation, technicism is the view that a prime role of government is to harness this power and channel these energies; a role which people's over-riding desire for increased material well-being gives it a man-date to perform. (How government is to play this role, whether as star of the show or discreetly from the wings, remains dis-puted.) In its educational form, technicism is the view that the main purpose of schools and higher institutions is to train people to contribute and accommodate to a society governed by the general technicist idea. It is not that everyone is to be a trained technologist, but that everyone is to be trained or prepared for filling the roles demanded in a technicist society. Hoteliers and caterers are not technologists, but there is an increasing demand for them in a technicist society; so that, in keeping with this educational idea, we find it urged that people be trained in these jobs at colleges and universities, at the likely expense of more traditional subjects deemed less relevant to modern life.

Bismarck's Germany was still a predominantly agrarian one, even if the growth of iron and blood, of industry and the armed forces, was rapidly transforming it. It is not surprising, therefore, that Nietzsche had little to say about technicism directly. But he did say some things, and much else that he says is transposable; for example, his attack on the yoking of education to the alleged needs of the state - which, in our times, has taken the form of technicism in education.

Nietzsche's central contention is that technicism is 'hostile' to both Life and Nature. If so, and if the aim of education is

that a 'man before all else learns to live' and to do so 'in the
workshop of the only mistress there is, Nature', then technicist
training is not education.(2) The notion of Life is discussed in
the next chapter; in this one we concentrate on technicism and
Nature.

The remarks on Nature in the early writings are punctuated
by metaphysical assertions that do not appeal to the modern
ear. We are told, for example, that it is 'unnatural' to pursue
individual aims like personal wealth, since the world is 'One'
and 'Subjectless';(3) and that Nature is purposive, aiming at
understanding of itself and at the redemption from suffering
such understanding will provide. This is why educators must
help Nature by producing the 'geniuses, saints, and artists'
who, through their understanding, will redeem.(4) It would be
exaggerated to say that Nietzsche did not mean these assertions
seriously; but it is easy to get the impression that they are
inserted less for the contribution they make to his critique
than out of loyalty to his early idols, Schopenhauer and Wagner,
from whom they derive. Assertions resembling these survive,
moreover, into the later writings; but in refurbished and more
appealing forms.

One thing Nietzsche did not mean by Nature was the primitive,
the pre-social, the pre-cultural. The demand that we learn from
'the only mistress there is, Nature' is not the demand that we
'imitate the actions of the tiger' or look to the Wild Boy of
Aveyron for guidance. On the contrary, it is only with the
arrival of 'those true men, those who are no longer animals
(*Nicht-mehr-Tiere*), the philosophers, artists, and saints' that
Nature is first realized.(5) If Nietzsche had meant the primitive,
then he would not have regarded technicism as being hostile to
Nature at all. Like Ortega y Gasset, some years later, he saw
technicism as the continuation of primitive pursuits by sophisticated means. Ortega writes: 'the type of man dominant today is
a primitive one, a *Naturmensch* rising up in the midst of a
civilized world . . . he does not see the civilization of the
world around him, but he uses it as if it were a natural force.'(6)
Ortega means several things in calling the technicist man
'primitive'. Not only does he continue by other means the
primitive's preoccupation with the material and the acquisitive,
but does so by a crude *assault* upon the natural world. Moreover, although the technicist must have an interest in theoretical
matters that the primitive could not, it is of a severely practical
kind, having little in common with that civilized interest in the
natural sciences which, for Hegel or Matthew Arnold, should
be ways of understanding men through their relation to nature.
Finally, like the primitive, the technicist man is submissive,
taking for granted his way of life, and as given the goals of his
society. He is easily drawn on, by the leaders of the pack or by
the captains of industry. Nietzsche, I think, would subscribe
to all of this, in which case his 'natural man', the *'Nicht-mehr-
Tier'*, cannot be the primitive *Naturmensch* or his technicist

descendant described by Ortega.

One notion of Nature, involving the idea of the primitive, Nietzsche is especially keen to dissociate his own from. This is the Romantic notion found in some of Rousseau's writings, especially *Emile*. Nietzsche's Nature, he insists, is not the fictitious Rousseauian world of 'idyll and opera'.(7) On the contrary, the natural world is a cruel, brutal, and highly *inefficient* place; it is likened to a bad archer who has to shoot many arrows before hitting the target. It is a place of waste and superfluity, so that not only would an upbringing which tried to emulate it fail to turn out such nice young men as Emile, but its methods would be extremely uneconomic and hit-and-miss.(8) Nietzsche sympathizes, to be sure, with the 'cries for light, sun, forest, and cliff', and with the disgust for the 'gaudy finery' of social life, which inspire Rousseau's homilies to Nature;(9) but he sees these homilies as misunderstanding the sense in which Nature is indeed something to be honoured and learned from.

It is important to stress the contrast with Rousseau, if only in order to scotch the idea that in appealing to Nature, and in attacking technicism and 'scholarship' alike, Nietzsche must belong to that tradition of 'child-centred' horticultural pedagogy which portrays the teacher as a discreet nurseryman gently tending the natural growth of the budding child. I have already quoted a passage (p. 5) which should scotch this idea, as should the following remarks: 'correct and strong education [*Bildung*] is above all obedience and custom'; 'indulgence of the so-called "free personality" [by teachers] is nothing but a sign of barbarism'; it is a crime to 'have incited someone to "autonomy" at an age when subjection to a great guide [*Führer*] . . . is to be cultivated'.(10) These remarks are only apparently contradicted by a rousing passage which could be mistaken for the words of a disciple of Pestalozzi: 'Your educators can be nothing but liberators . . . [education] is liberation, clearing-away of weeds, rubbish, and vermin which attack the tender buds of the plants. . . . It is the imitation of Nature where Nature is motherly and compassionate.'(11) To begin with, education should only imitate Nature where it is 'motherly and compassionate' – which, we have seen, is not too often. Second, it would reflect a confusion on the part of 'child-centrists', not Nietzsche, to suppose that 'liberation' of the child entails the methods they typically advocate. It is the confusion, roughly, between result and means. That the aim of teaching be some state of freedom cannot entail that its methods be those of the gentle nurseryman leaving the child as free to his natural inclinations as possible. Sometimes a plant is freed by a gentle tug at a weed; but sometimes by wielding a machete. Nietzsche leaves us in no doubt that the 'free spirits' to emerge from a true education will have been submitted to a thoroughly disciplined schooling.

We have not yet identified what, for Nietzsche, that Nature is

which is to act as an educational guide, to which technicism is
hostile, and which only the *'Nicht-mehr-Tier'* realizes. But it
has surely emerged that he does not mean the natural order,
or the world of nature as studied by zoologists, physicists,
and others. It is not Nature as a sum of natural forces, laws,
and phenomena he has in mind. (Clearly the word 'nature'
does bear other senses. The natures of numbers, love, or
democracy are not physical structures.) It is not, though, that
the natural world does not figure in what he has in mind; for
what he means by 'Nature', in the present context, is men's
relation to the natural order. In virtue of having – perhaps,
in some sense, being – bodies, men have innumerable natural
connections with the world. For example, they are nourished
by some bits of it. Such connections are as much part of the
natural order as spatial or causal connections between mere
physical objects. It is not these connections Nietzsche has
in mind, but rather the kind of relation some philosophers have
called 'intensional' or the one we have to the world as it is 'for
us' rather than 'in itself'. It is that umbrella relation which
covers more specific ones such as taking an interest in, having
concern for, interpretation of, or planning for. The natural
connections just mentioned are not of this sort, but are instead
among the objects of such intensional relations – as when someone takes an interest in how he is nourished. These connections
are part of the natural order, not of men's intensional relation
to it.(12)

Technicism, then, will be 'hostile' to Nature if it is incompatible with how men are, or should be, related in the relevant
sense to the natural order. And it would follow, if it is, that
it would also be 'hostile' to Nature in the sense of *human*
nature. This was understood in terms of a capacity for self-
concern, which devolved into such powers as those of reflecting
on one's situation in the world, planning and 'projecting', and
evaluating and interpreting. But these powers are among the
most important relations falling under Nietzsche's notion of
Nature; so that whatever distorts these distorts it. We are
returned, of course, to the topic of authenticitiy; and the
claim that technicism is 'hostile' to Nature involves, or is perhaps identical to, the claim that it is incompatible with
authentic living. We can therefore read the following discussion
in a triple way; it is about technicism's hostility to Nature,
to human nature, and to authenticity.

Two remarks of Nietzsche's set the scene for the discussion:

> *Hubris* is, today, our whole stance towards nature, our
> violation of her with the help of machines and the heedless
> inventiveness of technicians and engineers. . . . *Hubris* is
> our stance towards ourselves, for we experiment with our-
> selves in a way that is not allowed with any animal.(13)

how many young people are not allowed to grow up close to, personally related almost to nature! The rest must, early on, learn a new truth: how to subjugate nature. . . . What is lost through this new form of thinking . . . is the instinctively true and individual understanding of nature. In its place has now entered a clever calculativeness and outwitting of nature.(14)

The four features which best characterize the technicist idea are found here. First, the calculative mentality it reflects and reinforces. It is not simply that technicist investigation of nature is conducted with the devices of calculation and measurement, but that the questions raised are to be settled by calculative, means-end reasoning. They take the form, broadly, of asking how nature's resources are to be most efficiently utilized to achieve certain results, especially the overarching one of increased material wealth. The forest becomes something to measure: it consists of x units of material, the cost of whose utilization will be y, yielding z by way of benefit. Second, large chunks of nature become viewed as fit for 'subjugation'. As Heidegger puts it, nature becomes 'standing-reserve' *(Bestand)*; its contents are viewed teleologically, as resources, reserves, stocks, that we must 'challenge' in order to extract what we can.(15) Energy is not simply used, as the windmill used the wind, but stored up, kept on tap, controlled and let out at the technician's order.

Third, there is the *hubris* Nietzsche mentions. Nature is treated as 'ours', to do with as we please: and the more we do to it, the prouder we are to be. 'Make Britain proud again!' gets read as 'Improve Britain's technological performance!' It is in the transformation of nature that the great endeavour of men resides, the endeavour of *homo faber*. Finally, there is the modulation of these attitudes into ones directed towards men themselves. Men become units in technicist calculation, or dissolved into more convenient units: man-hours, consumer preferences, and the like. Men, too, become 'standing-reserve' - a labour force, manpower, the unemployed, human resources. And *hubris* modulates into pride in the ability to organize and co-ordinate vast numbers of people across oceans, or to devise ingenious work incentives. Human energy is part of the energy which technicism is proud to have harnessed.

There is nothing 'mistaken' in these attitudes. Manifestly, nature can be quantified, utilized, and put on 'standing-reserve'; men can be viewed as integrated components in technological enterprises, and those who integrate them can congratulate themselves on their administrative skills. Not only is there nothing mistaken in these attitudes, but elements of the technicist idea can appear exhilarating. Certainly, this was how the embryonic technological age was greeted by many writers and artists earlier in the century. The sinister Spengler welcomed the technologist as the new 'Faustian man', while the

scarcely less sinister Le Corbusier saw 'the spirit of the
modern age' as the equation of the aesthetic with the precision
of the technical. Marcel Duchamp gave up painting on seeing
the 'perfection' of an aeroplane propeller; and Marinetti's
Futurist Manifesto of 1908 urged people 'to hymn the man at
the steering-wheel whose ideal axis passes through the centre
of the earth'.(16) In some fine passages from *The Flight to
Arras*, Saint-Exupéry describes the exhilarating sense that
his, the pilot's, personal identity is inextricably enmeshed
with the instruments in the cockpit, the aircraft itself, and
the rest of the squadron, its mechanics and hangars. For many
people, clearly, there was the feeling that authentic life in
our century must be one deeply engaged with the technological;
that it must swim with technical advance, and not resist it
with that 'nostalgia for Homeric cheeses and legendary spinning
wheels' of which Marinetti accused Ruskin.(17)

But Marinetti died a jaded man, for already by the 1930s a
car was more likely to be a Model-T stuck in an urban traffic
jam than a Bugatti flying along the open road. His enthusiasm,
moreover, had not been for an industry that would subjugate
nature, by relieving men from the need to walk or ride, but
for something that would bring a person closer to it, with his
steering-wheel joined to the centre of the earth. And for Saint-
Exupéry, it was not technical mastery as such which created a
new sense of identity, but the opportunity it ideally afforded
for emotional ties – love, as he calls it – between people, great
distances apart perhaps, who are engaged in a common enterprise. What men work with or upon, he insists, should never
be viewed merely as materials and machines. To some a farm
may be simply a collection of tools, animals, and stocks to be
utilized; but to others 'there must be something which escapes
material analysis, since there are farmers who are ready to ruin
themselves for their farms'.(18)

For these writers, then, enthusiasm for the technological
was conditional: grounded in the belief or hope that 'living with
machines' would complement, and deepen, attitudes towards
nature and men that should never be lost. They could not have
enthused, therefore, over a society in which the technicist idea
takes over from and drives out these attitudes. And surely the
proper criticism of this idea is its claim to dominance, its
tendency to drive out others. It is not the 'mistakes' in the
technicist idea which depress, but its monopolization of the
contemporary outlook. It would be facile, however, to hold that
it is not the idea as such, but only the idea gone wild, which is
the monster; to trot out the old adage that a gun is only as bad
as the man who wears it. For it is inherent to technology, and
the technicist idea which gives it pride of place, that it should
go wild. The nature of technicist attitudes is to drive others
out, to become exclusive. Nietzsche saw this happening in his
own day, when he expressed the fear that the 'very technical
mastery' of scientists and technologists has as its 'purpose that

of not allowing something to become visible to oneself . . .
[of being] a means of self-narcosis . . . (for) stunned, heed-
less men who fear only one thing: to become conscious'.(19)
Calculative thought threatens to become *the* mode of thought,
and 'standing-reserve' to become *the* concept of nature; pride
in technological achievement becomes *the* form of pride – and
the modulations of these attitudes into ones directed towards
men emerge as the most conspicuous ones of our times. As
Heidegger puts it, it is inherent in the technicist way of
'ordering' or 'destining' our view of nature and men that 'it
drives out every other possibility of revealing [*Entbergung*]
. . . There is then *danger* in the highest sense.'(20)

The danger, ironically, is best confirmed by the many denials,
by its spokesmen, of the dominance of the technicist idea. We
are told, for example, that far from being blind to other human
concerns, the technicist society can alone provide the leisure
time in which people can indulge their interests. Or that, far
from ignoring moral problems, technicism promises, for the first
time perhaps, to solve these. But the very terminology of
these protests betrays the stranglehold of technicist thinking.
Leisure, says the OED, is 'unoccupied time', 'free time'. (The
German word for leisure, *'Musse'*, is a close relative of
'müssig', meaning 'lazy', 'idle'.) To refer to those periods of
life not taken up by contributing through work to society as
'leisure' is already to reveal a stance on what is really reckoned
to be valuable – the occupied periods which leisure punctuates.
It is already to think about men in the ways one does about
non-human ingredients in the productive process, which also
require their rest, their fallow times, before returning refitted,
well-tuned, or relaxed to the real business. Nor, of course, is
it necessary to emphasize the degree to which leisure itself has
become fair game for the application of technology. (The film
critic Pauline Kael attributes the huge spate of 'disaster' and
space movies to the technically oriented training of budding
directors, who are left unable or unwilling to make films that
are not series of technical effects.) Imbued with technicism, too,
is the ubiquitous reference to matters of concern, including
moral ones, as 'problems'. Problems are what can be solved;
insoluble ones being those, simply, which have not yet been
worked hard enough upon. Problems have keys to unlock them,
which the clever can find, and typically they have causes
which, if operated on, get rid of them. To describe the anxieties
and difficulties people encounter in their lives as 'problems'
is already to be on a particular tack: that of looking for keys
or causes, like unemployment or housing conditions or
recreational facilities, to be operated on as the technician
handles the snags and hitches he runs into. The thought that
the anxieties or moral concerns may be part of the human condition, or the condition of technicist society itself, is conveniently suppressed. For it is convenient, besides being generative
of further technicist projects, to suppose that a malaise is due

to some operable factor rather than to technicism itself.
Nietzsche had already observed how comforting it had become,
for the scientific mentality, to treat suffering as 'at most
another problem to be solved'.(21) We see the grip of the
technicist idea when 'moral problems' are given a public airing,
on television say, where the moral aspects are quickly suppressed, mentioned with a certain embarrassment, *sotto voce,*
so that one may get on to the considerations and 'solutions'
which are congenial by the less shamefaced criteria of technicism. A debate about vegetarianism, for example, tends to
become one about the economic and dietary advantages and
disadvantages of meat-eating. RSPCA spokesmen, I believe, are
encouraged not to hark upon the cruelties of farming, but upon
the economic drawbacks of cruel methods. This is not a criticism:
one must commiserate with those who publicly discuss moral
matters in a technicist climate.

How is it that the technicist tends to 'drive out every other
possibility of revealing'? Mainly, no doubt, through people
simply living their lives in an increasingly technicist society;
through going about their business in an environment where
everything, from shop-window to leisure-centre, from factory
to video-cassette, bears witness to its being that kind of society.
But of great importance is the power of technicism to take over
elements of the 'superstructure', the organs of opinion and
ideology. If technology is to grow - and it must if it is not to
collapse - people must want it to; and there are many ways in
which this desire is stimulated. Advertising is only the most
obvious one in which people are brought to place paramount
value upon material possession. In political debate, since the
parties must outbid one another in their promises to further
the economic enterprise, attention is increasingly focused upon
just that: thereby entrenching the idea that here indeed is the
prime concern of government, and thereby either pushing
other matters of debate - education, say - to the sidelines
or translating these matters into predominantly economic terms.
'Do we pay enough attention to education?' comes to mean 'Do
we spend enough upon it?' The time is long past, of course,
when the lieutenants of technicism need consciously to curry
favour for their enterprise, for it is one which feeds on itself,
swells, and digests many ready recruits. In the field of popular
entertainment, for example, *humour* readily enlists. Those who
reject, or try to stand outside, the enterprise are made gentle
figures of fun - 'cranks', 'eccentrics', 'dreamers'. A favourite
comic figure in television series is the person who 'opts out', to
become self-sufficient, or set up a little community of idealists.
The laughs come from the insuperable difficulties he faces, and
the 'happy ending' is his surrender of the attempt, his return
to the suburban house and family business.
    One of the most powerful allies won over to technicism is
language. Philosophers sometimes speak of 'essentially contested

concepts' - like democracy, or education, or insanity - which
have a vague empirical content, but carry strong evaluative
flavour. If I persuade you that such a concept has a particular
content then, *ceteris paribus*, I get you to evaluate that content
in a certain way. The most effective means for 'winning' a
contested concept is not rhetoric or blarney but constant
repetition, constant association of a word with the content,
policy, or whatever that one favours or disfavours. The mass-
media, through advertising, political debate, and much else,
provide previously unparalleled opportunities for those who
speak most and loudest to win such concepts for their own side:
and it is the spokesmen of technicism who speak most and loudest. The results are familiar. Some time ago Kenneth Galbraith
noted that 'progress', unless qualified, had come to mean for
viewers or listeners something like 'growth in GNP'. A 'better
Britain' is a wealthier one; and a 'crisis' - in education, the
arts, football, or wherever - is an economic one.(22)

It is not only individual concepts like 'progress' which get
captured, for the whole circle of terms usable for criticial
evaluation of such concepts also narrows. One is in danger of
running out of terms that have not had their senses closed off.
Someone who tries to query whether technicist advance is
really of paramount value, or something people genuinely want,
or a valid goal of life, is likely to find - unless he is given the
time and sympathy which probably he will not in public forums
- that these notions, too, are closed off for his audience.
Reference to values, wants, and goals is refracted through the
technicist prism.

A pervasive linguistic device, of the first importance, which
technicism wins over is *metaphor*. I do not mean isolated metaphorical uses of individual words, but whole fields or systems of
metaphor in terms of which we talk about, conceptualize, and
display attitudes towards, the world. For example, those
systematic metaphors which constitute 'organic' and 'contractual'
theories of the state. In good times, people are free to create
new metaphors, thereby suggesting new perspectives, dissolving old associations, and paving the way for new conceptions.
But in bad times, when mass-media, public spokesmen, advert-
isers, and other mouthpieces share an outlook, metaphors can
become one-sided and are warped to fit the outlook.(23) Two
examples: forty years ago in his criticism of technicism, Heidegger used the metaphor of 'dwelling' and 'being at home'. In
a technicist society, he wanted to say, where people's roots are
cut, traditional loyalties dissolved, the pace of change is
enormous, and lives are controlled by great impersonal forces,
individuals no longer have a sense of dwelling or being at home
in their world. But such metaphors, like so many, have been
taken over *for* the technicist idea. The 'home' is now a module
within the technicist society, not a refuge from it. Television
brings events 'into your home'; a hamburger restaurant is
'a home from home'; house loans are 'home loans'; discarded

executives find 'new homes' in other firms; caravans are 'mobile homes'. Or, think of the technicist exploitation of military meta-phors: governments 'fight for the £'; industry needs 'the Dunkirk spirit'; people travelling on British Airways are 'flying the flag'; overcoming an economic difficulty is 'winning through a crisis'; successful firms are awarded 'medals'; and we are asked to 'make sacrifices' this year for the sake of next year's, or some year's, GNP so that we may 'beat' the French, Japanese, or whomever. Such metaphors conspire to produce the impression that working for the technicist cause is a life of valour, chivalry, sacrifice, danger, and much else that stirs the soul.

I take it as evident that the attitudes which characterize tech-nicism should not become exclusive and drive out 'other possibilities of revealing'. Calculative thinking should not become the only mode; for it presupposes ends whose attainment is calculated – ends which themselves should be thought about. Nor should nature be simply 'standing-reserve': it should remain a source for rich human emotions, elation or terror; and a place to be studied for its own sake; and an inspiration for analogies and metaphors with which to describe ourselves; and the pro-vider of impressions whose recording is sometimes great art. When nature is utilized, this can be in a spirit of co-operation not subjugation; and those who grow organic foods or build mills in their streams should not be treated with condescending amusement, nor be judged by the criteria appropriate to tech-nicist enterprises, for they are trying to live, partly symbol-ically, in a relation to nature that is different from the technicist. Nor should pride in technicist achievement become the sole kind: there should also be pride in what were once meant by 'the achievements of civilization'.

Ernst Jünger remarked that what makes some lives seem wrong to us, even sinful, is their 'automatism'. The prostitute lives wrongly because she becomes 'a pleasure-machine'; and the miser because he has 'put his heart into matter and lives in metal'.(24) There are obvious ways in which lives become more 'automatized' in technicist society, the ways depicted with suit-able artistic licence in Lang's *Metropolis* or Chaplin's *Modern Times:* but this is not what Jünger meant. We must live with metal, no doubt, but not *in* it. A modern individual cannot keep 'yearning for Homeric cheeses', but nor should he become immersed in the technicist idea, to the mechanical exclusion of those attitudes to the natural world, to human achievements, and to himself, which contrast with the technicist. To do so is to surrender that capacity for reflection, and for openness to 'projects', interpretations, and emotional variety which is exer-cised in an authentic human life.

I have said little about another powerful ally that technicism is increasingly able to call upon – the education system. It is worth noting that the general technicist idea does not entail that edu-

cation should be technicistically bent. Adaption by the young to
a technicist society, it might be argued, is a fairly automatic
process wrought by simply living within it, and does not
require a curriculum with a strong technicist slant. And while
technologists must be trained, this is best done, it might be
thought, through an apprenticeship system or in special institutions outside the main educational stream. Certainly, it would
be a fallacy to suppose that because society has technicist
needs, then all or even very many young people must receive
a technicist education.(25) Security is a national need, but we
are not all to be trained as spies or Special Branch men.

Be this as it may, there is no denying the increasingly technicist appearance and aspirations of our own educational system,
which thereby reinforces the set of attitudes that anyway press
in upon people as they go about their everyday business, read
newspapers, watch television, and simply hear the language
which bombards them. It was the need to devise a curriculum
allegedly suitable to the expectations of a technicist society that
dominated Mr Callaghan's 'Great Debate'; and as R.F. Dearden,
in a sensitive survey of recent government papers, has pointed
out, the technicist idea soon creeps in even when lip-service is
being paid to seemingly contrasting educational goals. For
example:

> *The School Curriculum* (HMSO 1981) affirms in its second
> paragraph the apparently child-centred principle of develop-
> ing individual potential to the full. In the following paragraph
> it defines that potential with reference to the realities of adult
> life, and in the paragraph next after that, adult life is
> defined in terms of a technology-based economy.(26)

Although, as he also points out, much noise is made, in various
reports, about the need for a 'balanced' curriculum, the recom-
mendations which emerge are so biased towards the technological
that the notion of balance is only 'being used to express a wish
for chips with everything, and for everyone'.(27)

The effort to defend education against a take-over by the
technicist idea would be a formidable one, for not only is
government policy shot through with it, but it is the idea which
dominates the wider society in which schools operate. It is
strengthened, too, by the organization of the school system;
in particular by examinations, the need for certificates to be
got or diplomas won. One learns, it seems, in order to get; and
in ways that place a premium upon acquiring and storing information. The task, of course, is not that of promoting the 'arts'
against the 'sciences'; for physics need not be taught as a
handmaiden to technology, while history can be. Even less is
it that of making noises to the young about the profitable use
of leisure, the importance of hobbies, or about taking doses of
culture. The very terminology of leisure and hobbies, and the
association of culture with these - culture as a 'spice', Nietzsche

would say - merely deepen the impression that real life is useful life, the life engaged in the technicist enterprise. But it is not an effort to be shirked by anyone who places the value of authenticity close to the centre of educational concern. An education which meshes too closely with the technicist idea is not compatible with that value, for it is one which stifles or excludes many of those powers into which the capacity for self-concern devolves. It would be an education which, in Nietzsche's sense, is 'unnatural'; an education only in name. Some of my remarks later in the book may be read as suggestions on the form of an education which is not thus enmeshed. Indeed, I shall make one or two now in connection with Mary Warnock's discussion in her influential *Schools of Thought*.

In what she says, or fails to say, about notions like work and leisure, there are weaknesses which make her concept of education less free of the technicist idea than perhaps intended. Work, in her view, is one of the three elements - alongside virtue and imagination - of 'the good life' which schooling must, above all, educate for. She twice invokes Nietzsche's name in support of her contention about work, and it is in connection with these invocations that its disturbing features can be brought out. She is sympathetic to Nietzsche's account of motivation in terms of a 'will to power'; and argues that, if Nietzsche is right, there must be both a will to, and pleasure in, work - all of which would support the view that training for work is a main educational aim. Her reasoning is that work involves 'mastery, or reducing things to order', which is just the sort of thing Nietzsche meant by 'power'. 'The will to power', she suggests, 'is perhaps identical with the will to work.'(28)

But this appeal to Nietzsche is misconceived. First, his 'will to power' is intended as a global explanatory concept, covering the will to lie on a beach or to reflect while taking a country walk as much as the will to use tools, plan towns, or manage factories. Some of the most interesting passages in *The Genealogy of Morals* are those where he tries to show that behaviour like that of the hermit, which at first glance seems unrelated to willing power, is actually saturated with it.(29) Second, Nietzsche was almost as insistent as Marx that most work is distinguished more by the way *it* masters than by the manner in which men exhibit mastery through it. No doubt even the most humdrum work involves some 'mastery' of materials; but the impression much of it gives is that of the labour being one of the materials which are mastered.(30) Finally, in so far as the 'will to power' can, for Nietzsche, take the form of an admirable 'will to work', this is not work in the sense of employment. Despite her comment that 'not all work . . . is, or could ever be, paid',(31) Warnock does seem to confuse work as employment with work in contrast to idleness. It must be the former she has in mind when she says schools should attend to preparing for leisure as well as work, and when she offers as a main reason for the value of work that people find it important to be paid rather than be objects of charity. Work, in this sense, is not something whose merits as such were ever praised by Nietzsche. The most important type of work, indeed – philosophical – is not to be professional nor paid at all.(32) He did not, of course, favour idleness, nor have a dilettante's disdain for activity and effort, whether physical or mental. He was no advocate of buddhistic quietism or epicurean·indulgence. It is simply that, unlike Warnock, he consistently rejected an equation – of a type that falls neatly in line with the technicist idea – of work which is necessarily of value with professional employment or labour.

Warnock makes several proposals for a curriculum in which preparation for work is a major objective. It must include the '3 Rs', teaching about social institutions, preferably a second language, and 'a certain understanding, part practical, part theoretical, of the physical sciences and technology'.(33) I wish only to point to what is omitted here; for nothing is said about the manner, the 'ethos', in which these ingredients are to be taught. Yet this is of the first importance if there is to be resistance to a technicist takeover of education. For example, the manner and spirit in which biology and zoology are taught will affect whether animals become regarded from an instrumental standpoint alone – as items to be worked on, whether in the research laboratory of a cosmetics firm or on the farm – or as more than 'standing-reserve' to be drawn upon for profit or pleasure. Again, mathematics taught one way is an effective bludgeon for shaping a narrowly calculative mentality, for which questions and solutions are cut and dried, and next to which other modes of thought seem stigmatized as 'woolly'; but it can be taught so as to stimulate a questioning, open, imaginative, and creative attitude towards what, at first sight, look to be closed mechanical procedures. (Warnock, I should add, does have a good deal to say about the need for imaginativeness in other sections of her book.)

People, we can agree, must work – be in employment, that is; and they must do so in a society that defines the kinds of work to be done. But we are not obliged, in the ways in which we prepare people for work, to reinforce those features of society and technicist thought which little enough, outside of education, is willing or able to stand against.

4   Life and Liberal Education

We have seen that, for Nietzsche, the 'old maids' of scholarship and the technicist 'breadwinners' may belong to different regiments, but it is the same army. Both aim to make men 'current', both are hostile to 'Nature' and to 'Life'. The critique of technicism implicit in his writings was developed in the last chapter; I now turn to his critique of Liberal Education.

It is not surprising that so many of Nietzsche's arrows were aimed at the dry scholar, devoted to learning for no end beyond itself, for to gauge from the novels of, say, Raabe, this was indeed a familiar figure in nineteenth-century German education. But it is clear that Nietzsche's target was much larger, and included Liberal Education. He refers to his time as one which 'suffers from Liberal Education [allgemeine Bildung],(1) and many of his remarks are directed as much against 'Wissenschaft' - theoretical knowledge and the sciences - as against Gelehrsamkeit. ('Wissenschaft' is usually translated as 'science', but unlike the English word, does not connote natural science in particular.) The target is the idea that the primary aim of education should be to initiate the young into the knowledge and procedures incorporated in a variety of disciplines - such as physics, or history - which purport to explain our experience. The target, for example, that the influential pedagogue, Herbart, presents when he wrote: 'to present the whole treasure of accumulated research in a concentrated form to the youthful generation, is the highest service which mankind . . . can render to its successors'.(2)

Nietzsche's charge is that such an education would fail to help people to 'live'. In his autobiographical Ecce Homo, he reflects that the aim of his early educational writings was 'to bring to light what is dangerous, what gnaws at and poisons life, in our kind of knowledge-industry [Wissenschafts-Betrieb]'.(3) And in one of those early writings, revealingly titled 'Science and wisdom in conflict', the distinction is that wisdom, unlike science, 'displays itself in the applicability of its results to life'.(4) Such a remark is intelligible only if Nietzsche had something special in mind by 'Life', for in some obvious ways, science is clearly applicable to life. Nowhere, however, in the early writings, does Nietzsche offer a succinct characterization of 'Life'. No doubt he had much in mind, but he certainly intended at least what we have been calling 'authentic life'. So to charge that Liberal Education is hostile to Life is at least to accuse it of being inimical to the potential for authentic living.

There is plenty of evidence that this is what he meant. At the beginning of *Schopenhauer as Educator*, he describes con-temporary culture or education as the 'least human' in history, one ruled not by *'living* human beings, but . . . sham ones'.(5) We have already seen how the 'truly human' is tied to the notion of authenticity. At the end of his essay on history, he exhorts the young to 'overcome' their present culture, to submit them-selves to Life, and to do so by following the Delphic oracle's prescription 'Know thyself'.(6) We have seen, too, how Nietzsche's interpretation of the oracle relates to the idea of authenticity. In later writings, the statement 'Life is will to power' is frequently encountered. This does not contradict the suggestion that by 'Life', Nietzsche meant at least 'authentic life', since as we shall see in later chapters, the will to power itself is not to be understood without reference to authenticity.

The concern for authenticity, I argued, devolved into two related ones: the concern to estimate and assess one's 'situation' - how one is, how one is placed: and a concern to make one's beliefs, values and projects 'one's own'. Both of these are to the fore when Nietzsche accuses Liberal Education of being hostile to Life. Pursuit of the kinds of knowledge advocated in such an education not only threatens to distort people's under-standing of their 'situation', but ill-equips them to live in a proper relation to the beliefs and values they confront. On p.30 I listed some of the vituperative epithets Nietzsche hurls at 'scholars'. Some of these, 'idiots', 'flatheads', mere 'chatterers', pertain to the 'scholars'' understanding; while others, 'old maids', 'decadent', 'mirrors' 'herd-animals', 'players on only two strings', pick on their deficiencies as men, as livers of life. The initiate into the established disciplines faces the dual danger of misunderstanding and a distorted life.

Three important preliminaries must be gone through before Nietzsche's critique is unfolded. First, we must identify his target more carefully. It is not restricted to any single view of Liberal Education and the curriculum - to Herbart's 'reader's digest' version, for example, or to Paul Hirst's idea that the curriculum should contain exemplars of each allegedly distinct 'form of knowledge'. It would be possible to hold that *Wissenschaft* should be the primary educational aim without subscribing either to the distinct 'forms of knowledge' hypo-thesis, or to the view that this aim is best achieved in a curriculum divided into traditional disciplines. The target is the following, more general idea. Over the past few centuries, men have developed disciplined, interpersonal ways of arriving at, testing, and critically appraising claims to knowledge that purport to explain the phenomena and experiences men most want explained. These ways include canons of evidence, criteria of verification and of sense, rules of intellectual con-duct, and procedures of enquiry which together have succeeded, over a large area, in producing theories which, if only pro-visionally, promise explanations of what needs explaining.

Moreover, rationality, objectivity, critical awareness, and rigour of thought are only to be attained through initiation into these ways. An educated person is one who has gone through this initiation, in sufficient depth and breadth, to have developed those virtues which constitute 'the development of mind'.

This rubric is sufficiently general to encompass a wide variety of views adopted by those thinking of themselves as Liberal Educationists, yet sufficiently narrow to be pitted against some alternative educational ideologies - against the idea, say, that the primary aim should be character-formation, or the acquisition of common, everyday knowledge that neither belongs to, nor issues from, any disciplines. From now on I shall use 'Knowledge'(capital 'K' and inverted commas) to refer to the kinds of knowledge, understanding, criteria, canons, and procedures which Liberal Educationists consider it to be the prime educational aim to initiate people into.

Second, it would be grossly unfair to portray recent Liberal Educationists as being indifferent to the values Nietzsche has in mind by 'Life'. Their position is not that 'Knowledge' is valuable only for its own sake, unless the point of that flexible slogan is simply to contrast Liberal Education with narrow, vocational training. Richard Peters, in particular, has urged that the values of 'Knowledge' are not merely compatible with, but implicit in, those that are often pitted against them - 'wholeness' and 'self-realization', for example. It is through 'Knowledge', so he urges, that men will become 'whole', and 'realize themselves'. In his most recent writings, indeed, Peters's main argument for 'Knowledge' is the ability it confers to 'cope' with life and the human condition.

> my argument has been that there is a body of knowledge . . .
> that is extremely significant, or 'relevant' to a person in so
> far as it determines his general beliefs, attitudes and reactions
> to the general conditions of human life.(7)

> education should not consist of the accumulation of 'inert
> ideas'. . . . Towards what situations, then, is the develop-
> ment of awareness to be directed . . .? The answer can only
> be 'the human condition' . . . education is concerned with
> learning how to live.(8)

The argument, then, is not whether education should teach to live, but over the form it must take to succeed in this - over, for example, the importance of acquiring those 'essential elements of the different conceptual schemes by means of which various items of information are given a place and organized'.(9) Since education can hardly be conceived as a means, in any straightforward sense, of achieving crystal-clear goals of 'Life', 'wholeness', 'self-realization' and the like, the argument about the proper form of education is bound, in large part, to be one

about what these goals actually consist in. The agreement
between Peters and Nietzsche on these lofty goals may be, and
in fact is, largely illusory.

Third, the critique unfolded in this chapter is independent of
attacks on the possibility of objectivity, truth, and knowledge.
It is not one which is fired by scepticism or by relativism.
(Nietzsche has much to say on these matters, as we shall see
in the next chapter, but they are not the present business.)
It is perfectly possible to think that objectivity and truth are
attainable, but that the chase after their attainment should not
be the main educational enterprise. Truth, someone might
think, is usually too terrible a thing to encourage men to
pursue. Conversely, it is possible to deny that objectivity and
truth are attainable, but to insist - for therapeutic reasons,
perhaps - that it is a good idea to persuade people that they
are attainable, and to exhort them to go in chase. It's the
game, not the victory, that matters.

After a severe cull of Nietzsche's many hostile comments on
'Knowledge', or, better, upon the claims made on its behalf
by educators, I focus upon three themes. In each case, the
theme is that 'Knowledge' is inimical to authentic living. Some
notes sound the idea that 'Knowledge' cannot provide understanding of 'situations', others that it distorts people's relation
to their beliefs and values, or to their 'projective' freedom.
Like Kierkegaard in his *Journals*, Nietzsche would both 'recognize an imperative of understanding', yet insist 'it must be
taken up into my life, and *that* is what I now recognize as the
most important thing'.(10) No less than Goethe does he emphasize
right understanding, but it is with the following remark of
Goethe's that he begins one essay: 'Everything is hateful to me
which merely instructs, without increasing or directly enlivening
my activity.'(11) I dub the three themes 'Understanding as
philosophy', 'Orthodoxy and intimidation', and 'Mind and Heart'.

According to Liberal Educationists, 'Knowledge' offers explanations, along many dimensions, of our 'situations', of the 'human
condition', thereby enabling us to 'cope'. Here, we saw, was a
main defence of 'Knowledge' as a central educational aim. For
Nietzsche, bluntly, 'Knowledge' does nothing of the sort. The
only understanding of 'situations', of the 'human condition', which
is essential to the lives of people in general is *philosophical*
understanding. To the extent that 'Knowledge' tends to drive
out philosophy, or to warp it into something else - history of
ideas, a science, a word-game - it is thereby inimical to the
enterprise of understanding.

The person is so beleaguered by the most serious and difficult
problems that, guided in the right ways, he will succeed to
that philosophical astonishment . . . upon which alone . . . a
deeper and nobler education [*Bildung*] can grow . . .
especially in the stormy days of youth, almost every personal

problem is reflected in a double light, as an example of something everyday and, at the same time, as an eternal, astonishing problem requiring interpretation and understanding.(12)

With their growing emphases upon history and the sciences, schools and universities, he believed, were stifling philosophical thinking, which is the 'highest need' and 'natural instinct' of the young.(13)

To grasp what Nietzsche means, let us first look at some predictable objections that will be raised against the idea that philosophy alone can provide the right understanding our experiences require. Surely, someone will cry, the sciences very often provide results that are of the first importance to our understanding of 'the human condition', of the kind of creatures we are, of our place in the order of things. Think of the impacts of Copernicus, Darwin, Freud, or Gödel. Each of these has, for example, taught us to think more modestly of ourselves. The reply to this is that it is not such discoveries as such which have dictated revisions in our conceptions of ourselves, but philosophical reflection upon the discoveries. That men have developed through a process of natural selection, or that there are mathematical truths which cannot be proved within a complete and consistent mathematics, are as they stand totally neutral to any estimate of our 'condition' or worth. No doubt people have erected models or images of themselves which such discoveries can indirectly disturb, but investigating the sense or otherwise of such models and images, as well as the endeavour to erect more cogent ones, is a broadly philosophical enterprise. Even the creeping tendency to subsume mental activity under physicalistic explanations is, or should be, neutral in its impact on human beings' estimations of themselves. If Shakespeare's genius turns out to be a function merely of his cerebral make-up, it would be just as sensible to raise our estimation of matter as to lower that of genius.(14)

The objection will now be that we are in fact conceding that 'Knowledge' is vital to understanding: for if, as the above examples show, philosophy proceeds by reflecting on the deliverances of the other disciplines, then philosophical understanding must presuppose other modes of understanding. Mary Warnock reflects a popular view when she writes that philosophy is 'to some extent parasitic on other subjects. There is no interest in a theory of knowledge without any knowledge to have a theory about.'(15) But there are misunderstandings here. Certainly Nietzsche never denies that philosophy frequently proceeds by reflection on the deliverances of the sciences. We find him, for example, welcoming the contributions of medicine and biology in preparing 'for the future task of philosophers' - that of 'solving the problem of values'.(16) And there are countless passages where he stresses the need for information which only detailed, empirical research can provide. But such 'admissions' are perfectly consistent with the idea that such information, and the disciplines that generate it, do not provide understanding, but only germane inputs into the philosophical reflection which does. And they are perfectly consistent with the denial that initiation into 'Knowledge' should be a main educational aim or instrument. For appreciation of the impact of certain information on our conception of ourselves and on our understanding of 'the human condition' may require *very little* by way of initiation into the disciplines which provide the information. Certainly the information from medicine and biology which Nietzsche welcomed as being germane to philosophical reflection upon values is not of a kind that only those 'on the inside' of medicine or biology, only those for whom these subjects are encountered as 'Knowledge', can fathom. Nor, to take another example, does one have to be a mathematician to grasp how Gödel's proof dashed the hopes of Formalism. It would, of course, be a giant error - parallel to the 'technicist' one identified on p. 46 - to suppose that, because it is essential for some people to be initiated into a certain discipline, it should be an educational aim to initiate all people into it.

Finally, someone will object that philosophy itself is a discipline belonging to 'Knowledge' - so it remains that one area of 'Knowledge', at least, remains educationally fundamental. The less important reply to this objection is that it would surely be cold comfort to the Liberal Educationist, with his stress upon breadth as well as depth, if just *one* of the disciplines belonging to 'Knowledge' should exhaust the educational enterprise. The more important reply is that philosophy is not a discipline at all. It could be that only if we were talking, not merely about 'professional philosophy', but about some identifiable movement among professional philosophers. For only then would it be feasible to characterize it in terms of some agreed ways of proceeding, criteria of truth, rules of correctness, canons of argument, basic categories and the like. The idea that philosophy at large is *a* discipline, characterizable in such ways, is absurd. A day-trip to Le Havre, where Sartre taught, would soon cure the belief that the 'interpersonal' criteria identifying how philosophy is done at Oxford or London at some particular time are sufficiently interpersonal to span the channel. Whatever Nietzsche meant by 'philosophy', it was not some professional discipline. Indeed, the last chapter of *Schopenhauer as Educator* is an impassioned plea against the professionalization of philosophy. Once it becomes a 'subject', taught by professionals, tested by examinations, it is already dead.

Replying to these objections has only provided a limited grasp on the idea that understanding 'situations' and 'the human condition' must be philosophical. Our grip tightens if we look at the connection which obtains, for Nietzsche, between philosophy, understanding, and values. A 'situation' differs from a mere state of affairs in its relation to choice - of attitude, if not always of action. 'Situations' are, precisely, what call for attitudes or action to be adopted, and in the face of which the failure to adopt one is just that - a *failure*. Falling in love, encountering persecution, being faced with the possibility of great wealth or poverty, 'feeling a book trying to get out', finding oneself in a position of political influence, to be dying: each of these is to be in a 'situation' in the relevant sense. 'The human condition' is constituted by those 'situations' which human beings in general find themselves in. To understand a situation is to have an understanding that can guide one's adoption of attitude or action. A person suddenly confronted with wealth is 'lost', 'confused', 'overwhelmed', 'doesn't know what is happening to him', until he has settled on an attitude towards his wealth and a course of action. Understanding the 'situations' one encounters, or is simply in, is to grasp the attitudes and actions they call for. It is understanding which is at once a response to, and a guide in, positions which demand choices to be made. Necessarily, then, understanding 'situations' and 'the human condition' is understanding that all men must value, and which therefore has a powerful claim to being the kind that education must seek to foster.

For Nietzsche, a primary concern of philosophy is the setting of values, those values which must be set if attitudes and actions are to be adopted in the face of 'situations'. For when a person understands his 'situation' as calling for *this* action, he is placing a value upon it that he does not place on alternatives. In his earlier writings, Nietzsche contrasted 'Knowledge' unfavourably with myth, religion, and morality precisely because the former is not concerned with the setting of values, the guidance of actions: 'The Sciences [*Wissenschaft*] explain the course of nature, but can never give men orders. . . . Religions [and myths] have their strength through being measures of value, yardsticks.'(17) Education centred on *Wissenschaft* is also condemned because 'students and teachers simply neglect *moral* education'.(18) In his later writings, when religion, myth, and morality are no longer accepted as genuine viewpoints, it is philosophy alone which can serve as a 'measure of value', as 'judge of culture', as the provider of understanding that can guide. It is 'true' philosophers alone who are 'the givers of commands and laws: [who] say "This is how it should be."'(19) His point, incidentally, has nothing to do with the so-called 'Naturalistic Fallacy' of deriving value-judgments from factual premises. He is not concerned to deny that there can be such derivations, but to insist that they can only be recognized through philosophical reflection.

The idea that the understanding we require is that of 'situations', and that philosophy, as the setter of values, alone can provide this, gives us part of the explanation of what is meant by 'understanding as philosophy'. The other part of the explanation involves the notion of *meaning*. For Nietzsche, as for many others, philosophy has a distinctive concern with meaning. It is occupied with 'the hieroglyphics of existence',

with providing 'a picture of life as a whole . . . [to] learn from
it the meaning of your life', with being 'the interpreter of
action'.(20) Understanding of meaning, indeed, is a necessary
prelude to the setting of values. 'What men live and experience,
they must interpret for themselves somehow, in order to
evaluate.'(21) Understanding 'situations', then, requires understanding their meanings, their significance; it is, in some sense,
conceptual understanding.

The remarks just quoted show that, for Nietzsche, the
meanings with which philosophy is concerned are not, or not
primarily, word or sentence meanings. The task is not the
'linguistic analysis' or 'conceptual analysis' of terms like 'love',
'wealth', or 'death'. Nietzsche is not wedded to, and is in fact
hostile to, the kinds of distinction which must be taken seriously
if labels like 'linguistic' or 'conceptual analysis' are to be taken
seriously - distinctions between the analytic and the synthetic,
perhaps, or between conceptual and contingent truths, or
between criterial and evidential questions. If the 'linguistic' or
'conceptual analysis' of, say, 'death', were thought to aim at
providing a definition of the word, or criteria for its proper
use, then Nietzsche's interest would be in both more and less
than this. Some attempts at definition - in terms, perhaps, of
brain-function - would be beside the point, while some information, definitely not of a definitional or criterial kind - about
attitudes towards burial, for example - could be highly pertinent
to the understanding being sought.

Although philosophical understanding is not 'linguistic
analysis' in the familiar sense, it will be peculiarly engaged in
the examination of language. This is partly because the best,
and sometimes only way of discovering what 'situations' mean
or signify for people is to look at what they say: in particular,
at the stocks and webs of clichés, metaphors, hyperboles,
analogies, slogans, chatter, and received truisms that attach
to and envelop the 'situations' which love, wealth, death, and
so on, present. But, more than that, these stocks and webs in
part constitute the 'situations', so that examination of them is
less a means to grasping how people conceive of objects than a
requirement for grasping what those objects are. Or rather,
there is no real distinction here. 'Situations' are encountered
only in so far as they are conceived of in certain ways by
people; and how they are conceived of - what they are - is
partly constituted by the talk about them. In a society where
death is not 'tragic', 'so final', 'a topic to avoid', what the
dying man faces is importantly different from what he faces in
our society. In Chapter 1 I urged that the language one is
brought up to speak - including these webs and stocks - is an
important element of the condition one is 'thrown' into, and
one that constrains any Dadaist attempt at sudden and total
overthrow of inherited beliefs and values. Part of what was
meant by this, we now see, is that the various 'situations'
people encounter are to a degree defined by the stocks and webs

embedded in that language. Whoever is to become clear about
the meanings of these 'situations' for him must inevitably confront, examine, and take a stance towards these webs and
stocks. It comes as no surprise to find Nietzsche treating
'practical training in speech' and 'linguistic self-mastery',
which will involve a sharp ear for cant, misleading metaphor,
and mere chatter, as a 'holy duty' of true education.(22)
   It is clear, I think, that 'Knowledge' could play only a modest
role in the understanding of meanings, in the sense sketched.
Its methods and deliverances would have almost as little relevance
to the concept of death, say, as the chemistry of paint does to
aesthetic appreciation. I keep mentioning death, not out of
morbidity or at random, but because it is a topic that R.S.
Peters has used more than once to illustrate how the various
disciplines belonging to 'Knowledge' may come together to
provide understanding. But I fail to see how. A person is faced
with the stance he should adopt towards dying and death,
especially his own. This will involve raising and trying to
answer many questions: 'Is it sensible to regard death as both
inevitable and tragic?' 'Does the fact that I shall die have any
bearing on the importance of my activities and achievements?'
'Should I today act with the full realization that I might die
tomorrow - or should I put that entirely out of mind?' 'Is it the
main job of doctors to save lives?' 'Do I want people to be
entirely honest about my illness?' These questions arise against
a background of received opinions - on the 'tragedy' and
'finality' of death, for example; and of practices - solemn
burials, whispering secrecy. It is, of course, true that reflection on these opinions and practices, and the attempt to answer
the questions just cited, will utilize various facts - about the
suffering a prolonged death may bring, for instance, or about
different burial practices in other cultures. But these are
facts readily available and intelligible to enquiring people, and
their bearing upon the questions cannot justify Peters's view
that here we have an example of 'integration . . . in which
different types of understanding interpenetrate in the spheres
of knowledge which are relevant'.(23) Were he right, the person
initiated into the various 'relevant' disciplines should have a
more intelligent understanding of, a more enlightened attitude
towards, death. But there can be no experts here - unless we
mean those, simply, who have reflected a good deal on the kinds
of questions mentioned. Doctors, for example, are in no better
position than others to answer these questions, not even the
one about whether the main job of doctors should be to save lives.
   Following Husserl, R.K. Elliott writes:

Science . . . no longer provides an understanding of the
reality with which it was originally concerned . . . it is far
from inconceivable that a discipline should go on using its
criteria effectively and all its practitioners be satisfied with
it, yet no one know exactly how it is 'organizing experience'

or exactly what it is they are understanding in depth.(24)

This may be taken to mean, perhaps, that there was a time
when the budding sciences, precisely through their discipline,
provided theory and information necessary to combat the sheer
ignorance of people about their 'situations' - a time, moreover,
when only those engaged in these disciplines could properly
appreciate the theory and information. Today, however, such
theory and information has either entered the common, everyday consciousness, or is readily available at the request of
the enquiring person. Today, it is simply untrue to pretend that
only those who are initiated into various disciplines are in a
position to 'organize their experience' about the 'situations'
they encounter. It is a pretence that is perhaps based on a
confusion: a confusion between our experience and the objects
we experience, or between our concepts and the phenomena
to which they apply. Clearly there is no limit to what 'Knowledge'
may have to tell us about these objects and phenomena. Experts
from all directions can tell us any amount about births, deaths,
orgasms, bankruptcies, brains, and books. But it does not
follow that we are being told anything about how we do or
should experience these things. An encyclopaedic knowledge of
hormones, glands, or contraception tells me nothing about my
experience of sexual pleasure, about how I should 'organize'
that experience in my life, the weight I should give to it, the
place it has in my marriage, the reaction I should have when
age reduces it. The world of 'situations', the 'human condition',
is *our* world - a world as experienced, conceived of, and spoken
about by creatures that must adopt attitudes and take actions.
It is not another world - either that of physics or metaphysics -
but it is the one which men most seek understanding of, and
the one with which education should hold out the hope of
helping them 'cope'.(25)

I now turn to the theme dubbed 'Orthodoxy and Intimidation'.
While, as we have seen, Nietzsche sometimes praises the usefulness of 'scholarship', and the sober virtues of 'scholars', he
also emphasizes its dangers to the person. Only the 'strong',
for example, can devote themselves to historical studies without
being diminished as persons.(26) It is no accident, perhaps,
that Michel, the hero of André Gide's novel, *L'Immoraliste*, is a
historian, for Gide was one of the first major writers to come
under Nietzsche's spell. Despite the title, the book is less about
Michel's revolt against morality than his disillusion with 'acquired
knowledge of every kind that has overlain the mind . . . like a
mask and paint . . . [hiding] the very flesh of the authentic
creature that had lain beneath it'. Michel has been 'strong'
enough to reassert his individuality against the dangers of
'scholarship',

I ended by despising the learning that had at first been my

pride: the studies that up to then had been my whole life now seemed to me to have a mere accidental and conventional connection with myself. I found out that I was something different . . . that I had a separate existence of my own.(27)

It would be wrong to think that Gide's target, any more than Nietzsche's, is 'scholarship' alone: both writers' warnings concern the dangers of 'Knowledge' for the individual.

One pair of warnings Nietzsche offers seems, at first blush, to be inconsistent. For he complains about both the constricting conservatism of the disciplines, and their excessive emphasis upon criticism. One feels like replying that criticism is an anti- dote to conservatism, while a dose of conservatism is an antidote to wild, untrammelled criticism. Can he be entitled to complain in one passage of 'dullness', 'habitualness', 'imitativeness', and failure to appreciate the 'great and the uncommon', and in another that 'criticism has no effect . . . [that] in the extrava- gance of . . . critical effusion . . . the weakness of the modern personality is betrayed'?(28)

I want to look at this dual complaint in connection with recent defences of Liberal Education; for if there is tension in it, this is fully matched by a tension in the dual defence of 'Knowledge', as a central curricular aim, offered by several writers. They stress, on the one hand, that initiation into 'Knowledge' is into *established, rule-governed* activities; and, on the other, that this is initiation into *critical* activity. Richard Pring, for example, says that a discipline is 'logically connected with following or submitting to rules', and refers to the 'rules of activities that scientists or historians or philosophers typically engage in', as well as to 'the rules to which the disciplined man submits'. Submission to such rules, indeed, is said to be essential 'in developing the minds . . . of pupils'. At the same time, he insists, 'openness to criticism, and respect for other people as the possible source of criticism, is the first of the intellectual virtues to be fostered through the curriculum'.(29)

Pring would deny that there is any tension in his position, for among the 'rules of a discipline' are what he calls 'rules of criticism': so that to submit to a discipline's rules is, *ipso facto,* to submit to critical openness. Like many other writers, including Paul Hirst, he is fond of analogies between disciplines and games or languages, or best of all, those popular hybrids 'language-games'. But, to the extent that these analogies hold, they make nonsense of the idea of 'rules of criticism'. There may be rules of English – such as that regular nouns take 's' in the plural – but English contains no rules of criticism. Those who enjoy criticizing English, because it isn't Latin or doesn't have the structure of predicate logic, may erect some rules, but these are not rules of the English language. No more do the rules of soccer include ones for criticizing the game. In general, an activity can hardly be *governed* by rules if some of them – the alleged 'rules of criticism' – allow the 'players' to dispute what the rules are.

Perhaps what these writers mean to say is that the disciplines have their rules - though not special 'rules of criticism' - and that it is by reference to these alone that methods, arguments, theories, and conclusions of the respective disciplines can be criticized. Criticism which does not proceed in accordance with these rules will either be wild, since it does not invoke rules at all, or it will be irrelevant, since the rules appealed to will be those of the wrong discipline. It would be like criticizing English either on no basis at all, or on some alien basis, such as the rules of Swedish.

I have three points to make; first that the disciplines are not governed by rules at all; second, that there is a strong tendency for people to suppose they are; and third that this tendency can at once stifle, yet produce the illusion of, critical openness. It is particularly young 'initiates' who are thus doubly threatened. When Nietzsche complains of the conservatism of 'Knowledge', he is attacking the idea that it is rule-governed and the constricting effect of this idea: and when he complains of 'critical extravagance', he is attacking the illusion of critical openness with which this idea is coupled - and which does its own job of constricting.

The studies of philosophy, physics, logic, history, and so on, are not, in any serious sense of the term 'rule-governed'. To suppose they are can only be the result of confusion about various ways in which rules do relate to disciplines. First, of course, it may be the aim of some disciplines - formal logic, say - to formulate rules. These are not rules *of* the discipline, but its output. Second, any activity which employs language, mathematics, or logical reasoning will, with a qualification, be bound by those rules (if one wishes to speak of them) which belong to language, mathematics, and logic. This, of course, will be true of all relevant activities - gardening and collecting antiques, included - not only of the disciplines. It would be quite wrong, as we have just seen in the case of logical rules, to suppose that the rules of a language, of mathematics, or logic belong peculiarly to the disciplines of linguistics, mathematics, and logic. The rules of English or of algebra are what are studied or formulated by those engaged in the disciplines of linguistics or mathematics - not rules of those disciplines. If Noam Chomsky says 'I eated a good breakfast', he has broken a rule of English, not of his chosen discipline. There may, third, be some very general 'rules' governing any serious intellectual activity; but if they are to receive the general assent required for them to count as rules, they must be, or border upon, the truistic. I mean such 'rules' as 'Try to gather good rather than bad evidence.' Even such advice as 'Make sure you avoid contradictions', or 'Don't accept conclusions until you have firm evidence for them', 'Never violate the truths of mathematics', do not express rules which practitioners of a discipline must follow on pain of being branded a non-practitioner. This was why a qualification was needed to the claim that, in any discipline, one must be bound by rules of language, mathematics, or logic. When an empirically well-founded theory, such as quantum mechanics, seems to run foul of normally accepted rules of logic, or when a plausible theory of meaning seems to run counter to some traditionally accepted bit of mathematics, it is not obvious that it is the theories which must be sacrificed. And it would be merely absurd to suppose that those who hang on to the theories, even if mistakenly, are failing to practise within a discipline.(30)

It is true, finally, that within a discipline, at a time and place, certain procedures or approaches become so popular among certain practitioners, and their students, that they begin to get looked upon as rules - as procedures or approaches that must be adopted if one is to remain within the discipline. Perhaps, for example, the practice of looking at the functions of behaviour, and not at the explanations offered by agents, became among some sociologists, in certain places and for a certain period, a 'rule of sociological method'. And perhaps among some philosophers in some parts of England for some years, the close examination of the use of words in everyday contexts became a 'rule'; those who did not go in for such examinations simply weren't 'doing philosophy'. But these are not examples of 'rules' of philosophy or sociology, except in an ironic sense. They are examples of policies favoured by . . . , at . . . , in. . . . This is not to castigate, or even to criticize, the policies: maybe they were, and are, the best ones. But it should not be pretended that those who did not favour them were, by 'breaking rules', thereby placed in some limbo outside of the disciplines. Surveyed as a whole, and over a reasonable timespan, a discipline will only display a variety of procedures, methods, styles, presuppositions, and fashions - each with its champions and opponents. (The reader may wonder, if all of this is so, why I talk of 'disciplines' at all. I do so only because everyone else does: it is not a way of talking I like, being only marginally more fortunate than the talk of 'rules'.)

There is an unsurprising tendency for people to elevate their procedures to the status of rules. If they do things a certain way, for sufficiently long, and with sufficient reinforcement from colleagues and pupils, they may lose the sense that there could be other ways. Habit, as Hume noted, breeds a sense of necessity. Nor are the propagandist advantages of this elevation to be overlooked. To be persuaded that one's way of doing things is demanded by 'the rules' is to exonerate oneself and others from having to come to grips with other ways - for these are the ways of those who do not play the same game, who are not engaged in the discipline at all. This is why the talk of a discipline's rules, metaphorical as it is, is a serious matter, for like many metaphors it can be a dangerous one. It can only contribute to that 'scholarly' conservatism that Nietzsche attacks. The more practitioners convince themselves that their way of

proceeding is 'rule-governed', the more they insulate themselves from the objections of mavericks within their field, from
criticisms stemming from other fields, and from the doubts
expressed by everyday, unprofessional thinking. The maverick
becomes a professional fouler, the critic from another discipline
becomes like someone who complains of what happens at Wembley
because it differs from what happens at Lords, and the 'man
in the street' becomes the callow tourist, equally lost at
Wembley and at Lords.

It is no reply to cite examples where the maverick, the outsider, and the amateur have had their impact, for this impact
must be *despite* the awesome armour that the disciplines wear in
the minds of those who view them as systems of rules. More
important, we have no way of telling how many potential mavericks, outsiders, and amateurs have been stunted. I say 'more
important', since our concern with 'Knowledge' is in connection
with education. It is not the unfortunate effect that the 'rule'
metaphor may have upon the disciplines themselves, but upon
those who are to be 'initiated' into them as the fundamental
part of their education, which is our main worry. R.K. Elliott
puts it well when he says we must encourage the young to
'develop points of view of their own without first having to
confront the intimidating power of orthodoxy'. Yet to teach the
disciplines, as bodies of rules, is precisely to conjure up that
power, and to constrain the young mind 'to adopt contemporary
attitudes . . . concern himself with fashionable problems . . .
to follow accidental conventions as if they were essential means
to understanding'.(31)

If there is the powerful tendency suggested for practitioners
of 'Knowledge' to see and promote their activities as rule-
governed, then it will be disingenuous to hold that it is not
'Knowledge', but only some particular and mistaken conception
of it, which threatens to intimidate the young. For such
intimidation is an endemic tendency, especially when 'Knowledge'
is presented to the young as the fundamental moment in the
'development of mind'. It is not some unsightly growth that can
be conveniently cauterized. This intimidating orthodoxy will
be particularly acute in schools, where the practitioners -
teachers and pupils - lack the time and freedom of those at
universities, or of those outside the official educational system,
to encounter and explore the unorthodox.

This 'intimidating power of orthodoxy' is disguised, and hence
abetted, by a sense of there being, at a certain level, a
feverish amount of critical activity going on. The disguise is,
ironically, a consequence of the emphasis upon rules - for the
more rules there are, the greater is the scope for deviation
from them, and hence for criticism. When a language becomes
more rule-bound, then what had been different ways of talking
within the community now become deviant, mistaken ways. Of
course, the deviations must not be too gross, for then they
cease to be deviations: a different language is being spoken, a

different discipline engaged in. But deviations of the right size provide unlimited scope for criticism within a discipline, or within a certain group of its practitioners, however orthodox things seem from a more removed vantage-point. A 'school of thought' within sociology, say, or philosophy may conduct itself within narrow limits, yet simultaneously generate journals packed with comments, and comments on comments, on the exact ways to proceed by its rules. There may, at least for a time, be a great sense of excitement, the smell of blood, and flexing of intellectual muscles; while from only a slightly wider or later perspective, the buzz of activity can appear almost embarrassingly parochial. The hunt that is on is not Nietzsche's 'great hunt'; much of it is 'mere virtuosity'. 'Nothing leads to a result, but only to another criticism: this criticism itself has no effect, but only undergoes criticism.'(32) But, for the young mind, this 'extravagance of critical effusion' creates the sense of a critical space that may be no more than a clearing within a stockade. The exercise of the interpretative, creative, 'projective' capacity has become illusion.

'Surely you are not suggesting that anyone who is not "inside" a discipline is in a position to offer serious or radical criticism!' In a number of ways, I would want to suggest precisely that. The insider, for example, is not in a sovereign position to judge the importance of some theoretical enterprises, unless importance is completely, and unwarrantedly, relativized to the discipline. Nor is only he in a sovereign position to assess the 'translation' into more ordinary language that his professional pronounce- ments must undergo if they are to be intelligible to people at large. It is not, for example, the computer scientist who is necessarily best placed to assess the mentalistic language used to describe the operations of computers in popular expositions. Nor is the insider the one best placed to engage in that 'genealogical' reflection on the motives, ideological assumptions, and pragmatics of 'Knowledge' which can be a more effective counter to passive acceptance of prevailing trends than inter- nally generated criticism.(33) But even if criticism of disciplines had to be 'internal', it would not follow that the best way to foster critical thinking was *via* initiation into the disciplines. That would only follow if it was held that the most important dimension of criticism to foster was in the terrain occupied by the disciplines. If the argument of an earlier part of this chapter is correct, this is not so: it is with philosophical under- standing, in the sense sketched, that the fostering of critical openness among the young is most vital - and these are not questions belonging in the province of any discipline. A hawk- eye for the errors of one's fellow mathematicians or sociologists could coexist with a total blindness towards the cant and confusions embedded in talk about 'the human condition'.

Authenticity, we decided in Chapter 1, belongs to lives, and therefore embraces more than the beliefs, interpretations, and 'cognitive' activities of men. Feelings, emotions, and the 'affective' are also to have their place in authentic living. In this final section, which I dub 'Mind and Heart', I touch briefly upon what, for Nietzsche himself, is perhaps the most worrying danger presented by 'scholarship' and 'Knowledge': the impact upon men's emotional attitudes towards their world and one another. My treatment is brief, because Nietzsche's contentions belong at a level of speculative psychology where the nature of assessment is obscure. His remarks are, however, perceptive, and no account of Nietzsche's critique of 'Knowledge' could simply leave them out.

The 'scholar', says Nietzsche in the sixth chapter of *Beyond Good and Evil,* runs the risk of becoming 'cold and closed-in', 'his eye like a flat reluctant sea, in which there is no ripple of delight or compassion', of losing 'the bold joy in wanting', and of having to feign emotions as a *'tour de force'*. These comments belong with many others whose drift is that 'Knowledge' threatens emotional capacity. This contention, with its Romanticist roots, is at some odds with the prevailing view that it is precisely *through* 'Knowledge' that emotional attitudes are to be best shaped. This is a view manifested in many ways: for example, in the increasing tendency to respond to difficulties in personal relations between different groups of people – racial groups, say – by immediately calling for more information, by setting up committees, and by hauling in experts who will provide the antagonistic parties with the under- standing that will reduce or abolish the antagonism. Typically, of course, it remains obscure what the nature of the relevant information and knowledge is supposed to be; and when 'dialogues' between the parties do seem to have some success in improving relations, the suspicion is that this is due less to what anyone *learned,* than to the simple phenomenon of rubbing shoulders together. Schiller was perhaps right in attributing to 'the egoism of reason' the idea that it is knowledge, and more knowledge, which is required in such cases, rather than encour- agement of 'the capacity . . . to take up strange natures . . . into ourselves . . . to make alien feelings our own'.(34) Certainly we should not confuse being understanding of people with piling up more information about them.

A different manifestation, this time at the theoretical level, is R.S. Peters's influential account of the education of the emotions as a thoroughly cognitive endeavour. If it were not, he says, there could be no educating the emotions at all, only training people into 'appropriate appraisals and habits of response'. His argument is that since emotions are 'differentiated by their cognitive core, by the different beliefs that go with them' then, 'if . . . we are contemplating changing people's emotional attitudes . . . our main task consists in trying to get them to see the world differently in relation to themselves'.(35) Unless this claim is to be tautologous, 'see the world differently' must refer to a cognitive change in beliefs. Peters's account is not, naturally, without its critics. It is hardly obvious, for example, that all emotions are, or are mainly, distinguished by the beliefs 'that go with them'. More important, it would anyway remain unclear that the 'main task' must be to change emotions *via* changes in beliefs. In some cases, surely, the more vital task would be to put someone in the way of those experiences - musical ones, say - which might elicit feelings of which he had hitherto been incapable. Of course, if 'educating the emotions' is defined in cognitive terms, then eliciting feelings through musical experience will not belong to it; but the question would then be whether *education* of the emotions is the teacher's 'main task'.

Nietzsche's view is that an education of the emotions through 'Knowledge' would threaten the very emotionality it purports to direct and refine. And this is because 'Knowledge', generally, threatens emotional capacity. His points are best grasped in connection with two metaphors he borrows from a long tradition in German thought. There is, first, the metaphor of 'Knowledge' as 'destructive' and 'dissolving'; and second, the metaphor of it as placing a 'screen' or 'veil' between the individual and his world. The 'scholar', he says, wants to 'kill [and] dissolve' by his analyses; especially to 'dissolve' people who, like so many Humpty Dumptys, cannot then be put together again by subsequent syntheses. And the 'screen' metaphor is illustrated in this remark: 'Whoever lets concepts, opinions, past events, books enter between himself and things . . . will never see things for the first time, nor ever be one of those things seen for the first time.'(36)

The point about 'dissolution' was touched upon during the discussion of technicism in Chapter 2. It is the way of calculative, technicist thought to 'dissolve' or 'reduce' natural objects and people to units fit for quantification, cost-benefit analysis, and the like. But reductionism of some sort, and to some degree, is characteristic of each main empirical discipline, and not only the overtly technicist ones. Nor is it confined to the natural sciences, for the social sciences with their treatment of people as bundles of roles, drives, preferences, or whatever, follow the same recipe as analysis of objects into collections of particles or cells. Nietzsche's point is not that there is anything mistaken, for certain purposes, with such analyses - though no doubt people make mistaken claims about their status. It is, rather, that immersion in disciplines which conduct these reductions has an irretrievable impact upon emotional attitudes towards the objects and persons variously 'dissolved' by them. They become viewed as 'points in a process' - or, better, points at which several processes intersect - and thereby lose their flavour of individuality. The world, it seems, can be described without reference to *them*, but only to the process of which they are the temporary intersections.(37) If in one lesson a person is treated as a bundle of cells, in the next as a conglomeration of drives, there is difficulty in returning to that image of

him as a unitary individual which is the foundation for adopting
personal feelings towards him. It is not that, for Nietzsche,
the person is a metaphysical entity transcending whatever can
be described in terms of cells, roles, and the like, but that such
descriptions are privative and abstract, obtained in a parasitic
way from the notion of a person as a unitary whole. It is as if
one were to view a sonata as a collection now of notes, now of
chords, now of progressions, and never as a musical whole.
And just as an overdose of musicology might destroy a student's
ability to retrieve his original, emotional encounter with the
sonata, so, thinks Nietzsche, immersion in the reductive disciplines may sever affective ties between persons. Whether any
loss in emotional attitudes is a rational response to scientific
dissection is not what is important. The important thing is that
there is this loss; and the attempt to defend against it explains
a number of Nietzsche's quite specific educational proposals,
for example his insistence that education must grant a large
place to good, especially good classical, literature. For in the
best literature, people are treated as whole persons, in the
round as it were; and not taken to pieces in the manner of the
sciences, or that of the 'naturalistic' novels Nietzsche detested,
where the characters are reduced to points in (usually seedy)
psychological or social processes.(38) He was hostile, too, to
that kind of art history which proceeds by delving into the
lives of the great artists; for by turning the artist into a set
of hereditary traits, psychological urges, or manifestations of
social trends, such studies dissolve the affective relation that
should exist towards the artist and his work.(39)

Reductions in the sciences are not normally pursued for their
own sake, but as preludes to generalization, to subsuming the
particular phenomenon under general laws or tendencies.
Objects are first broken down into elements about which generalizations are feasible; then, ideally, these generalizations are
fitted together to yield ones about the original objects. It is
this urge to generalize which characterizes, and is perhaps
definitive of, the disciplines that is the main culprit in placing
a 'screen' or 'veil' between the individual and his world. There
is, thinks Nietzsche, a directness of contact between people
and the objects of their experience, including other people,
which can be destroyed by the interjection of generalizations.
Objects and people get viewed as instances, or examples, of
something more general, and are thereby deprived of that
uniqueness and immediacy which is the source of emotional
effect. His point, here, is not a philosophical one; at any rate,
he is not (as we shall see in the next chapter) claiming that
there are 'raw' experiences, intuitive acquaintance unalloyed
by concepts. He is drawing attention, rather, to a familiar,
yet pathological kind of experience which is most acute among
those 'ruined by scholarship'. A good example of such a victim
would be Mr Casaubon in *Middlemarch*. On his visit to Rome
with Dorothea, Casaubon is totally unable to enjoy the Raphael

frescoes, or anything else, since he can see them only as
instances - and only then through the estimations and opinions
of others. His dry, generalizing replies to her question 'But
do you care about them?' do not 'give her the hope that if she
knew more about them the world would be joyously illuminated
for her'. For Casaubon - 'a mind in which years full of knowledge seem to have issued in a blank absence of interest or
sympathy' - even Dorothea has become an example: she was
'not only his wife: she was a personification'.(40) Nietzsche,
in fact, invents his own Mr Casaubon when he imagines a
'scholar' who tries to force himself to think on certain of his
personal problems, such as his state of health and lack of
companions - 'But in vain! Already his thoughts wander away
to the *more general* case . . . he has lost seriousness, and
time, for *himself.*'(41) He is a man, no doubt, who when faced
with the personal problems of a friend will soon be talking about
'cases like yours', 'people's problems', or 'one's difficulty'.

I do not know how to assess the claim that immersion in ways
of thinking whose aim is to reach generalizations, to discover
what items are instances of or data for, helps to produce the
Casaubons who are unable to enjoy, or relate in any direct
manner to, people and things. The same is true of the previous
claim about the impact of analysis and reduction. They are
vague claims, but I think perceptive ones. Individual readers
must consult their own experiences, of themselves and their
acquaintances, to judge how apposite they may be.

Nietzsche's contentions about the impact of 'Knowledge' upon
the emotions do not directly contradict Peters's point about
educating the emotions through understanding. But there is a
tension, which soon becomes extreme when understanding is then
interpreted in terms of 'Knowledge'. For, if Nietzsche is right,
whatever might be gained by way of *educating* the emotions
would be more than offset by losses in the emotions themselves.

5 Nietzsche's philosophy of truth

The preceding chapter was about 'Knowledge', not knowledge, and the criticisms brought against the former as a central educational aim were more or less independent of views on the nature, or availability, of the latter. To charge that the kinds of knowledge provided by the disciplines are not of the educational moment often assumed is not, of course, to deny that what is provided is indeed knowledge. Nietzsche does, however, have a great deal to say about the nature of knowledge, truth, objectivity, conceptual schemes, and scepticism: in short he has an epistemology and metaphysics. They are, moreover, of striking and stimulating originality. (One result of the strange neglect, in the English-speaking world, of Nietzsche's views on truth and knowledge is that several of these are wrongly thought to be the original creations of later philosophers.) In this chapter, I hope to provide a sympathetic account of these ideas, one which will lend order among claims that, at first blush, seem barely reconcilable. It is never easy to assess, though always easy to exaggerate, the impact of deep philosophical theses upon practice; but I think it will emerge, towards the end of the chapter, that Nietzsche's philosophy of truth harmonizes well with the critique of 'Knowledge', and that it both complements and enriches the idea of an education revolving about the notion of authenticity.

An account of Nietzsche's philosophy of truth must begin with the central role he ascribes to language, for only with this does there 'emerge for the first time the contrast between truth and falsehood'.(1) The starting point is the Kantian thought that experience is only possible for self-conscious beings, for only these can distinguish states of themselves from objects they experience, how things seem from how things are. The drawing of these distinctions requires that our 'sensations' and 'sense-impressions' be brought under concepts, for they will not otherwise display the order and recurrence which provide the essential background against which the distinction between 'seems' and 'is' can gain purchase. To this thought, Nietzsche applies a linguistic turn. 'Concepts', he says, '[are] only possible where there are words.' 'We cease to think when we try to do so without the constraint of language.' We can only 'fix' experiences, and 'as it were place them outside of ourselves' when we 'communicate them to others through signs'.(2)
The central thought here is the one attributed to Wittgenstein

in his attack upon 'private language'. To have a concept is to
classify distinct items of experience as being similar; but
criteria of similarity are the interpersonal ones provided by a
public language. Only, says Nietzsche, where there is 'a
uniformly valid and binding designation of things' is a concept
possible.(3) In an early article, the claim is that items in
reality are not similar, so that 'every concept originates through
making alike what is not [really] alike'.(4) In later writings,
this is replaced by the better idea that no sense can be given
to the notion of similarity except in terms of items being brought
under concepts by us. For Nietzsche, as for Wittgenstein,
concepts do not emerge through paying private attention to
inner experience, on the contrary, 'inner experience enters
our consciousness only after it has found a language the individual understands'.(5) There are no 'raw' experiences waiting
to be classified according to their natural similarities. 'I also
maintain the phenomenality of the inner world: everything of
which one becomes conscious is thoroughly arranged, simplified,
schematized, interpreted'.(6) It is, for example, only *pleasure*
that I experience on an occasion because there is a public
language by whose criteria this experience is classified along
with some, and not other, experiences.

Since conceptualization and consciousness are functions of
language, then the communicative needs to which a language
answers, and the constraints these impose upon it, will pro-
foundly shape our conceptual scheme. 'The refinement and
strength of consciousness always stand in relation to the
communicative ability of a man . . . and the communicative
ability in turn to communicative need'.(7) Originally, that
'most endangered animal', man, needed to communicate to
secure help and defence. Certain 'sensations' induced someone
to call out 'Tiger!' as a cry for help; the practice spread, so
that 'tiger' eventually became a referential term for the alleged
cause of these 'sensations'. The 'sensations' are now experiences, since they are now related to similar objects - tigers -
the concept of which has entered the public language. As men
become more co-operative, new communicative needs are
generated, to which language responds. For example, some
tribesmen will be perceived as dangers to the community, so
that it becomes vital to be able to communicate about these
individuals: hence the emergence of a terminology of 'persons',
'intentions', 'right', 'wrong', etc. A term like 'honesty' arrives
to refer to what is allegedly common to a host of actions which
it is convenient to bring together. As men become more sophisticated and less endangered, they engage in long-term projects
for mastering and taming their environment, so that reference
to tools, quantities, weather conditions, invisible forces, and so
on, grows up. Predicting, inferring, postulating causal chains
are now challenges that language rises to meet. All through
this process, from the fear of the tiger to the sophistication
of science, 'it is our needs which interpret the world: our

drives For and Against'.(8)

These needs and drives are subsumed under the heading of 'will to power'. Even at the earliest stages, it is not mere self-preservation which explains the development of concepts; while at the later stages, it is still the urge for greater power that is the inspiration for further development. 'The measure of the desire for knowledge depends on the degree of the growth, in a species, of its will to power: a species grasps *just so much* reality, in order to become master over it, to take it into service.'(9) In broad terms, what happens at each stage, when concepts answer to the dictates of power, is the same: disparate items of experience are grouped together, schemata imposed, according to the (supposed) value this will have in granting us power over our environment and future. Or, as Nietzsche puts it, in Heraclitan vein, 'to impose upon becoming the character of being - that is the highest will to power'.(10)

Philosophical accounts of the world, according to Nietzsche, are disguised descriptions of the *grammars* of languages which have succeeded in their mission. Traditional ontological talk of 'substances', 'properties', 'classes', or 'numbers' merely reflects that these languages contain subjects, predicates, species-terms, and numerals - all of which are necessary to a language's performing an efficient job. It is no more surprising, therefore, that philosophical systems have tended to be markedly similar than that grammars, responding to similar human needs, should themselves be alike. Philosophical systems merely give explicit expression to the '*Volks-Metaphysik*' embodied in grammar.(11)

From this account of how thought, science, and philosophy emerge in harness with communicative need, Nietzsche draws radical conclusions. In the early paper mentioned, where he still allowed that our concepts just might correspond to similarities in reality, he also therefore allows the possibility of a real world distinct from our conception of it - though, if there is one, we can know nothing of it. But when the idea of real similarities is rejected as senseless, so is the idea of an objective world of which our conception might or might not be an 'adequate expression'. Kant's structure is dismantled brick by brick. The senseless question of what reality must be like for synthetic *a priori* judgments to be possible is replaced by the sensible one of why we need to make such judgments. Why, for example, is the notion of causality so vital to us?(12) Things-in-themselves, of course, disappear. 'The psychological derivation of the belief in things forbids us to talk of things-in-themselves.'(13) Things are constructs which collect together, and so enable prediction and regulation of, our 'sensations'. Since the *Ding-an-sich* could perform no such functions, it is an empty notion. If there were a transcendent reality, then *nothing* could be said about it, not even something as bare as that it contains things, for that is already to be engaged in human conceptualization and interpretation.(14)

Along with 'real' objects standing against experience, the

'subject' or 'substantial self' standing behind experiences also disappears. Nietzsche writes that the 'subject' is 'the fiction that many similar states in us are the effect of a single substratum'; though to this Humean point it is quickly added that it is anyway we who have 'first created this "similarity" of states'.(15) It would be misleading to conclude that, with the disappearance of both 'objects' and 'subjects', we are therefore confined to 'the world of appearances'. On the contrary, thinks Nietzsche, such a 'world' requires both a 'subject' for whom appearances are appearances, and 'objects' against which their appearances may be contrasted. Nor is Nietzsche suggesting that we give up employing object-terms like 'tiger', or subject-ones like 'I'; only that we clearly register that these stand for 'fictions' constructed for organizing the 'medley of sensations'. 'The antithesis to the phenomenal world is *not* "the true world" but the formless-unformulable world of the chaos of sensations.'(16) There can be no description of 'the true world', because there is no such world; and there can be no description of that 'other world' of 'the chaos of sensations', since to be able to describe is already to have risen, irreversibly, out of that world. We cannot think how it would be to be without thought.

Where do truth and knowledge take their places? Nietzsche's many comments on these notions have, unsurprisingly, confused many readers, leading some of them to think that he goes out of his way to antagonize through paradox and contradiction. Certainly there are moments when he denies the very existence of truth, but others when he is telling us what makes some beliefs true. There are passages where the possibility of knowledge is dismissed, but places where the quest for knowledge is hailed as men's most noble task.

   The difficulties subside if it is realized that Nietzsche is trying to do three very different things, without always making it clear which task he is engaged upon. First, he is offering an *analysis* of truth and knowledge as they are, in his view, standardly conceived. Second, he is offering a *genealogy* of truth and knowledge: this is an account not only of how and why people have held various things to be true or knowable, but of why their concepts of truth and knowledge are the ones revealed in the preceding analysis. Finally, he is offering a *reconstruction* of these concepts; new concepts of truth and knowledge. The three tasks are intimately connected. The analysis reveals that truth and knowledge, as standardly conceived, are necessarily unattainable, hence there is a problem – to be tackled by the genealogy – as to why people have nevertheless held things to be true and knowable. For, given the results of the analysis, the reasons they usually give cannot be the real ones. Because the old conceptions of truth and knowledge are incoherent, we require new, reconstructed ones: but if these *Ersatz* notions are to go by the old names, then they must be securely tied to the actual practices - as revealed by the genealogy - which have induced people, however mistakenly, to suppose that things may be true or knowable in the standard way. What confuses the reader is that a passage in Nietzsche beginning 'Truth is . . .' may belong to any one of these tasks. What follows those two words may belong to the analysis of the everyday notion of truth, or it may belong to a genealogical account of why people have held something to be true, or it may be an exhortation to embrace a new, reconstructed notion of truth. Let me develop these remarks.

A question frequently posed by Nietzsche is why we seek truth at all. 'Granted we desire truth: why not rather untruth?'(17) The question seems an odd one; indeed, taken one way, it sounds absurd. One cannot, surely, opt for a belief one takes to be untrue; for to regard what it expresses as untrue is equivalent to not believing it. For any proposition, p, surely the following familiar equivalence holds:

It is true that p if and only if p.

For example: it is true that Wagner was a composer if and only if Wagner was a composer. Hence, wanting to find out if it is true that p is the very same as wanting to ascertain whether p. If we take the question another way - as asking why we ever conceptualize and form beliefs at all - then it is surely one Nietzsche has already answered: we do so to lend order to 'the medley of sensations', to predict, control, regulate, in short to get power. But Nietzsche does *not* take this answer as the answer to why we desire truth, but only as the answer to why we conceptualize and form beliefs. The power that concepts and beliefs confer, he insists, is independent of the question of their truth. It is the power certain beliefs confer, not their truth, which explains why we value and 'desire' them. In dozens of passages, Nietzsche separates a belief's pragmatic value from its truth.

> The falsity of a judgement is for us no objection to the judgement.(18) That a great deal of belief must be present . . . that is a precondition . . . of life. It is necessary, therefore, that something be held true - *not* that it be true.(19)

As if truth could be proved by the fact that men remain preserved!(20) This separation is intelligible, of course, only if Nietzsche's *analysis* of truth is not a pragmatist one in terms of power, preservation, and the like: if it were, those beliefs which are 'preconditions of life' would have to count as true. It is clear, indeed, that he analyses truth as a thoroughly 'Realist' notion - as correspondence to the facts, to reality. For example, to ask if the axioms of logic are true is to ask 'are [they] adequate to reality?'(21) To ask whether language equips us to state truths is to ask 'do designations and things

correspond [*sich . . . decken*]? Is language the adequate
expression of all realities?'(22) To these questions, Nietzsche's
answers are predictably negative. Since, in reality, there are
no things, numbers, classes, selves, or the like, because they
are 'fictions', then the terms in our language, and therefore
our concepts, have no objective references. Hence the propositions formed out of these terms cannot correspond to objective
facts. Nietzsche sometimes puts this dramatically by saying
that all propositions are false; or that 'truths are illusions of
which one has forgotten that this is what they are'.(23)
A *priori* truths, for example, are 'purely false judgements',
which serve, none the less, as 'regulative articles of belief'.(24)
Even if, perchance, there were a real world independent of our
conceptualizations, there could be not the least reason to think
it is structured in a way that corresponds to our scheme of
things, selves, numbers, and so on.

Knowledge goes the way of truth. To count as knowledge,
beliefs would not only have to be true, but somehow be 'caused'
by the facts they correspond to. But there are no such facts,
and even if there were they could not cause our beliefs, since
causality is a relation between items in experience, not one that
could obtain between experience and a reality beyond its ken.
'The greatest fable', Nietzsche concludes, 'is that of knowledge.'(25)

The 'silly' question of why we should value truth now becomes
the deadly serious one of whether we should care if our
efficacious beliefs, those which enable us to deal with the
'medley of sensations', correspond with objective reality.
Nietzsche's answer is that we should not. 'I don't care if my
beliefs are true' now expresses the sensible, and admirably
nonchalant refusal to speculate on a reality transcending human
experience. There are now two ways of taking the familiar
equivalence 'It is true that p if and only if p'. Either it reflects
our standard, 'Realist' conception of truth, and means something
like 'p' corresponds to reality if and only if 'p' - in which case
it is discredited along with that conception of truth. That 'p'
is not true - i.e. does not correspond to a fact - is no reason
for not holding that p. Or, it may simply encapsulate a dull and
harmless feature of the everyday use of the expression 'is
true' - its use as a redundant device for making assertions.
You say 'p': I reply 'That's true.' I am not saying anything
about 'p', such as that it depicts a fact, but merely making the
assertion that p. People tend to continue using 'That's true' in
this way even when the propositions in question are ones they
refuse, in their philosophical moments, to ascribe a truth-
value to. For example, a mathematical conventionalist who thinks
that mathematics is a collection of rules, not truths, will no
doubt go along with the everyday practice and say 'That's
true' when his child asks him if 2 + 2 = 4. So if the equivalence
is read as 'Whenever you assert that p, then you must also be
willing, as a matter of everyday conversational practice, to say

"'p' is true" - and vice-versa', it is unobjectionable. At the
same time, it provides no objection to believing that p without
holding that 'p' is true in the 'Realist' sense.

Jürgen Habermas, whose account of the relation between
needs, power, and knowledge is in some respects akin to
Nietzsche's, nevertheless takes Nietzsche to task for denying
the possibility of truth and knowledge. In his view, Nietzsche
comes close to, but unfortunately fails to accept, a 'transcen-
dental-logically determined pragmatism' *within* which the
distinctions between truth and falsity, or knowledge and
illusion, can be made.(26) Rightly enough, he attributes the
'failure' here to Nietzsche's 'classical', 'Realist' idea of truth.
But, considered as a criticism of Nietzsche, there are two
replies to make. First, as we shall see, Nietzsche *does* embrace
pragmatism - only this belongs in his *reconstruction*, not his
analysis, of truth. Second, as I shall now elaborate, Nietzsche
might surely have been right in thinking that the standard
notion of truth is a 'Realist' one.

Let me mention three pieces of evidence, out of many, which
suggest that ours is a 'Realist' notion of truth; that we take
statements or theories to be true or false in virtue of a relation
to objective states of affairs, independent of any pragmatic
value attached to accepting or rejecting the statements and
theories. First, our usual talk allows sense to the idea that
even the most efficacious theory, the most pragmatically
warranted one, might none the less be false and one of its
rivals true. This could hardly be if truth were actually understood in terms of pragmatic warrant. Second, there is the
common, though not unchallenged, assumption that all statements with a determinate meaning are either true or false.
Applied to so-called 'undecidable' statements, for which there
is no method of verification, this assumption seems to carry
with it an assumption of 'Realism'. Goldbach's conjecture that
every even number is the sum of two odd primes is undecidable,
and nothing surely turns on whether it is accepted or not. The
insistence, therefore, that the conjecture either is or is not
true is hard to fathom unless the idea is that there is a transcendent mathematical reality to which it either does or does not
correspond. Finally, the common-sense view has it that where
a statement or theory is the best one to accept, in virtue of
such pragmatic criteria as predictive power, this is *because*
it is true. Modern genetic theory, we will be told for example,
works because it tells us something true. Such explanatory
claims could make little sense, or would be tautologies rather
than explanations, if the common-sense notion of truth were
itself pragmatic.(27)

I doubt if all these and other pieces of evidence are produced
by Nietzsche himself, though when he says that only in 'five
or six heads' has it dawned that 'physics is only an interpretation
and arrangement of the world . . . and not an explanation of
it', he is surely criticizing what he takes to be the normal,

'Realist' assumptions of science.(28) And when he says it is
in the nature of thought to engage in 'metaphysics as the
derivation of the conditioned from the unconditioned', he is
drawing attention to the engrained tendency to explain the
empirical success of theories by their correspondence to what
goes beyond experience.(29) The fact is, though, that Nietzsche
is less concerned to demonstrate that ours is a 'Realist' notion
of truth – something he takes as obvious – than to explain why
it is; to show why men have not been satisfied with a frankly
pragmatist notion. This explanation belongs in his genealogy
of truth.

Before we turn from analysis to genealogy, however, let me
record my disagreement with Mary Warnock's account of
Nietzsche on truth.(30) Habermas, we saw, was right to think
that Nietzsche's analysis of truth is a 'Realist' one, though
wrong to ignore that he advocates a pragmatist notion.
Warnock's is the opposite mistake of thinking that Nietzsche,
at least some of the time, actually analyses truth pragmatically.
According to her, a confused Nietzsche uses 'truth' in a
'Realist' sense when talking of individual propositions, but
in a pragmatist sense when talking of scientific theories. It
would be strange if there were this bifurcation in Nietzsche's
use since, in many passages anticipating the views of Quine,
he is keen to deny any sharp distinction between belief and
theory. 'There are no isolated judgements! . . . Only in
connection and relation to many judgements is there surety.'(31)
The fact is, anyway, that whether he is speaking of individual
propositions or of theories, we find the same mixture of claims,
some denying the possibility of truth, others allowing it. The
explanation, whether in the case of propositions or theories,
is that sometimes he is using 'truth' in accordance with his
'Realist' analysis, sometimes in his reconstructed pragmatist
way.

Turning to the genealogy, we find Nietzsche offering three
nested explanations of why we have come to have a 'Realist'
conception of truth and knowledge. First, there is the power of
grammar to foist upon us a view of the world as containing
persistent objects and substances distinct from our 'sensations'
and experiences. 'Why shouldn't the world which concerns us
not be a fiction? . . . May not the philosopher raise himself
about the belief in grammar?'(32) The subject-predicate structure of grammar generates referential terms which encourage
us, constrain us almost, to seek objects for the terms to refer
to; and because of the sharp grammatical distinction between
subject and predicate, we think of the objects as substances,
distinct from the properties predicated of them. This is so even
in cases where, quite obviously, the object/property distinction
is artificial – as in the instance of flashing lightning, where
grammar seduces us into speaking of an agent, the lightning,
and what it does, flash. The tendency to look for things named

by names is so great that 'I am afraid we are not free of God,
because we still believe in grammar.'(33) It is such a tendency
which makes it so hard to view objects as fictions, constructed
to organize our 'sensations' and to group experienced properties
together.

Grammar, however, could only encourage such a tendency if
it were already there; if there were some rather special terms
where it seemed quite essential to postulate corresponding
substances. For Nietzsche there is indeed a group of such
special terms: 'I', 'ego', 'self'. What grammar does is encourage
us to generalize the idea, originating with these terms, that
names require corresponding substances. Like Leibniz,
Nietzsche sees the 'self' as the prototypical substance:

> The concept of substance [is] a consequence of the concept
> of the subject: not vice versa! If we give up the soul, 'the
> subject', the precondition for a 'substance' in general is then
> missing . . . we leave behind that which has being [*man
> verliert das Seiende*].(34)

It is because of the tremendous need men have to think of
themselves as persistent, unitary beings, and not as mere
Humean 'bundles of perceptions' or artificial 'fictions', that the
link is first forged between terms and substances.

But - and here we reach the third ingredient in Nietzsche's
account - whence comes this tremendous need? The reasons,
Nietzsche says, are moral ones. Passing moral judgment on one
another requires us 'to interpret events . . . as events caused
by intentions', those of a 'self' which can be held responsible,
praised and blamed, for the events.(35) One way this requirement works is described in a brilliant section from *The
Genealogy of Morals*. Those who have most to gain from morality,
the 'weak', must not, partly for reasons of self-esteem, see
themselves as being 'weak'. This requires them to separate the
person from his actions, otherwise his 'weak' behaviour would
mean that *he* was 'weak'. The method of separation is this:

> people exploit the seduction of language . . . which under-
> stands and misunderstands all effects as determined by an
> agency . . . popular morality [*Volks-Moral*] separates
> strength from its manifestations, as if behind the strong
> person there were a neutral substratum, which is free to
> express strength or not to.(36)

The 'weak' can now congratulate themselves for being people
who simply choose not to express 'strong' behaviour, and
condemn others for being tough and aggressive. 'Realism', like
morality, is born in sin, because people 'need the belief in the
neutral independent subject out of an instinct for self-
preservation and self-affirmation, in which every lie can be
sanctified'.(37)

There are other ways in which 'Realism' serves to answer to moral needs. An extreme form of 'Realism' is the ancient idea of an unchanging world of essences, of which the world of experience is but a poor and temporary reflection. But this idea is morally motivated by the 'wish that there should be such a world; . . . hatred against a world which produces suffering is expressed by imagining another, *more valuable* one'.(38) Elsewhere, explaining 'How we, too, are still pious', Nietzsche argues that the scientist's insistence that he is discovering truths, not constructing 'regulative fictions', displays a 'faith in science' that cannot be reduced to a faith in its 'utility'. If it could, the scientist would be able to accept the 'fictional' interpretation, provided his 'fictions' worked. The root of the insistence, according to Nietzsche, is the principle 'I will not deceive, not even myself' - and with this, he adds, 'we stand on moral ground'. The 'deception' the scientist fears to commit cannot be that of producing theories which he, or anyone else, could detect as wrong, in the sense of pragmatically inadequate. It must, rather, be the heir of an earlier notion: deception as the failure to live in the truth of God and to have produced an account of reality that matches the divine conception. Thus it is a moral, a 'metaphysical faith upon which our faith in science rests'.(39)

Nietzsche has now explained why our standard notion of truth and knowledge is a 'Realist' one, but it remains to be explained why people hold as true just the beliefs they do and not others. Clearly, it cannot be because these have been checked off against objective reality and found to fit. The next component in Nietzsche's genealogy attempts an explanation. The central point is stated succinctly in many passages: for example, 'will to truth is - *will to power*', or 'the criterion of truth lies in the increase of the feeling of power'.(40) He means that people tend, without generally realizing it, to accept those beliefs and theories which give them power. This conferment of power is the effective, though not official, reason for holding things true. Nietzsche hopes to explain many features of belief and claims to knowledge in these terms.

For a start, he can explain why there is a logical, as well as temporal, order among beliefs: why some beliefs, for example those of theoretical science, can only arise on the foundation of everyday, humdrum empirical beliefs. This is because the kind of power 'to master the multiplicity of sensations' which the latter confer is required before we can progress to those organized, co-operative activities, like science, which then confer power in the form, say, of technical mastery of the environment.(41)

Two related features Nietzsche also hopes to explain are, first, the common people's (*Volk*) test for knowledge - that 'something unfamiliar be reduced to something familiar'(42) - and, second, the rugged persistence of many beliefs in the face of apparent refutation. In both cases, what is operative is the need to overcome the impotence brought on by 'fear of the unknown', 'intellectual confusion', or 'intellectual chaos'.(43) We are ever-ready to accept as true a theory which renders initially unfamiliar phenomena familiar, or a belief which can be fitted smoothly into our already established set of beliefs: and we thereby lend unity to our view of things, a unity that is itself a form of organizing, of centripetal power. By the same token, once a belief has been forged, people are resistant to giving it up in the face of apparent refutation; for that would mean a return to the 'intellectual' chaos which stymies thought and action alike. 'Man is like this: an article of his faith can be refuted a thousand times, but given that he needs it, he'll continue to hold it "true".'(44) A crucial point - to which we return later - is contained here. The power which beliefs and knowledge confer is not always extrinsic, not always a causal result produced by the knowledge, but intrinsic. Knowledge is itself a form of power, since it is a form of ordering and intellectually regulating phenomena: an antidote, therefore, to that crippling suspension of belief which leaves people in 'intellectual chaos'. Nietzsche, then, is far from claiming that men generally accept just those theories which have the best extrinsic, efficacious results: for it often happens that the power obtained through merely holding a coherent set of beliefs outweighs the extrinsic advantages there might be in giving these up in favour of some others.

Finally, he explains why some conceptions are engrained in the thinking of all of us, while others are found accepted by only some people. The former conceptions, those of material objects, say, or of persons and actions, have won their spurs so thoroughly that it becomes hard to imagine how experience could be organized without them. He points out, as Wittgenstein did later, that some of these conceptions are so engrained that it becomes peculiar to speak of them as beliefs or knowledge at all: rather they are preconditions for the making of such claims - the 'unmoving foundations' of Wittgenstein's language-games. Thus he writes: 'The word "I", the word "do", the word "suffer": - these perhaps are horizons of our knowledge, but not "truths".'(45) Conversely, where a conception confers power only on some, and not others, because of the different estimates and values people have, we should expect no general agreement on its validity. Thus it is only some - the 'weak', 'envious', 'resentful' - who have anything to gain in the way of power (both psychological and social) from Christian or socialist faith: and it is only these people who are predisposed to swallow such faiths.

As these last examples suggest, Nietzsche is hardly happy with some of the ways considerations of power have influenced beliefs and claims to knowledge. Nevertheless, he is insistent that if we are to retain the terms 'truth' and 'knowledge' at all - the old 'Realist' notion having been discredited - we must understand them, frankly and explicitly, in terms of power and

pragmatic yield. Only then will their meanings have any genuine
connection to the ways which have in fact governed their
employment - disguised as that employment has been from most
of us. Since claims to truth and knowledge have always been
generated by pragmatic considerations, it is time we adopted
such considerations as the conscious measure of truth and
knowledge.

> The 'criterion of truth' was in fact . . . biological utility:
> and since a species of animal knows nothing more important
> than to preserve itself, one may indeed speak of 'truth'
> here.(46)

> The meaning of 'knowledge': as with 'good' and 'beautiful',
> the concept is here to be taken in a strongly and exactly
> anthropocentric and biological way.(47)

Here, then, we have Nietzsche's reconstructed notion of truth:
one which, according to him, fits actual human practice much
better than the old 'Realist' one. We should have no difficulty
now in dissolving some of Nietzsche's apparently paradoxical
remarks; for example 'Truth is the kind of error without which
a certain kind of living being cannot live. The value for *life*
is the final determinant.'(48) Here 'truth' is being used in the
new, reconstructed sense, as a frankly pragmatic concept:
while 'error' is still being used in the old 'Realist' way. Life-
serving beliefs are still 'errors' in so far as they do not
correspond with any objective reality of the sort postulated by
'Realists'.

Where does Nietzsche's theory of truth - analysis, genealogy,
and reconstruction - leave us? How might it impinge on our
lives, and our attitudes towards claims to truth and knowledge?
What should its impact be upon the teacher's presentation of
claims to truth and knowledge; how should he prepare young
minds to handle them? Let us approach these questions by
looking at three reactions to Nietzsche's theory which would
be clearly misplaced. I call them the reactions of 'despair',
'license', and 'conservatism'.

The reaction of 'despair' is poignantly illustrated in a letter
Kleist wrote his fiancée:

> We cannot decide whether what we call truth really is truth,
> or only seems so to us. If the latter, then the truth we
> collect on earth will be nothing after death, and every
> effort to earn a possession which follows us into the grave is
> in vain. If the point of this thought does not touch your
> heart, do not laugh at one who is wounded by it in his holiest
> sanctum. My single, highest goal is sunk, and I have no
> other.(49)

This despair, which led to Kleist's suicide a few years later, is one Nietzsche was inclined to share as a very young man: at the time, in fact, when he shared the idea of a transcendent world. For, as he later saw, such despair is brought about precisely by the thought of a reality whose nature, tragically, can never be known to us. Kleist's letter was written on reading Kant, and like many German readers, he was more impressed by what the first *Critique* rendered unknowable – *noumena*, *Dinge-an-sich* – than by the consolation it offers that at least the course of our experience is, in broad terms, knowable. For Nietzsche, the cure is to jettison Kant's unknowable world, and frankly embrace a pragmatic notion of truth which makes speculation on transcendent reality nonsensical, rather than tragically uncertain.

Equally misplaced would be the emotionally reverse reaction of 'license': an orgiastic, nihilistic delight that 'anything goes', that 'everything is permitted'. If beliefs do not, indeed cannot, match objective reality, why not believe whatever tickles one's fancy? According to Nietzsche, though, it is the 'Realist' notion, and not his own, which breeds such license; for it allows people to speculate at will, without constraint, on how things might be with this unknowable world. The notion of a 'true world', he says, licenses us to 'invent fables about "another" world . . . phantasmagoria of "another", "better" life'.(50) Criteria of power, preservation, and communicative advantage, on the other hand, provide severe constraints on what can be accepted and rejected. Science may indeed invent fictions 'for the purpose of mastering nature', but the achievement of that purpose requires rigour, so that 'we find consistency here . . . [and] it yields a kind of practical reflection'. Much of our rational thought, far from being flippantly discardable, constitutes 'an interpretation according to a scheme which we cannot cast off'.(51) Nietzsche's pragmatism permits no one to divest himself of that 'intellectual conscience' which makes it 'despicable to believe this or that, and to live accordingly, without first becoming conscious of the final and most secure reasons for or against'.(52)

We must not now, though, veer towards another extreme reaction, that of 'conservatism', and imagine that Nietzsche's account 'leaves everything as it is'. The phrase is one associated with Wittgenstein: philosophy, since it must not interfere with ordinary language, only describe it, 'leaves everything as it is'.(53) It is puzzling, *prima facie*, that the reaction of Wittgenstein and that of Nietzsche – who clearly thinks many of our ways of talking must be overturned and reconstructed – should be so different, given their remarkable kinship on so many large matters: the rejection of 'private languages', denial of the sense of comparing language and reality as wholes, the emphasis upon behavioural criteria for psychological concepts, the idea of logical grammar, and so on. One writer implausibly suggests that the difference which makes the two men 'as far apart, almost, as it is possible to be' is that, whereas for Wittgenstein it is philosophers who misconstrue ordinary language, for Nietzsche it is language itself which misleads.(54) Given their equal stress on the intimate connection between grammar and thought, this could hardly be a difference which puts two men 'as far apart, almost, as it is possible to be'. But anyway, it is a difference I find hard to grasp. Unless philosophers are simply buffoons, who gratuitously misconstrue, then surely language must set its own traps. Moreover, if Wittgenstein's point were that *only* philosophers succumb to temptations - like that of looking for something essentially in common to all those things called by the same name - he would be simply wrong.

There are a number of reasons Nietzsche thinks his accounts of truth and knowledge do not 'leave everything as it is' - and, of these, only the first finds an echo in Wittgenstein. First, for all the talk of some of our conceptions being 'necessary' - principles of logic, for instance, 'have to be believed true for the purpose of maintaining our kind of existence'(55) - the necessity is not absolute. However engrained certain concepts are, and however strong the related constraints on talking with the same tongue as others, there remains the possibility of slow revision and rejection. One cannot, on pain of intelligibility, commit sudden and total violence on ordinary ways of speaking, everyday beliefs, but new 'perspectives', as Nietzsche calls them, might gradually emerge to challenge the old.

> I think we are today at least far from that laughable immodesty which decrees from our corner that only perspectives from out of this corner are allowed. The world has once again become 'infinite' for us, in so far as we cannot dismiss the possibility that it contains infinite interpretations.(56)

As he puts it, we need to let 'the ambiguity of the world' reappear. It is not obvious, for example, that we are forever committed to an ontology whose basic items are medium-sized physical objects - rather than particles, perhaps, or quanta of power, or Leibnizian monads, or Heideggerian 'beings-to-hand'. Again, however great the grip of causal thinking may be, it is surely possible, and desirable in some cases, to struggle out of this grip where the cause-effect model can be misleading - as in psychology, perhaps. There must, to be sure, 'be no haste to go forward'; but, as with the ship of Theseus, new perspectives can be gradually built. Even logic may not be sacrosanct: we have seen in recent times attempts to construct new logics better able, allegedly, to handle problems in special areas, such as quantum physics.(57)

Second, and of greater everyday impact, the criteria of power, which are henceforth to be the criteria for truth, can be of great revisionary and critical force. The point is not, or not mainly, that ideas and theories get accepted only if they 'pay off'; for, according to Nietzsche, this has always been the case, though only in an unconscious, haphazard way. The point is, rather, that in many cases, whether or not some belief or conception confers power depends on the people in question. Different people derive a sense of power from different things and different conceptions: and this is because they evaluate aspects of life differently. If it were possible, therefore, to adjudicate between senses of power, different evaluations of life, it would then become possible to adjudicate between beliefs and conceptions according to the kinds of power they confer on what kinds of people. A religious interpretation of the world, for example, confers a sense of power - but upon the 'weak' and 'resentful' whose self-esteem is raised; whereas a materialistic conception of the world will serve those stronger individuals who have no need for the sops of an afterlife and divine justice.

> [It is] not 'truth' in struggle with life, but one kind of life with another. - But it wishes to be the higher kind! - Here one must furnish the proof that a rank-order is necessary - that the first problem is that of the rank-order of kinds of life.(58)

We shall return to this point in later chapters: for the moment, we leave it as the idea that if power is to be the new criterion of truth, and if there can be adjudication between kinds of power, according to the kinds of life they reflect, then this new criterion offers vast new critical possibilities.

But - and here is the final point - we can easily guess what, for Nietzsche, is the most sublime form of power. It is the power of the interpretative, creative free individual. Nietzsche himself uses the term 'leave everything as it is', when he unfavourably contrasts 'the men of knowledge [*Erkennenden*] who leave everything as it is' with the artists who 'fix an image of what should be - they are productive, insofar as they actually change and transform'.(59) His point is that, while knowledge has always and necessarily been a matter of interpretation, people have succumbed to the temptations of the 'Realist' picture and envisaged knowledge as something imposed by a 'true world' which thereby closes off possibilities for interpretation. Thus rejection of 'Realism' will bring in its train a forcible reminder of that power and scope which knowledge shares with art - interpretative, creative power. 'What a feeling of freedom resides in sensing, as we freed spirits sense, that we are not harnessed in a system of "purposes".'(60) By way of example, Nietzsche cites the liberating sense of realizing that 'the concepts of "reward" and "punishment" do not reside in the essence of being'; that we are free to twist, pummel, mould, or reject these concepts, and are not doomed to taking over everyday, settled beliefs about these notions.

The important idea mentioned on p. 78 is at work here; namely that power can be intrinsic to an activity. Just as the power the artist derives from painting or composing is not an effect or product like money or station, but resides in the work, in the creative activity, so the sublime power of interpretation, adopting perspectives, forging new concepts is intrinsic to these. A new sense is given, perhaps, to the famous remark in *The Birth of Tragedy* that the world is justified only as an aesthetic phenomenon.(61) True, after the demise of 'Realism', beliefs and theories will be explicitly judged by reference to the extrinsic powers they confer - accuracy of prediction, for example, or technical mastery; but the greatest boon of its demise - of 'the death of God' in fact - will be the new appre-ciation of individual creation and interpretation of ideas.

> every heightening of man brings with it the overcoming of
> narrower interpretations . . . every strengthening and
> widening of power attained opens up new perspectives and
> means believing in new horizons - this runs through my
> writings.(62)

It follows that, for Nietzsche, there will be a sense in which truth and knowledge are unattainable. It is not the unattainability which drove Kleist to despair, for that required the notion of a transcendent world we are unable to fathom. Nor do I mean that even our best theories and schemes of concepts, pragmatically judged, might yet give way to better ones - though this may well be. I mean that there will be men who can never rest content with whatever theory and scheme is current. In them, the will to power is very much the will to interpret and to reinterpret. A perspective, once forged, will now be one that the will to power, in its urge to increase power, will strive to overturn. A dominant idea will for a time be 'freely subordinated to', and as much done with it as possible, but then it will be time to 'overcome' it.(63) If there is any element of tragedy in this sisyphean process of forever revaluing and reinterpreting, it is not a Kleistian one, but that of an artist who can never turn back or rest content with what he has hitherto created. There is one implication of this, incidentally, that Nietzsche takes on the chin: 'Suppose that this [i.e. the doctrine of the will to power] is also only interpretation - and won't you be eager enough to raise this objection? - Well, all the better.'(64)

At the beginning of this chapter, I said that Nietzsche's account of truth would harmonize with my critique of 'Knowledge' as an educational aim, and hinted it must have its impact on how teachers should handle claims to truth and knowledge. The nature of that harmony and impact will be as complex and indirect as the relation between epistemology and practice typically has to be. I content myself with pointing to two aspects of this harmony and impact.

The appeal of 'Knowledge', and 'initiation into the disciplines', as a prime educational goal derives in part from the idea that most of the disciplines have it as their job to tell us how the world and its contents actually are. (And, of those that do not, like philosophy or mathematics perhaps, some are treated as helpmates to those which do.) The educated person, it is tempting to say, is one who knows a good deal about how the world is; but this requires acquaintance with the various disciplines which have taken it upon themselves to treat of different areas of that complicated world in the appropriate ways. Brute, pre-scientific encounter with the world can reveal only so much of how it is: what is left untold is taken up by the sophisticated disciplines. The initiate into these is, quite simply, coming to know much more about how things are.

From a standpoint like Nietzsche's, the danger of such an idea resides in what we might call its exaggeration of the factual; in its suppression of that relativity which claims about the world have to the particular schemes of concepts we have forged in response to our purposes and values, our estimates of 'power'. Of course, many of these purposes and schemes are so universal and established that they can, so to speak, be 'bracketed', taken for granted as the backdrop against which various claims about the world are made – rather as we can often take a system of spatial coordinates for granted when saying where things are. There is little harm in saying that claims of this sort 'give us the facts'. It is a fact that tables are solid: that is, we do not call into question the concepts, or the purposes they serve, which enable us to classify certain recurrent chunks of experience as perceptions of solid tables. But, even here, it requires only a maverick's jolt to remind us of the relativity. Eddington, when he denied that tables were solid, was not making a big mistake about the world, but trying, as he saw it, to bring our classifications into line with molecular physics – unsuccessfully, since the aims of the everyday classifications are too different, and too engrained, to be touched by considerations about gaps between molecules. (It is as if someone tried to get Australians to join with cartographers, so as to refer to their heads being beneath their feet.)(65)

The danger becomes live when we turn to those many, important areas of discourse and theory – with which an education should surely treat – where there exists no similar, venerable agreement on the purposes and values to be served by schemes of concepts and classifications. Here there is the obligation, however much we may ignore it, to attend to the relativity of claims about how things are to those purposes and schemes. Without such a relativity, there is no sense to talking of the claims as true or false, as providing or failing to provide the facts. I have in mind, by way of a few examples, discourse about health, intelligence, criminality, grammaticality, insanity, or love. Questions like 'Has there been a decline in mental

health?' 'Are blacks as intelligent as whites?', 'Do Harlem
blacks speak ungrammatical English?', or 'Can there be asexual
love?' have no true-or-false answers except relative to a
contested choice of concepts serving contested purposes of
classification, ordering, treating, controlling, appraising, and
policy. The notion of mental health is to serve us to differen-
tiate among people for purposes of treatment, care, sympathy
and the like; so that without agreement upon the value or per-
missibility of treating these rather than those people, there is
no saying, with any degree of exactitude, what that notion
amounts to. The notion of grammaticality is tied to the appraisal
of ways of speaking, so that without agreement on why and how
we should appraise there can be no truth-value to various
claims about when people are speaking grammatically. When the
socio-linguist, Labov, announces that it is 'bad observation'
and 'ignorance of language' which has led some people to the
'false' view that Harlem blacks speak ungrammatically, he is
simply ignoring the series of decisions and stipulations that are
required before there is anything to observe, well or badly
(in particular the decision, hardly 'discovery', that Harlem
talk is a 'separate language'). (66)
    Labov, like so many, falls prey to just the danger that the
model of 'Knowledge' presents, the exaggeration of the factual.
Faced by the difficulty of assessing competing claims in the
problematical areas, the reaction, too often, is that 'we don't
have enough data', 'it's just very complicated', or 'we need
some new studies'. But these are not the main difficulties: for,
lacking agreement on the purposes to be served by the discourse,
lacking criteria of success, we do not know what kind of data
to seek, what further research would be germane. It would be
superficial, too, to think the problem was simply one of vague
concepts, which a good dose of 'conceptual analysis' would
clear up. 'Table' and 'solid' are vague - and we would not want
them otherwise, given the role such concepts play in accommodat-
ing new, unpredictable experiences. It is not the vagueness of
'grammatical' or 'criminal' or 'mental health' that renders so
much of our talk indeterminate in truth-value, but the lack of a
firm relation to agreed judgment on the appraisals, policies,
controls, or whatever, that lend point to the forging of such
concepts in the first place.
    What is required, then, and what the pragmatist conception
pushes into the foreground, is reflection on the purposes, the
'powers', which we should want our conceptual schemes to
serve. Much, no doubt, will be involved in such reflection: not
least, a genealogical eye for the wrong, fishy purposes that
some people have for pressing schemes into their service. We
must, to take a clear example, beware of those who, pretending
to discover the nature of intelligence, are forging a notion to
have a desired, ideological outcome: whether it be that racial
groups must be, or cannot be, of similar intelligence. (67) And
such reflection will involve everything I included, in the previous

chapter, under 'philosophical understanding'; 'situational' understanding, attention to the 'webs and stocks' of everyday, clichéd talk, and so on.

On a Nietzschean account, the whole 'Knowledge' idea not only exaggerates the factual, but also the rule-governed nature of the disciplines: hence it complements my criticism on p. 60 ff. The disciplines, from any pragmatist standpoint, must be viewed as more or less groping, more or less successful attempts to lend order and coherence to the 'medley of sensations' and data encountered by the investigators. But imposition of such order will rarely, if ever, be an end in itself: it will be relative to further purposes and interests of the investigators. I do not have in mind the rather fashionable point, urged by several sociologists of knowledge, that the conduct of a discipline will be due, in part, to jealous professional interests, considerations of prestige and reward, or the like. I mean that the direction of the discipline, the ordering concepts it employs, will be relative to valuation of the kind of prediction and explanation which might be sought after. It will be this difference in goals pursued, typically, rather than intrinsic differences in the data studied or the facts revealed, which keep two disciplines apart. Donald Davidson has argued that the events studied by psychology and physiology are no different: my pains, thoughts, and depressions are not distinct happenings from ones in my brain. Nevertheless, psychology does not collapse into physiology, because it aims at quite different explanations, quite different predictions. The aim of the former, and of its battery of concepts, is to make sense of behaviour, to render it - as far as possible - rational: and this is an aim alien to the apparatus of physiology.(68)

It follows that the direction of a discipline, and its proximity to others, can radically change through a shift in the valuation of what it is to do, what it is to explain. Such a shift, I guess, took place in social anthropology some years ago, when the emphasis moved from observation of behaviour and its social functions to enquiry into the 'native mentality'. Instead of notions like 'function', 'social cohesion', or 'exchange' dominating the literature, those of 'rationality', 'belief', or 'mental structure' came into the foreground. The discipline had changed orbit, circulating closer to psychology and linguistics than to political science and economics. It is not, as friends of the factual might have it, that the older approach had failed, had got the world wrong: what had changed was the conception of success and of what it was important to be right about.

It follows that the rule-government of a discipline could at best be a fragile, threatened thing, liable, at any moment, to be rendered archaic by a shift in aim and value. Durkheim's 'rules of sociological method' are scarcely those that a Schütz or a Goffman feels obliged to follow. But, of course, why speak of rules at all? Strategies, policies, approaches, and styles that can be scrapped by a change, which they are powerless to prevent or check, in conceptions of what is to be achieved, do not deserve such a label.

Nietzsche's epistemology and the idea of authenticity as a central educational goal touch, penetrate, and colour one another at various points. This must be so, given that the epistemology stands opposed to those conceptions of the disciplines and knowledge which, we saw in the previous chapter, threaten that idea. It stands against the exaggerations of the factual and of the rule-governed, These two exaggerations have a similar source: the failure to countenance the degree to which claims to truth and conceptual adequacy are relative to the values and purposes of enquiry - a failure whose effect is to immunize enquiry against that concern for values and purposes which belonged in our notion of authenticity. If Nietzsche is right, this is not a concern that can be isolated from the pursuit of truth, since claims to truth are, *au fond*, not to be assessed without reference to the objects of that concern. Only in areas where the guiding values and purposes are so established, obvious, and unobjectionable that they can be 'bracketed', is there excuse for entertaining at least the semblance of an isolation.

One important point at which the epistemology and the idea of authenticity touch is where they lend prominence to 'genea-logical' considerations. The authentic person is to make his beliefs and values his own, and this must involve the attempt to see how he has come by and retained the ones he has: for if he has simply taken them on board, or begins to see them as having been thrust upon him, then they cannot - yet, anyway- be his own. But if truth has a relativity to the values and 'powers' served by theories and conceptual schemes, then a 'genealogical eye' for what these are, how they come about, and how they sustain a theory or scheme, is required for any investi-gation into truth. We are not constrained to accept as a correct taxonomy a way of classifying which only survives because of the role it plays in serving purposes that should not be ours.

Those of a Dadaist inclination (see p. 10 ff) are wont to pit authenticity against knowledge, and the rational in general. 'We want to demolish museums and libraries', proclaimed the Futurist Manifesto.(69) Truth and knowledge, they say, are either illusions, or at any rate of insufficient moment when matched against the authenticity of the creative artist or spontaneous man of action. This is a view which many have attributed to Nietzsche - both acolytes like Stefan George and his circle, and detractors like Lukàcs. And it is indeed a view which Nietzsche came close to in his first book, *The Birth of Tragedy*, where the intoxicating, the aesthetic, the Dionysian are favourably contrasted with the 'Alexandrian' or Socratic pursuit of know-ledge and reason. But it is not, as we have seen, a view that persists in his writings; and one of the most striking features of his mature philosophy is the attempt to reconcile the authen-ticity that the creative artist or man of action might be held to illustrate with the pursuit of truth. Truth is no illusion if it is understood in terms of the order, coherence, and power over 'the medley of sensations', which beliefs and theories can afford. But, so understood, the pursuit of truth is assimilated to the activity of the creative artist. No more than art is knowledge a mere response to what is given, a record of what there is to register. It is moulding, interpreting, taking perspectives, and refusing to rest where others have stopped. At least this is how it should be; for like a style of architecture or convention of painting, a body of beliefs and concepts can be a deadweight that drags people below that level of vision at which new possibilities are visible. The artist and the theorist, far from being at opposite ends of a pole, together represent the highest form that the will to power can take: for they are both, in Nelson Goodman's term, engaged in 'ways of worldmaking'.

Nietzsche's attitude towards the place of the intellect and the pursuit of knowledge in human life is best indicated, perhaps, by the title of one of his most important books, *The Gay Science*. It derives from the Provençal *gai saber*, which referred to the poetic art of the medieval troubadours from that region - an art, distinguished for Nietzsche and others, by its inventiveness, exuberance, lightness, and *élan*.(70) Nietzsche's point is that the pursuit of truth should, in various regards, emulate this *gaya scienza*, whether at the global level of systematic philosophizing, or at the level of particular detailed enquiries. The spinning of new metaphors, the suggestion of new analogies, the cutting across old classifications, the refusal to be opposed by the weight of tradition and orthodoxy: these are some of the ways truth should be pursued and educators should encourage. This is not, of course, to be the exuberance of license, and educators are not to be the preachers of a free-for-all. A poem in the book insists 'Our science shall be gay!' (Fröhlich - unsere Wissenschaft),(71) but the book also contains the section on 'The intellectual conscience', from which we have already quoted - that conscience which regards it as 'despicable' to accept a belief that has not been thoroughly investigated and weighed. And we have seen how, for Nietzsche, ways of conceptualizing can be so engrained in our language that to attempt to obliterate them in a trice, as an artist might try to overturn a tradition at a stroke, is to divest one's endeavour of intelligibility. Unlike the painter with his brushes and palette, the thinker is forced to take his tools in trade - words and concepts - from the very stock he wants to reorganize.

Writing about *The Gay Science* in his autobiographical *Ecce Homo*, Nietzsche refers to a poem from the former - *An den Mistral: Ein Tanzlied* - as a 'perfect Provençalism' which 'dances right over morality'.(72) It is to Nietzsche's moral Provençalism I now turn.

6 Genealogy, values, and the teaching of morality

Time was when teachers and educational thinkers viewed moral betterment as the principal purpose of schooling. A teacher asked to justify his choice of career might appeal to his contribution to the moral development of the young and so to the moral improvement of society. He might have taken his cue from Fichte, who considered it a criterion of proper education that it should make it impossible for a child to prefer, knowingly, the bad over the good; or from Dewey, who insisted that 'the moral purpose [is] universal and dominant in all instruction - whatsoever the topic'.(1) There are signs, in very recent years, of a renewed emphasis upon this goal of moral betterment. Mary Warnock, for example, includes virtue as one of the three ingredients in her 'good life' which it is the aim of schools to promote. 'Morality, or virtuousness', she says, 'should be taught, and can be learned' - though not, she adds, 'in special lessons'.(2) There has even been a revival of sympathetic interest in Fichte's views, at least as represented by English philosophers like T.H. Green who were influenced by him, and who themselves influenced generations of teachers and civil servants by bequeathing to them a lofty moral conception of their professions.(3)

For a considerable period, however, fashions in both educational and ethical thought conspired to produce a climate hostile to this emphasis upon the moral. The ideology of 'child-centredness', with its stress upon what the child demands as against what society demands of him, contributed to this climate; as did the well-subscribed view that any attempt to teach virtue must belong to indoctrination, not education. Reinforcement came from influential trends in moral philosophy; especially from the 'Emotivist' doctrine, and its various offspring, according to which moral judgment cannot express objective, teachable truth, but only the subjective, personal feeling of the person making it.(4) To be sure, there were philosophers, in broad agreement with this outlook, who emphasized that moral judgments must display consistency with one another and with the more general principles guiding them, and who argued that moral judgment, to count as such, must meet certain formal requirements. This allowed for the presence in the curriculum of something that could be labelled 'moral education'; but this would eschew the teaching of virtue and centre instead upon encouraging consistency and an awareness of the formal, methodological conditions which moral judgment must meet.(5) Nor should one overlook the influence of various 'radical' educators, for whom 'teaching virtue' could only mean either teaching children to share the values of a rotten society or teaching them to reject those values. The former, clearly, would be intolerable; while the latter would not only produce impossible friction with parents and government but, to judge from the events of 1968, results sufficient to shock even those who had advocated it.(6) Better, then, to leave moral education altogether alone.

What has revived the aim of teaching virtue? Partly, no doubt, the demand by large sections of the public that in a society of growing violence, hooliganism, alcoholism, racial hatred, or unwanted pregnancy, the school should again assume the responsibility for moral conduct which many feel it has abdicated. But there have been changes in the realm of ideas, too. 'Child-centredness' is not the banner it was, and if there is a new orthodoxy, it is that the child's self-development requires his rigorous subjection to the methods of the disciplines. The idea that teaching virtue must be indoctrinatory is now seen by many as exaggerated to the point of simple falsity. Is it not the case in all areas of learning that children must first be told what is so, before they can proceed to assess matters for them-selves? And, as Dewey asked, can the teacher avoid teaching virtue (or vice), through his demeanour, attitudes towards his subject, disciplinary methods, and the ethos of the school in which he works? If not - if he is bound to pass on some values rather than others - is it not best that he takes on a self-conscious concern to promote those which he thinks are right and adjust his teaching accordingly?(7) Finally, there has been a powerful resurgence of the idea that morality must, as it is put, have a 'content': that moral principles cannot be identified as such unless they enjoin certain kinds of conduct.(8) If so, moral education could not consist solely in teaching consistency and the formal requirements moral judgments have to obey, but must in addition encourage those modes of behaviour that are partially constitutive of moral understanding.

Any serious discussion of moral betterment as a goal of school-ing must honour a distinction, however rough, between moral education and training. For many of the arguments about this goal have little or nothing to do with educational matters. The demand that schools do something to stem the tide of hooliganism, mugging, or whatever, is not, as it stands, one that pertains to education. The imperative is that schools employ the most effective means to stop people behaving in certain ways, and it is hardly evident that these means would be educative ones. Schools, after all, do much besides educating - for example, trying to ensure a level of physical fitness - and perhaps the moral training or conditioning demanded by sections of the public belongs in this domain. The distinction in question is bound to be rough, and where one draws it will be contested. Someone who thinks teaching which goes beyond explaining 'the

form of moral reasoning' is indoctrinatory is likely to condemn
as mere training that teaching of virtue which, for others, constitutes the essence of a moral education.

Rough and contested it may be, but there is the distinction
to be made, and my discussion in this chapter will focus almost
entirely upon moral education, not training, for it is only with
this that the organizing theme of the book, authenticity, can
interestingly engage. To opt exclusively for moral training is
to abandon a concern for authenticity, at least in the realm of
moral beliefs and choices. Such questions as whether authenticity
and morality require one another, or whether they exclude one
another, or whether authenticity is itself a moral value, can
only be live questions if it is morality as 'the moral point of
view', and not a set of instilled habits, which is meant. Unless
the goal of moral betterment involves the attempt to foster
critical, self-conscious, independent moral choice, it cannot
figure in an education revolving around the notion of authenticity. To put things truistically: if the teaching of morality
belongs in an education for authenticity at all, it could do so
only as moral education.

These remarks must not be taken as any rejection of moral
training. Circumstances may - and, according to many, do -
make moral training an overriding imperative, for those who
need it, and for the sake of society. Moreover, if conditions in
some places are as grim as they are sometimes painted, it could
be merely frivolous to gear one's efforts either to fostering
authenticity or to the development of a critical moral point of
view. Inculcation of acceptable behaviour, by whatever non-
educational means, might remain the only attainable or sensible
goal. My interest, however, is in schools where moral education
would not be a sisyphean enterprise, and where a concern for
authenticity has some viability. The questions I ask concern
the relation between moral education and authenticity; and I
discuss them in the light, indeed glare, of Nietzsche's famous,
but frequently misconstrued, 'critique of morality'.

In his early educational writings, a main target of Nietzsche's
was the failure of German schools to pay due attention to moral
matters. Both *Realstudien* and 'scholarship' were 'a deviation
from true education as a moral phenomenon'.(9) A few years
later, he was still insisting that 'education should enforce the
virtues'.(10) And in one of his late notes, he could also say
that handing on the moral ideals of Christianity 'belongs among
the most desirable things there are. . . . We . . . require the
power of morality.'(11) But between the early and the late
remark, something had intervened - the critique of morality:
and a proper understanding of the late note will not disappoint
those who know of Nietzsche as the great moral iconoclast.
For alongside his demand that Christian ideals be handed on, he
was also insisting that the educator be 'beyond good and evil'(12);
and the reasons he gives for why we require the power of

morality are of a thoroughly non-moral kind. The passage runs:
'We immoralists require the power of morality: our self-
preservation drive wants our opponents to keep their strength -
it only wants to become *master over them*.' Morality, that is,
must be preserved, so that 'we immoralists' have opponents
against whom to test our mettle. And there are other reasons.
Among 'sturdy' and 'simple' people whose moral principles are
deeply ingrained, it would be merely disruptive and confusing
to challenge their attitudes.(13) More important, civilization
and its benefits - science and art, for example - have depended,
and continue to depend, on the majority of people obeying a
moral code. The 'superiority up to now of men over other
animals' has been due to the stability afforded by a common
morality and its chaining up of potentially dangerous 'barbarians'
and 'blond beasts'.(14) Even when morality threatens to become
a 'burden', we must express 'the deepest gratitude for what [it]
has hitherto achieved'.(15)

Nietzsche, then, is plainly an advocate of moral training - but
with the major qualification that this be only for the majority
of ordinary people, the 'herd', and not for exceptional individuals. 'The mentality of the herd should rule in the herd, but
not reach out beyond it.'(16) He is in qualified agreement with
the 'morally concerned' public which regards it as imperative to
encourage, by whatever means, that general conformity to a
moral code which is a prerequisite for social stability and
civilized existence. What must be done, according to Nietzsche,
is not to get rid of the moral code, but to 'end its tyranny'
over those who are capable of arising out of the 'herd'.(17)

For Nietzsche, of course, there is nothing educative about
moral training; and here his view parallels the one he adopted
towards *Realstudien:* practical studies are of great importance
for a community, but they have no place in a 'true education'.
What about moral education, then? Nietzsche's answer is that
the very notion is a contradiction in terms - and in more than
one way. To begin with, education is to be on the side of 'Life',
whereas morality, bluntly, is detrimental to 'Life'. 'The anti-
natural morality - that is, almost every morality . . . which has
so far been taught . . . is directed *against* . . . the instincts
of life.'(18) Moral education, then, would have, impossibly, to
be both for and against 'Life'. Second, the attempt at moral
education would of necessity employ means that were dishonest,
disingenuous, and hence *im*moral. 'One cannot establish the
domination of virtue by means of virtue itself.'(19) The main
point here is not that teaching morality ought only to employ
morally acceptable means: after all, moral training, which
Nietzsche allows, typically does not. The point, rather, is that
to count as education, moral teaching could not employ the lies,
illusions, and other immoral devices which it is, none the less,
constrained to do. When Nietzsche proclaims 'No "moral education" of the human species!'(20) he has both types of incon-
sistency in mind. Neither in what it aims at, nor in the way it

must proceed, can the teaching of morality belong to education.
It is upon this dismissal of the very notion of moral education,
and not upon the qualified advocacy of moral training, that I
shall concentrate. It is important, though, that we do not lose
sight of the latter, as too many commentators on Nietzsche
are prone to do. Thomas Mann, for example, thinks he is
criticizing Nietzsche when he writes: 'Life and morals . . .
belong together. Ethics supports life, and a man with good
morals is an upright citizen of life - perhaps a little boring, but
extremely useful.'(21) By 'life' Mann clearly means social life,
and is therefore saying nothing which Nietzsche would not
endorse. Society certainly requires the 'power of morality'; the
'man with good morals' is indeed 'extremely useful'; and ethics
indeed 'supports [social] life' - that is its function.

To understand the rejection of moral education, we need first
understand Nietzsche's critique and genealogy of morals. He
offers a number of, by and large, compatible scenarios for how
morality came into being and is sustained. Here is the well-
known one from section 201 and thereabouts of *Beyond Good and
Evil*. A community whose energies are taken up defending itself
against hostile surroundings and neighbours has no morality,
merely a set of regulations for facilitating this defence. The
admired men are the warriors and strong individuals who lead
the battle against these external threats, and they will be
referred to as 'good' in a non-moral sense such as 'noble'. But
as the safety of the community becomes ensured, it is precisely
these individuals who pose a threat to the community; for they
are likely to turn their powerful energies and aggressive nature
inward, against their own weaker brethren. It is from fear
of this that the weaker band together to set up a system of
rules which, it is hoped, will constrain the behaviour of all,
but in particular that of the potentially dangerous, powerful
individuals. Fear is thus 'the mother of morality'.(22) The
values codified by the system of rules will be ones like pity,
charity, humility, meekness, equal rights, and turning the other
cheek; for it is these which serve to emasculate the powerful
to the advantage of the weaker. Since the strong man hits
harder, it will be as well for the weak if he can be persuaded
not to punch back - or, in case he does, to treat his victim
with sympathy and charity. This 'slave-revolt' of morality has,
by and large, been successful: partly because the 'slaves'
have number on their side: partly because they are more
prudent, calculating, and shrewd; and partly because they
have consolidated the victory of erecting a set of convincing
illusions and myths to bolster up the new moral code. In
particular, they have constructed religions devoted to the
worship of vengeful Gods who side with the weak. Morality,
then, is a device used by some to assert or maintain their
power against others; either in a fairly direct way, as with
the 'turn the other cheek' maxim, or in subtly indirect ways -

as when the weak exploit the idea of free will so as to pride
themselves that they simply do not *choose* to exercise individual
strength.(23) In crude or subtle ways, morality is, in
Nietzsche's frequently reiterated phrase, a form of 'the will to
power'.

Someone whose acquaintance with Nietzsche's critique does
not go beyond such scenarios would be right to raise two
queries. First, why do they constitute a critique of morality
in general? After all, Nietzsche himself refers to a 'master'
morality whose nature and roots are very different from the
'slave' or 'herd' morality just sketched. Second, why do such
scenarios constitute a *critique*, even of 'slave' morality? Is
Nietzsche not guilty of a 'genetic fallacy' of confusing issues
of truth and validity with ones of history? It may well be that
altruistic principles took root through a defensive response by
the weak and were then nourished by various illusions. But
how can all of this bear upon the rightness or otherwise of the
principles?

We need, clearly, to examine what, for Nietzsche, are the
fundamental features of morality, its essence. Only then will it
emerge why he thinks that the reasons people have for embracing morality provide a critique of it, and why he thinks it is
morality as such, and not some parochial version of it, that
stands condemned. It is vital to realize that Nietzsche in fact
operates with two main concepts of morality: a 'thin' and a
'rich' one. It is the first which tends to dominate in earlier
writings, such as *Human, All-Too-Human,* where he writes:
'To be moral, ethical, means to be obedient to old-established
law or custom. Whether one submits to it with effort or gladly
is indifferent: it is enough that one does so.'(24) In these
writings, a recurrent phrase is *'die Sittlichkeit der Sitte'* -
the morality of mores, or better perhaps, morality *as* mores.
Here is the 'thin' concept of morality as a set of practices and
customs subscribed to by a community; morality in the sense
that an anthropologist describes it when he lists the various
taboos and traditions which govern a tribe's social life. There
can, in this sense, be a wide variety of moralities - as many as
there are distinctively different societies - including 'master'
moralities which enjoin practices far removed from those which
flourish where the 'slave-revolt' has been successful. The codes
of the Samurai warriors, the Homeric heroes, or the Nordic
'robber-barons' might be 'master' moralities in this sense.

In *The Genealogy of Morals* and other later writings, however,
we find morality as mores treated as something belonging to
the 'pre-historical work' of men. Morality in a 'rich' sense only
emerges when it becomes tied to notions like free will, responsibility, and conscience, which had no place in the 'pre-moral'
era of mores. In that era, recall, the motive for submitting to a
code was irrelevant: it was enough that one did so. The relevance
of motivation, however, to the assessment of an action now
becomes 'the sign of a period that one may call "moral" in the

narrower sense' - the 'rich' sense.(25)

Nietzsche's critique is directed against morality in this 'narrower', 'rich' sense, for it focuses upon those features which had no place in the 'pre-moral' era of morality as mores. These features, moreover, are not ones peculiar to only some brands of morality, but belong to any form of evaluation that can count as moral in the 'rich' sense. 'Master morality', which does not display enough of these features, or not to a sufficient degree, is now a misnomer. Nietzsche stresses that 'good', in the mouths of 'masters', does not contrast with the moral expression 'bad' *(böse)* but with 'bad' *(schlecht)* used in a non-moral way. Hence the 'master's' 'good' is not the moral term it is in the mouths of the 'slaves', but means something like 'noble' or 'of a superior nature'.(26) Nietzsche's tendency is now to equate morality as such with what he had previously qualified as 'slave', 'herd', or 'Christian' morality. It is the use of 'morality' in connection with values other than the 'herd's' which now gets qualified, as when he refers to the 'so-called morality' embodied in the Law of Manu.(27) A variety of moralities is still allowed for, but these must belong within a fairly close-knit family. It is totally wrong, therefore, to suppose that Nietzsche is the moral relativist he is often portrayed: for him there cannot be that degree of incompat-ibility and rivalry between widely different moralities which relativism presupposes.

It is not Nietzsche's way to supply neat definitions - 'Only that is definable which has no history'(28) - but he does provide a list of features enough of which and to a sufficient degree must belong to anything recognizable as morality in the 'rich' sense. There are at least four such features. First, the moral point of view must lend a central place to notions of blame, responsibility, and conscience, drawn from a philosophical psychology which attributes free will to people and explains their behaviour in terms of intentions and volitions. Concepts like 'guilt' and 'duty', for example, only become genuinely moral ones 'with their being pushed back into bad conscience'.(29) Second, it is only 'selfless' or 'altruistic' behaviour and attitudes which can have moral value. 'What is the criterion of a moral action? . . . its disinterestedness'.(30) Next, the moral view-point requires certain beliefs in human equality: the belief, at the very least, that there are principles binding upon all men as such. 'The essence of the moral [is] "universal and general".'(31) Finally, morality must enjoin the removal or mini-mization of suffering. Morality is 'a principle of preservation . . . advantageous to the "suffering".'(32)

Nietzsche's claim is that each of these features represents false beliefs that owe their entrenchment to the manner in which they bolster up the values which the weaker need to impress upon a community in their power-struggle against potentially dangerous, powerful individuals. The value of charity, for example, is reinforced by the idea that uncharitable behaviour

is at once blameworthy, selfish, a denial of equal human rights
and of the necessary evil of suffering. Nietzsche offers many
considerations in support of such contentions. He notes, for
example, how as the weak become more secure, the premium
upon holding people blameworthy diminishes; so that *inter alia*,
not only do punishments become less severe, but the very
notion of punishment begins to give way before that of 'treatment', and the idea of the responsible criminal before that of
the victim of social conditions.(33)

It is essential to grasp, however, that Nietzsche does not
hold the crucial beliefs - in free will, altruism, equality, and
the necessary evil of suffering - as false *because* they serve
to bolster up the values advantageous to the weak. If any
'genetic fallacy' is present, it is not at this level of crudity.
Indeed, Nietzsche is insistent that 'the question of the origin
of our evaluations and tables of the good is not at all equivalent
to their critique, as is so often believed'.(34) In the case of
each bolstering belief, reasons are offered as to why it is false,
which have nothing to do with matters of origin or function.
The belief in free, blameable actions rests on a mistaken
philosophical psychology which posits a mythical subject, self,
or ego distinct from, and somehow responsible for behaviour.
The distinction between selfish and selfless, altruistic action
collapses for the same reason, for 'there is no such thing as the
ego of which one speaks when one censures egoism'.(35) In
another sense, however, all actions are egoistic, since they aim
at preserving or increasing the agent's power. Will to power is
the universal explanatory factor. Since all actions take place
within a deterministic scheme, there is no sense to the practice
of condemnation which is integral to moral evaluation: for to
condemn an individual action would be to condemn the world of
which it is an inextricable part. 'A reprehensible action means:
a reprehensible world.'(36) (This somewhat Leibnizian point,
incidentally, is the sense of Zarathustra's puzzling insistence
that one must 'affirm' the whole of existence if one is to 'affirm'
anything.)

As for conscience, this is not, as moralists claim, a voice
informing one what is right and wrong, but the directing
inwards of cruel, aggressive instincts that no longer have
an external outlet: a sort of self-directed *Schadenfreude*.(37)
The belief in equality and the universalizability of values is
absurd on a number of counts. It ignores the 'rank-order'
among men; those fundamental differences in abilities, character,
and powers which make it perverse to suppose that all men owe,
or are owed, the same. It ignores, too, the particularity and
uniqueness of the situations in which men are called upon to act.

Whoever judges 'This is how everyone should act in this case'
has still not taken five steps towards self-knowledge: otherwise he would know that actions neither are nor can be the
same - that every action [is] done in a unique and irretriev-

able way . . . that all prescriptions for actions relate only
to their coarse exterior.(38)

The belief, finally, in the inherent evil of suffering rests, like
the practice of blaming and condemning, upon a failure to
appreciate the integrated nature of existence. For suffering is
often a precondition of individual achievement, greatness, and
self-realization. 'I do not count its evil and painful character
as a reproach against existence.'(39) It would, for example, be
incoherent to be grateful for the literary achievements of,
say, Kleist, while proclaiming oneself against the type of
anguish that can alone give birth to such writings. Nietzsche,
of course, sees no value in pointless suffering: one of his main
criticisms of pity is that, since this is a kind of suffering that
in itself helps no one, it merely reduplicates the stock of
suffering to no purpose.

Readers will agree, I hope, that it would be frivolous to try to
assess Nietzsche's arguments in the space available. The point
about blame alone would at once embroil us in no less than the issues of free will, behaviourism, and determinism. I simply record
my view that none of his arguments is less than serious, and are
not to be dismissed (nor accepted) in any cavalier fashion. With
this on record, I proceed to examine the exact place of these
arguments within the critique of morality and of moral education.

Granted, someone might say, that the beliefs which support
moral evaluation are, or involve, illusions, this does not constitute a criticism of the values themselves: and this is so, even
if both values and illusions are subscribed to, ultimately,
through fear, *ressentiment,* or the demand for power. Nietzsche's
reply to this charge moves in two stages. First, once values
like charity become unhinged from the (false) beliefs which
buttress them, there is no longer reason to count them as moral
values. Politeness is a value, but not a moral one: not only are
we generally unconcerned with why people act politely – it is
enough that they do – but its value is not grounded on considerations of selflessness, equal rights, the evil of suffering, and
so on. If charity were similarly advocated solely on grounds of
social cohesion, smoothness of personal relations, and the like,
there would be no reason for counting it as a moral value either.
We would have moved, in Nietzsche's terminology, to an
'extra-moral' perspective – and sensibly so. The second stage
in his reply is that once people recognize the usual reasons
given in support of moral values to be false, they are forced to
admit that the real reasons for having subscribed to these
values have been of a shadier type – a type, indeed, which
makes their subscription *im*moral by their own criteria. Having
been forced to see morality as 'the work of error', they must
also view it as 'the work of immorality'. For example: envy
and *ressentiment* are attitudes condemned by morality; so if it
turns out that subscription to the value of equality, say, is
founded on such attitudes, then this subscription stands con-

demned - morally condemned by the moralist's own lights. Or
again: since the attempt to dominate others is morally censured,
a person could see no moral worth in performing charitable
actions if their real motive is the will to dominate.

Nietzsche is no Kantian, but shares with him the view that
actions, to be of moral worth, must be brought about in certain
ways - by Kant's 'good will', or something akin. For Kant, it
was a puzzle how actions could be so brought about. For
Nietzsche, there is no puzzle, just an impossibility. What goes
for actions goes for values and beliefs as well. Those who
accuse Nietzsche of a 'genetic fallacy' overlook an important
point he is making here: that it is integral to the acceptance of
a moral belief - in the value of charity, say - that not only the
actions evaluated, but the belief itself, be thought of as generated in some ways and not others. I cannot continue to ascribe
moral worth to my charitable actions, nor validity to my belief
in this worth, if I come to see actions and belief alike as fully
explained by *ressentiment*, the will to dominate, and the like.
Such explanations are not of mere external or sociological
interest: for acceptance of them cuts into the very possibility
of continuing with the beliefs.(40)

If my reading of Nietzsche is correct, his critique requires
both that the usual reasons given in support of moral values
are false, and that the real reasons for subscribing to these
values are anyway of a different order. Were it simply that the
reasons usually given by the moral man were not his real ones,
he could comfort himself that, whatever his reasons, there may
be some good ones around - and isn't that enough? Were it
simply that the proffered reasons were bad ones, it would
remain that people who subscribed to moral values on their
basis do so in good faith, and hence have a genuinely moral
viewpoint, however shaky the supports may look to an outsider.
But if the proffered reasons are bad ones and, to boot, not the
operative ones anyway, no such comforts remain. There are no
good reasons for subscribing to moral values, and the real
explanation of why people adopt them renders that adoption
condemned by the light of those very values.

We are now in a better position to understand why Nietzsche
thinks the notion of moral education is incoherent. But, first,
a preliminary point. Earlier I drew attention to a distinction
between teaching virtue and teaching the 'form' or 'essence' of
moral evaluation. This distinction, on which much weight has
been placed by several moral educationalists, must be an
artificial one for Nietzsche. If teaching virtue is simply the
instilling of mores, then it is not the teaching of morality, in
the 'rich' sense, at all; for it would not incorporate teaching
those fundamental features without which mores still belong to
the 'pre-history' of morality. But these fundamental features -
the idea of freely willed, blameable action, for example, or the
notion of universalizability - turn out not to be purely 'formal'.

On the contrary, they serve directly or otherwise to bolster up those virtues which the 'herd' requires a society to recognize.

Moral education, then, would have to go beyond the encouragement of certain mores, and initiate people into an understanding and acceptance of those features without which mores do not progress to morals. But in that case, Nietzsche argues, moral education must involve the teaching of illusions, the impressing upon the young of false conceptions of how men, their nature, and the world really are. Clearly this would be incompatible with an education which aimed to provide that correct 'situational' understanding which was an ingredient in authenticity. Since, moreover, the direction of these illusions is towards the buttressing of a set of values inimical to any individuality which the weak might view as a threat towards themselves, such an education would take us away from that 'projective' concern for individual purposes which was another ingredient in authenticity. Given that education is for 'Life' - which we interpreted to mean 'authentic living' - it follows, in a double manner, that moral education could form no part of a true education.

Worse still, perhaps, moral education could not be an honest and transparent enterprise. Part of what Nietzsche means here is that, as a matter of contingent fact, teachers of morality are typically constrained to employ means that stand condemned by the lessons they are teaching - flattery, threats, white lies, and so on. 'Whoever lacks the courage for immorality is suitable for anything, but not to be a moralist.'(41) More importantly, though, he means that no moral educator could sincerely engage in his enterprise whilst having a genuine understanding of its nature. Morality, and hence moral education, is the attempt to continue by other and more refined means the domination of some to the advantage of others. But such an attempt stands condemned by morality itself. No teacher of morality who understands this can regard his enterprise as morally justified; nor can he allow those he is teaching to share his understanding. He is forced to see that moral education, like morality itself, 'is always in contradiction with itself'.(42) The necessary duplicity and opacity of moral teaching, by those who understand its nature, disqualifies it as an ingredient in a true education. The mere instilling of mores - moral training - need not involve such duplicity; but since training, as such, does not incorporate the teaching of understanding, it forms no part of education anyway.

Nietzsche, we all know, did have his own 'table of values'. Indeed he thought the idea of a person without values was unintelligible, for in order to act one must will, and to will something is to place a value upon it. At various places - for example, in the list of 'our virtues' in *Beyond Good and Evil,* in the chapter on 'higher men' in *Thus Spake Zarathustra,* or in the occasional glimpses he gives us of the 'overman' - Nietzsche communicates his vision of how men should, if they are capable of it, be. It

is the 'breeding' of those who are capable to live in accordance
with this vision that is the aim of true education. I postpone
until the final chapters any detailed account of this vision: it
suffices for the purposes of the present chapter to list some of
these, 'our virtues'. Among them are: self-honesty; conquest
of fear; mistrust towards both received and 'scholarly' opinion;
despising the petty and mediocre; a developed sense of history;
self-discipline; willing nothing beyond one's capacity; full
awareness of what that capacity is; the ability to command –
and to obey; the refusal to regret or 'do the dirty on' one's
chosen and considered purposes; abstention from merely negative
criticism; the ability to 'laugh at', hence stand at a distance
from, hence be ready to alter how one has been; the power to
turn sufferings and illness into new sources of strength;
spontaneous, as against brooding, calculative responses to
treatment by others.

Several items on this list, unsurprisingly, belong to that
constellation of values grouped under our heading of 'authenticity'. Mistrust of received opinion, for example, is a condition
of 'situational' concern; while the refusal to 'do the dirty on'
one's own actions is a mark of the person whose purposes are
adopted only after due 'projective' concern. At a pinch we might
view each item as an ingredient in a life that is truly one's
own. If so, the questions I discuss in the remainder of this
chapter can be taken as ones about authenticity, even when they
are not framed in those terms.

One question is this: since Nietzsche does have his own 'table
of values', does it not emerge after all that his critique was not
of morality as such, but only of a general species which he wants
to replace by one of his own? (Or, if you wish, do the values
grouped under the heading of 'authenticity' not constitute a
morality?) Does not Nietzsche himself sometimes depict what he
is doing in this way, as when he speaks of advocating a 'healthy
morality . . . demanded by an instinct of life'?(43) Although he
does sometimes speak in this way, his usual practice is to refer
to his own values as 'extra-moral', or, in a nice phrase from
The Antichrist, as 'moraline-free', suggestive of the abstemious
Nietzsche's dislike of caffeine, nicotine, and other stimulants.
It would be a pity, anyway, if we took the main issue to be
whether Nietzsche, or we, should at the final reckoning *call*
by the name 'moral' a set of values that differ from the paradigmatically moral ones mentioned earlier. The important matter
is to become clear that Nietzsche's values do not share the
fundamental features of these paradigmatically moral ones; that
the differences between his values and these are not of the
relatively parochial kind that might separate the moral codes of,
say, two successive generations. The scale of these differences
should, I think, dissuade us from applying the term 'moral'
to Nietzsche's values; but it is appreciation of this scale which
is the real business.

There are, in fact, good pragmatic reasons for not wielding

the term 'moral' in as wide a way as many writers are prone to
do - a way so wide that it would, for example, contain
Nietzsche's values in its sweep. For one thing, it would scotch
the temptation to oscillate, unnoticed, between some very wide
use and a much narrower one. Dewey, a writer given to such
oscillations, provides a nice illustration. Having announced
that 'moral ideas' are any which 'take effect on conduct and
improve it . . . (whether arithmetical, or geographical, or
physiological [ideas])', we find him concluding, not unreason-
ably, that 'the moral purpose [should be] universal and
dominant in all instruction'. Shortly, though, he manages to
reach the thoroughly controversial conclusion that the 'moral
work and worth of the . . . school system . . . are to be
measured by its social value', and that therefore the primary
aim of instruction is to produce the 'good citizen . . . the
efficient and serviceable member of society'.(44) What has gone
wrong, of course, is an unannounced shift from an extravagantly
wide sense of 'moral', in terms of whatever improves or betters,
to a much narrower one, in terms of the socially useful. Another
danger in an over-catholic use of 'moral' is that we can be
blinded to the real nature of certain shifts in evaluations,
wrongly assimilating them to cases in which, fairly clearly, one
moral viewpoint gives way to another. The so-called revolution
in sexual morality, for example, may be less that than a take-
over of a moral perspective on sexual behaviour by an almost
medical one. The 'problem page' columnist, Marje Proops, noted
how, over the years, her readers' questions about the rightness
or wrongness of certain sexual behaviour had given way to
ones asking if the behaviour was 'natural' or not, 'inhibited'
or not. In the field of penology, too, we find the creeping
tendency, predicted by Samuel Butler and by Nietzsche (see
p. 96) for a quasi-medical viewpoint to replace a moral one,
with crime and punishment becoming increasingly categorized
as a social disease and hygiene respectively.

It is apparent, to return to Nietzsche's 'table of values', that
these exhibit few, if any, of the features he deemed essential
to moral values. They are not altruistic or 'selfless'; they pertain to the individual's good, not to the community's welfare;
they do not rest on a notion of equal humanity; conscience is
rejected as a form of self-betrayal; and suffering, in some of
its forms, is to be positively welcomed. If reference to
Nietzsche's own 'morality' tempts people to overlook or
minimize these differences, then it is a reference to be avoided.

These differences, of course, will seem less impressive to
those who think of morality as constituted less by the substance
of its values, and the beliefs they rest upon, than by rather
more formal conditions on moral judgments. Two conditions,
both deriving from Kant, which several philosophers have held
to be essential to, or even definitive of, moral judgments is that
these be 'universalizable' and 'imperatival'. If Nietzsche's own
evaluations are neither of these, then we have further reasons -

assuming these philosophers are right – for not counting his evaluations as moral. They will not have the right 'form', let alone the right 'content'.

We have already seen that, for Nietzsche, *universal* prescriptions are absurd, since they neglect both the 'rank-order' among men and the 'uniqueness' of their actions. In the same vein, he writes: 'what naiveté there generally is in saying "Man ought to be such and such"! Reality shows us an enchanting wealth of types, the luxuriousness of a lavish play and change of form.'(45) His own values are to apply only to 'free spirits', 'higher men', and those, however designated, who do not belong in the 'herd'. 'I am a law only for my kind', says Zarathustra, 'I am not a law for all.'(46) His own words notwithstanding, someone may object that Nietzsche's values do not transgress the 'universalizability' condition: for what this enjoins is that a judgment, to count as moral, must apply to all persons who are similarly placed in relevant respects. Without this caveat, it would be a silly condition – entailing, for example, that paupers have identical obligations to millionaires. Isn't Nietzsche's point, simply, that there are relevant respects, sadly overlooked by many moralists, in which men are not similarly placed? Some people are 'creative' and others 'uncreative', for example; some are capable of great self-discipline, others not. If the 'universalizability' condition is compatible with the rich having different obligations from the poor, why not with the 'creative' having different ones from the 'uncreative', or with the self-disciplined having different ones from other people?

The problem with this objection is that it threatens to reduce the 'universalizability' condition to vacuity; for if it is to place real limits on what can count as a moral judgment, there must be constraints on what can figure as the relevant respects in which people may or may not be similarly placed. Otherwise a person could pick any one of the innumerable features which distinguish him from other people as exonerating him from an otherwise general obligation – the number of wrinkles on his brow, say. It is notoriously difficult, of course, to settle just what these constraints are; but it is surely plain that the differences in 'rank-order' on which Nietzsche focuses are not of the kind that Kant and his successors could regard as making for differences in moral obligations. That one man is a 'creative' philosopher, while a second is not, could not constitute the type of difference which, for the Kantian, could exonerate the one from the duties incumbent on the other. To hold, as Nietzsche does, that the philosopher has duties which are not those of members of the 'herd', or vice versa, is not a claim which can be accommodated by a 'universalizibility' condition which hopes to place genuine limits on which duties may be deemed moral ones.

Various considerations underlie the suggestion that moral evaluations must be 'imperatival' in nature. One is that it seems to help distinguish moral from aesthetic judgments; for in

praising a masterpiece, I am hardly issuing a directive that
others paint like the master. It also seems to help distinguish
the moral from the merely Utopian meaning of a judgment like
'No one ought to be rich'; which is the distinction, arguably,
between something like 'The rich are under an obligation to
give their wealth away', and something like 'In the best of all
possible worlds, there would be equal wealth; but in the real
world of course . . . '.(47) (There is another consideration
which I shall come to in a moment.) Whatever the force of these
points, it is clear that Nietzsche does not regard his own
evaluations 'imperatively'. Consider the following, pregnant
aphorism: '"A man as he *ought* to be": that sounds to us as
insipid [*schmacklos*] as "A tree as it ought to be."'(48) Certainly,
one may say of an oak that it should be tall, leafy, and sturdy,
but it would be insane to think of this as a directive issued to
the tree. There are a number of reasons why Nietzsche does
not want his own evaluations construed imperatively. One has
to do with the point, already encountered, about the integrated
nature of reality of which a given person's life is an inextricable
part; for if this is so, Nietzsche urges, then to demand of a
person that he alters his behaviour is, absurdly, 'to demand
that everything be changed, even retroactively'.(49) More
importantly, he thinks that to direct people to live in accordance with his values would be either dangerous or superfluous.
The majority of people, the 'herd', are incapable of living
authentic lives; and it could be cruel, and certainly socially
disruptive, to try to get them to do so. On the other hand, those
'free spirits' and 'higher men' who are capable of realizing such
values in their lives have only to understand them, and to
understand the bankruptcy of other values, in order to want
to realize them. This point is linked to the doctrine of the will
to power. Higher individuals only attain their power by living
in accordance with a Nietzschean 'table of values'; and since
people cannot but aim at what they see as increasing their
power, then any individual who recognizes that his power resides
in authentic living is bound to want to live in such a way.
Telling him he should do, once this understanding and recognition has dawned, would be superfluous.

   The point is also linked to the perceptive one which emerges
in the following passage:

> What does the 'Thou shalt!' mean, which is even thought of
> by philosophers as 'given'? The apparently insane thought
> that a person should have greater esteem for the actions he
> performs for another than for those he performs for himself
> . . . does have a sense: namely as the instinct of the public
> spirit which rests on the valuation that the individual is of
> little importance.(50)

Nietzsche is drawing attention, rightly, to the difficult problem
of how moral imperatives - 'Thou shalt's' - are possible; how

directives which are not backed by punitive sanctions and
which typically demand behaviour against one's own interest
can take effect and secure obedience. Nietzsche's answer is
that training has instilled into people an 'instinct of the public
spirit', which places community welfare above the good of the
individual. Moral directives achieve uptake through touching
this instinct. Nietzsche's own evaluations, however, are almost
entirely devoid of 'public spirit'; nor, like prudential directives,
could they take effect by appealing to self-interest, for there
is no gravy in the Nietzschean life. It is obscure, therefore,
how Nietzsche's directives, if this is what his evaluations are,
could achieve any uptake. But the notion of imperatives which
no one can have reason to comply with verges on the incoherent.
If so, Nietzsche is right not to regard these evaluations as
imperatival, and to view the imperatival model as inapplicable
to the relation between these evaluations and the actions of those
who accept them.

   The imperatival analysis of moral judgments appeals, primarily,
to those who, on various grounds, are unable to accept that
these judgments can express true-or-false, fact-stating,
informative propositions. Not only does the analysis seem to
circumvent the danger which then threatens of treating moral
judgments as meaningless ejaculations but, in contrast to the
propositional account, provides a plausible model of their action-
guiding nature. If a moral judgment merely furnished information
how could it move to action? Now Nietzsche belongs among those
philosophers who deny that moral judgments have the nature of
informative propositions. One of his original insights, he boasts,
is 'that there are no moral facts'.(51) For this reason, we have
just seen, he agrees that moral judgments are imperatives, 'Thou
shalt's'. Were he to admit that his own evaluations were
imperatival, the force of the admission would be the denial that
these provide understanding and information - a denial Nietzsche
would certainly not make, since he regards his evaluations as
philosophical descriptions of the nature of authentic human
existence. It is, if you wish, a matter of philosophic fact that,
say, self-discipline is an ingredient in the authentic life.
Nietzsche's evaluations, therefore, have a totally different
grammar from moral ones. There cannot, as Nietzsche sees it, be
any problem as to how such descriptions and understanding
guide action - the problem which, in the sphere of moral judgments, the imperatival model was supposed to solve. For it is
not intelligible that a person who understands the nature of
authentic living should, provided he is capable of it, not try to
live in this way; not intelligible that a person should prefer to
live a life that is not his own to one that is. At any rate, such
a preference would betray that he is someone incapable of living
in accordance with his nature as a human being. Nietzsche's
style can blind us to the nature of his own evaluative remarks,
as he construed them; for, especially through the mouth of
Zarathustra, he often presents them in a thoroughly exhortative

way. But what he is exhorting is that we understand and grasp
something - what is involved in authentic living: once the
understanding is there, there will be no need for calls to
action.(52)

There is a further consideration, of some importance, serving
to emphasize the distance between Nietzsche's 'table of values'
and morality. If moralities are codes which aim at the well-being
of the community, then the central moral focus will be upon
what men do, upon their actions. This focus upon actions is,
of course, compatible with a derived concern for character,
attitudes, and motives, since these can be assessed according
to their contribution to behaviour. A motive is morally honour-
able, say, because of its tendency to issue in desirable behaviour.
But action is not Nietzsche's first concern. It is not what men
do, but what they are, which has value. Not even indirectly is
a man's worth derived from what he does; rather, the value of
his actions derives from his worth. 'An action in itself is totally
devoid of value: everything depends on *who* does it. One and
the same "crime" can in one case be the highest privilege, in
another a stigma.'(53) To take another example: the reticent,
self-effacing refusal to give commands may be justified for one
man, but not for another who is 'called to and made for
commanding'.(54) Again, self-sacrifice on the part of a person
who despises himself does not have the worth of the same action
performed by someone whose pride and integrity demand it.
(There need be no difference in motive here: both persons may
want, by resigning their jobs, to save a colleague's.)

At first blush, Nietzsche's focus here may seem to run counter
to his robust rejection of any mind/body dualism and of 'inner'
states identifiable except through behavioural criteria. He is
dismissive, as we saw, of the idea that 'strength' might be an
'inner' capacity which people simply decide not to exercise in
their behaviour. But there is no contradiction. It is indeed
behaviour alone which enables identification of character; but
once identified, it becomes possible to evaluate actions
differently relative to characters. If a person has shown, by
his behaviour naturally, that he is 'called to and made for
commanding', then his reticent self-effacement becomes a self-
betrayal which it would not be in the case of someone who had
shown nothing of the sort.

It would be misleading to conclude that, since character is
identified behaviourally, then it is, after all, behaviour which
is the true locus of value. For one thing, this would be to
overlook the degree to which many of Nietzsche's values are, so
to speak, 'second-order'. Persistence, creativity, self-discipline,
and the like, are not displayed in the doing of some things
rather than others, but in the manner or style in which almost
anything may be done - from drinking to writing, from love-
making to philosophizing. Such a conclusion would also encourage
a false assimilation of Nietzsche's views to those of Dewey. For
both writers, a prime educational aim is the 'harmonious develop-

ment of all the powers of the individual', but Dewey goes on to
add that this aim has no meaning except with reference to
'accomplishing certain definite kinds of [social] work'.(55) Here,
to be sure, we find a value cashed in behavioural terms; but
it is a transaction that has no analogue in Nietzsche's conception.

A teacher impressed by Nietzsche's critique of morality and
moral education might nevertheless feel the coldest of feet at
the prospect of what may seem to be the Nietzschean alternative.
For is that alternative not to teach *immorality*, egoism, rejection
of established mores, and lack of sympathy? If moral education
is to disappear, then surely silence on matters of value, and
not the Nietzschean substitute, is the only recourse.
We are in a position to see that this reaction would, in several
respects, be misguided. Nietzsche's critique, recall, is directed
primarily against the beliefs and attitudes which underpin mores,
and against a heavily camouflaged creature invented by and
for the sake of certain interested groups. It is less the particular
actions which morality enjoins than the nature of those who
utilize it that is his critical concern. Those same actions, performed by different men and on a different basis, would have
a different worth. Thus we find Nietzsche distinguishing
between at least two kinds of altruism and two kinds of pity or
sympathy. There can be a 'moraline-free', 'noble' pity, which
has a value that 'weak', 'Christian' pity does not possess. This
latter, which Nietzsche decries, is that of the man, convinced
by egalitarian cant and ashamed of his own advantages and
self-concern, who feels it a duty to give these up for the sake
of others. It is the pity referred to in the title of Stefan
Zweig's only full-length novel, *Ungeduld des Herzens (Impatience
of the Heart)*, and which is felt by the hero for a young crippled
girl whom, in a drunken state, he had asked to dance. His pity
is a 'weak-willed and sentimental' one, and an attempt 'to escape
as quickly as possible from the painful emotion felt at another's
misfortune'; a pity whose cloying and wavering nature drives
the girl to suicide and the hero to seek death on the battlefield.
It is contrasted with the 'unsentimental, but creative . . .
decisive, patient' sympathy of the Doctor, whose motive is not
horror but love of people, and whose aim is not to offer consolation but to return the girl to a properly human existence,
freed from her obsession with her useless legs.(56) This is
Nietzsche's 'noble' pity, whose goal is to confer pride and
dignity.

> *Our* pity is a higher, more far-sighted pity - we see how man
> belittles himself, how *you* belittle him. . . . In man, *creature*
> and *creator* are united. . . . *Your* pity applies to the 'creature
> in man'.(57)

> My kind of 'pity' . . . is a feeling . . . I feel . . . when I see
> precious abilities squandered . . . or when I see someone . . .

lagging behind what could have come of him.(58)

The teacher's reaction to Nietzsche's 'egoism' is also misguided. For one thing, Nietzsche advocates, like Aristotle,
only that *some* people be egoistic: 'Egoism is of as much worth
as the physiological worth of he who has it.'(59) Since most
people are 'indifferent egoists', they would soon go under if,
instead of obeying mores and following convention, they tried
to behave in self-consciously egoistic ways. For some, however,
egoism is a precondition of full personal development. Let me
elaborate.

We noted earlier a sense in which, for Nietzsche, all men are
egoists: for, like everything in nature, they aim at the
maximization of their power, even when, as in the case of
martyrs, they seem to be doing the opposite. If altruism is the
demand that people be otherwise, then altruism is a pipe-dream.
This doctrine of universal egoism is, however, at a far remove
from traditional versions, with their postulation of a 'self',
'ego', or whatever which always seeks to bring about actions
that will be to its advantage. For Nietzsche, this is psychological mythology. 'There is no such thing as the ego of which
one speaks when one censures egoism.' Nor is Nietzsche's
universal egoism of a traditional hedonist variety, for it is not
pleasure, happiness, or utility men are doomed to pursue. Nor
is it a hedonistic ethic he is advocating when he uses 'egoism'
to refer to a value that some men ought to pursue, rather than
as something which, in the form of will to power, characterizes
all of us. Hedonistic utilitarianism, he thinks, is a 'secret,
malicious, vulgar, perhaps self-deceiving instinct for diminishing
man'.(60) His advocacy of egoism has nothing in common with
Adam Smith's idea that, through the operation of a 'hidden
hand', the utility of all will be maximized by each aiming at his
own.

The fact is, Nietzsche is playing the *enfant terrible* in his
choice of the term 'egoism' as an evaluative one. What he means
by it are some of the main ingredients in our notion of authenticity - self-concern, for example, and a sense of one's
individual worth. Altruism, with its demand that we focus our
attentions on others, stems from the individual's sense of 'being
a miscarriage. The value judgment at bottom says here: "I am
not worth much".' The 'right to egoism', belonging to the 'well-
constituted individual', comes from his 'care for the future
promised in him'.(61) With such 'well-constituted individuals',
the 'most essential thing is the feeling "Who am I?"'(62) The
'egoist', then, is a person with a persistent, reflective concern
for himself, his values, beliefs, and purposes; one who will not
be deterred by the 'altruist's' insistence that he is of insufficient
worth to have a right to this concern. I return to Nietzsche's
'egoism' in the final chapter; but it should now be plain that his
advocacy of it has nothing in common with the call to rear a
generation of Sir Willoughby Patternes, whose main concern at

losing a wife is the bother of finding another.(63)

That 'egoism' is only being advocated for some should remind us of a point that is perhaps being overlooked by our teacher, frightened at the prospect of a Nietzschean alternative to moral education. If 'teaching morality' means something like moral training or encouragement to comply with society's mores, then it is not something Nietzsche wants to replace at all - not, that is, for the great majority of people, the 'herd'. Far from desiring a general breakdown in mores, Nietzsche, as we have seen, regards general compliance with them as a precondition of the pursuit, by some, of 'higher values'.

If the Nietzschean alternative is not an unbridled encouragement of immorality, it remains, of course, that the 'breeding of the higher man' is not the 'breeding' of the moral one. We must not ignore the divide I have tried to exhibit between Nietzsche's 'table of values' and morality. It is worth remarking on one respect, so far unmentioned, in which the individual 'bred' by a Nietzschean education would differ from the moral citizen representing the educational ideal of, say, Dewey. We 'free spirits', writes Nietzsche, are 'born, sworn, jealous friends of solitude'.(64) This need not, of course, be the solitude of the hermit: 'whoever does not have two-thirds of his day for himself is a slave, whatever in addition he may wish to be: statesman, tradesman, civil servant, scholar'.(65) Nietzsche himself spent the years preceding his breakdown alternating between the mountain wastes on Sils Maria and large Italian cities - though, admittedly, the nature of his Italian sojourns is best captured by the paintings they inspired, Chirico's haunting pictures of a shadowy, siesta-time Turin. The 'solitude' meant is a quiet distancing of oneself from the helter-skelter of everyday life, a refusal to become totally embroiled in job, duties, or social relationships. In Nietzschean 'solitude' there is no place for the life of total social and political commitment, for wholesale dedication to the welfare of others, for making of oneself the good Deweyan 'efficient and serviceable member of society'.

There are a number of reasons for Nietzsche's emphasis upon solitude. One is that it immunizes against the snares, seductions, petty self-interest, and mediocrity which surround us in our everyday dealings. More important, perhaps, it is a condition of honesty and authenticity; for a person must 'wear masks' if he is to be a readily acceptable member of society or groups within it. A 'free spirit', were he to come clean, would soon be regarded as a threat by those whose values and beliefs he questions or rejects; hence he must present himself as being other than he is, if he is not to be cast out. 'Every profound spirit needs a mask.'(66) This is not to condemn 'the profound spirit', for the mask is as inevitable as the fact that, to live among others, one must *speak* along with them, and so express oneself in ways that encapsulate the very beliefs and values one wants to challenge. Only in 'solitude' can the mask be shed; thus it is never shed by those who are fully integrated in, and totally comfortable

with, their social world. This is the great central theme of many
of Hesse's books, where the main figure's dilemma is whether
to remain, if not a solitary, then an 'outsider', or to return to
and identify with the everyday world. Siddartha can remain a
lonely barge-keeper or go into the towns; the Master of the
Glass Bead Game can stay in his esoteric little community, or
descend into the city and engage in a 'useful' life. For both
men, a crucial deterrent to the latter course is the impossibility
of speaking in the everyday world without forfeiting independence
and honesty; without replacing the masks they had managed to
shed.

7 The justification of society

There is a feature of Nietzsche's educational thought that will
be unpalatable to some. This is its 'aristocratic' nature: 'true'
education is only for the few. *Realstudien*, we saw, which do
not belong in 'true' education, are nevertheless appropriate for
the many; and for the 'herd', it is not an education in values,
but moral training, that is in order. This 'aristocratic' element,
perhaps because it has been found unpalatable, is ignored by
many commentators – or pushed to the sidelines, or treated as
an unfortunate growth that can be cauterized without damage
to the body of Nietzsche's educational thought.(1) But this
cannot be right. 'Aristocratism' runs through, even organizes,
the whole of Nietzsche's philosophy. It is not only 'our educational institutions', but socialism, religion, morality, popular
culture, everything that draws Nietzsche's fire, which are
decried because of their 'levelling' tendency, their threat to the
possibility of authentic living by the few capable of it.
Zarathustra descended among men to 'teach them the overman',
and there are few of Nietzsche's main ideas that are not geared
to this central lesson.

Whether or not to make it more digestible, I do at least want
to break down this feature of Nietzsche's educational thinking.
In particular, I want to show how, for Nietzsche, this special
concern for the few is compatible with, and in fact entailed by,
a concern for all men. Educating 'higher men' turns out, in a
sense, to be for the sake of all. The attempt to understand this
sense will take us into Nietzsche's philosophy of society and his
view of education's place within society. That place is absolutely
central. It is not by its political forms, its economic arrangements,
or its legal system that a society is to be judged – but by the
nature of its education. These two points – that 'aristocratic'
education is for the sake of all, and that education is absolutely
central – interpenetrate. It is partly because the 'true'
education of the few is for the sake of all that education is
central, that it gives 'sense' to society. And reflection on the way
education is central reveals that there must be a 'true' education
for only the few.

Before I proceed, however, it will be advisable to ward off a
couple of misunderstandings over Nietzsche's 'aristocratism'
and his division of people into such contrasting classes as
'strong' and 'weak', or 'higher men' and 'herd'. The first may
arise from Nietzsche's claim that there is a hereditary, genetic

element to these divisions. Two remarks need to be made about
this claim. First, Nietzsche's belief was the Lamarckian one that
acquired characteristics - mental as well as physical - can be
inherited. For example, it is 'commonly the ancestor in the blood
and instinct of the scholar' who 'expresses' himself in the
scholar's habits and opinions; like everyone else the latter
cannot be 'the child of his parents unpunished'.(2) This doctrine, it must be noted, is totally at odds with the genetic
doctrines proclaimed by the Nazis and by others intent on
dividing people into fixed classes on the basis of ancestry alone.
If acquired characteristics can be inherited, then those of
'inferior' races could be eradicated over the span of a few
generations - a possibility which, of course, Nazi theorists
rigorously denied.(3) Clearly a claim according to which people
can acquire important characteristics, through education for
example, and not simply inherit them, provides no warrant for
dividing children up at birth on grounds of heredity. Second, it
should be noted that the Lamarckian doctrine plays no dis-
cernible role in Nietzsche's educational or more general thinking.
His interest, rightly, is not in how children - at age ten, say -
have come to display the intellectual and educationally relevant
potential they do, but simply in the fact that some of them do,
while others do not. It would make no difference to Nietzsche's
insistence that the exceptional must not be sacrificed for the
sake of the average if it were to turn out that experience and
environment were alone responsible for there being exceptional
people. If this were so, then it would follow, I suppose, that
by equalizing everyone's experiences and environments, one
would equalize their potentials. Nietzsche would have at least
three comments on this. First, no one can have the slightest
idea in what respects experiences and environment would have
to be engineered so as to produce these equal products - let
alone how to proceed with the engineering. Second, any likely
moves in this direction - state creches, identical reading for
all, and so on - are too grotesque to take seriously. Finally,
one can only imagine any success (by egalitarian lights) being
achieved *via* arrangements which would make it impossible for
those who would have otherwise displayed superior potential
to do so.

The other misunderstanding encouraged by Nietzsche's use
of starkly contrasting terms is that these refer to distinct
natural kinds or species, between which there are no gradations.
In fact, he makes it clear in some passages - not enough,
perhaps - that terms like 'strong' and 'weak' mark opposite
poles of a human continuum. With reference, for example, to
'health' and 'sickness', as features of character as well as of
body, he writes: 'One must not make distinct principles or
entities out of them . . . in fact, there are only differences of
degree between these two kinds of existence.'(4) There are, I
think, two reasons, besides his stylistic predilections, why
Nietzsche none the less writes in such polar terms. First, it is

his belief, as we shall see later in this chapter, that in modern times people are gravitating increasingly towards one end of the pole or the other. Second, he thinks there is a tactical value in speaking as if men fell into different species, since it is an antidote to the creeping and dangerous egalitarianism which pretends there are no significant differences between them at all. 'If you would get rid of strong contrasts and differences in rank, you would also abolish the strength of love, the height of conviction, and the feeling of individual being [*das Gefühl des Für-sich-seins*].'(5) In particular, we should not let the fact that, in reality, there are only gradations seduce us into a policy of identical education for all. For while a degree of arbitrariness and perhaps injustice will accompany the educational differentiations we make, it remains that there are those with a special potential which only a special and 'true' education can realize; an education that it would be criminal to deny them.

Nietzsche belongs among a fairly small number of thinkers who reverse the standard ordering between social and educational philosophy. The standard view has it that questions of political and social aims have priority, logical and moral, over educational ones. We first settle the nature of our desired polity, then address the issue of how education can best fit people for it. Aside from a certain appeal to common-sense, this view has been reinforced from many intellectual directions: from the Enlightenment faith in the perfectibility of man through ingeniously devised political mechanisms, for example, or from the Marxist tradition in which education is pushed upstairs into the 'superstructure' of society, outside the economic 'engineroom of history' whose proper workings alone can bring about the betterment of men.

There is nothing absurd, however, in the inversion of this view; in the idea that education should be the axis around which political and economic arrangements shall revolve. The organization of *The Republic* is motivated by the primarily educative endeavour whereby some will come to know 'The Good'. And in Dewey's writings, it is certain educational aims that provide a justification for democracy, rather than vice versa. Democracy, he argues, supplies a maximally educative environment through its creation of 'shared common interest(s)' and 'freer interaction between social groups'.(6) Such inversions have been more frequent in the German tradition than elsewhere. For example, Fichte, perceiving that the two main bonds which have tied individuals to the political whole - 'fear and hope' - have lost their power, concludes that we must 'find a completely different and new binding agent, which transcends fear and hope . . . in a word it is the total change of the previous education system which I propose as the only means of preserving the German nation in being.'(7) And for Schiller, the issue of education has first priority. The modern sickness, he argues, resides in the various schisms that rend men's personalities and interests -

reason *vs.* feeling, work *vs.* enjoyment, business *vs.* religion,
and the like. The state, through the compartmentalization of
its functions and the blessing it has given to the division of
labour, has helped bring about the disease, and no remedy,
therefore, can be expected from its activities.

> One must regard any . . . attempt at a change in the state as
> untimely and any hope based upon this as chimerical, until
> the division within the inner man is again transcended and
> his nature sufficiently developed for this to be the creative
> agent and to guarantee reality to the political realization of
> reason [*die politische Schöpfung der Vernunft*].(8)

The required transcendence and development is to be through
'aesthetic education' (a notion I discuss in the final chapter).
   With Nietzsche the inversion of the standard view is complete.
It is educational aims that define what political and economic
forms and arrangements there should be – or, at least, should
not be: for the imperative is that nothing be done to embarrass
the pursuit of 'true' education. This outlook was due, in part,
to Nietzsche's total scepticism towards the social panaceas that
abounded in his times. Fourierists, Saint-Simonians, Cabetists,
Benthamites, Marxists, Blancists, and countless others, were
vying with one another to concoct infallible political and
economic remedies for the times. In the midst of this optimistic
cacophony, Nietzsche's was a dampening voice. 'Progress', for
example, in the form of economic and technological advance, was
merely chimerical, and could result only in the 'dwarfing' and
'homogenizing' of men. As for the 'democratic movement', this
was 'not merely a decadent form of political organization, but a
corruption and belittling of men'.(9) It is not, of course, that
Nietzsche held any brief for the Prussian brand of statism and
nationalism to be found in his own country – as we saw in Chapter
2. In fact, his attitude towards the state – Prussian, democratic,
socialist, or whatever – and towards the political in general
became thoroughly negative.

> As little of the state as possible . . . political . . . affairs
> are not worth enough for the most gifted spirit to concern
> himself with.(10)

> All states are badly organized in which people other than
> statesmen must trouble themselves with politics.(11)

The state should be little more than a protective organization,
a 'minimal' state, whose control over individual lives should be
as limited as possible. In particular, it must not extend its
control over 'true' education: 'The school system is always very
mediocre in great states, for the same reason that cooking is
mediocre in great kitchens.'(12) As several of these remarks
suggest, Nietzsche's turn towards education is not simply a

response to his negative assessment of the political and economic. That negative assessment is, in part, explained by the educational concern. Social remedies are not only chimerical but of the wrong type, since they treat men *en masse;* they make us avert our gaze from the special individuals who alone represent the 'enhancement of the [human] type', and who can be produced, in any number, only through education. 'What must we grasp with our hopes?' asks Nietzsche after his dismissal of 'the democratic movement'. Not socialist utopias or Treitschkean national states, but 'new philosophers . . . spirits strong and original enough to give stimulus to the most opposite valuations and the revaluation and inversion of "eternal values" . . . to teach man the future of man as *his* will.'(13) It is teachers, then, educators, and not forms of societal organization, which 'our hopes must grasp'. It is important, of course, to bear in mind Nietzsche's distinction between schooling and 'true' education. What we must grasp with our hopes is not some massive programme of expansion in schools and colleges: on the contrary, Nietzsche feared, the state embarks on such programmes only because it 'fears the aristocratic nature of true education'.

Nietzsche's claim for the centrality of educational aims in society devolves into two assertions: that the *purpose* of education is identical with that of society, and that it is the achievement of education's goals which can alone *justify* or *give sense to* society's existence.

In an early passage, from the preface to an intended book on the Greek state, Nietzsche agrees with what he takes to be Plato's view that 'the authentic goal of the state [is] the Olympian existence and the ever-renewed production and preparation of genius, for which all other things are only tools.'(14) As we have seen, before, 'the production of genius', in Nietzsche's early terminology, is the goal of education. Later he will speak of producing 'overmen', 'higher men', or 'free spirits' - but the broad idea of education's goal remains. The point about justification emerges in that important note where Nietzsche refers to the 'dwarfing' and 'homogenizing' of men by economic progress, and to the inevitable 'consumption of men and mankind', to their increasing 'adaption . . . to a specialized utility'. He pleads for a 'justifying man', a 'higher type' of man who must emerge out of all this if any sense, any justification, is to be given to these terrible processes:

> that total machinery, the solidity of all the wheels, represents a maximal exploitation of man: but it presupposes those on whose account this exploitation has a *meaning*. Otherwise, it would really be a mere total diminution, a value diminution, of the type Man - a regressive phenomenon in the grandest style.

And he adds: 'My metaphor for the [justifying] type is, as one knows, the word "overman".'(15)

I have said very little about the 'overman', and do not intend to say much until the final chapter. But we know this much: that 'overman' is also Nietzsche's metaphor for the totally authentic individual, and hence for the ideal product of 'true' education. So the point he is making is this: only if education's goal is achieved - if, that is, the 'overman' emerges - can there be any justification for, or sense to, the terrible mechanization and 'dwarfing' of men which are the inevitable processes of advanced societies. (The parallel with Marx can hardly be overlooked, and is nicely brought out by Camus when he writes 'Nietzsche . . . in his theory of the overman, and Marx . . . with his classless society, both replace the Beyond by the Later On.')(16)

Although, according to Nietzsche, the purpose of society is also what justifies it, his claims about purpose and justification are not synonymous. Purposes sometimes justify and justifications sometimes cite purposes, but there is no general coincidence. Someone might hold, for example, that while the emergence of a 'higher type' of man might justify society, this cannot be a purpose, since this emergence is a random, chance affair. Questions of purpose and justification typically arise against different backgrounds. We want to know of an institution what is its *raison d'être* and how it might best discharge the functions this dictates. These are questions about purpose. Then we encounter processes, social or natural, which seem senseless or evil, and we ask whether it is possible, nevertheless, to view them as preconditions for something of great value, so that we are spared a purely nihilistic judgment upon them. This is a question of justification.

The claim that the aim of education, to 'breed a higher type', is also society's purpose, introduces us to nothing new: it is composed out of themes already encountered. Nature, recall, is an inefficient archer, who has to fire many arrows to hit a target. Hitherto, therefore, the emergence of 'higher men' has been the occasional, lucky accident. If they are to emerge in any purposive fashion, and in any significant number, this can only be through education. This educative enterprise will require the co-operation of the state, if only in its role as protective guardian - for, of course, the state, organized society, is not to control education. In ensuring the conditions under which this enterprise can flourish, the state is only completing the task which it was brought into being to perform - that of affording the protection required for men to transcend their animal nature. It was the state which, supported by mores and religion, provided defence against the 'blond beasts' and *Raubtiere* who had outlived their usefulness to primitive communities. In Zarathustra's famous metaphor, man, as he now is, is on a rope slung between the beast and the 'overman'. It is only through the state and social organization that he has crawled thus far; and it will only be through their protective

agency - their only genuine role - that he will, if 'truly' educated, crawl yet further.

The claim that only the 'breeding of the overman' can justify
social existence is more opaque. To understand it, we need to
bear in mind the characteristically Nietzschean point that a
justification is not a discovery, but a conferment of value or
meaning. The justification of social processes cannot consist in
an end-state towards which we can see them moving. Nietzsche's
'Later On' is not, like Marx's, an inevitable destination that
lends direction to the journey. Even if there were an end-state,
it would have to be men who conferred value upon it. When
Nietzsche hails the 'overman' as the 'justifying man', he is
asking us to confer supreme value upon such an individual and,
through this, to confer meaning on the society from which he
might emerge. 'The overman is the sense of the earth. Let your
will say: *May* the overman be the sense of the earth!'(17)

It is essential that supreme value be conferred upon *something*
that might, albeit with trial and effort, emerge from a seemingly
senseless social existence. For the alternative is nihilism in one
or more of its myriad forms: jaded, passive *ennui*; beaverish
obsession with the immediate in order to anaesthetize the sense
of senselessness; escape into the illusory and transcendent, into
heavens imbued with a meaning lacking on earth; or nihilism à
la St Petersburg, wanton destructiveness that places a value on
nothing but that.

It cannot do, of course, to confer any old value on any old
thing. In particular, the justifying value conferred cannot be
one of those which reflect and serve the very existence we are
seeking to justify. It cannot, therefore, be a moral justification
we seek, for morality has played a leading role in those 'dwarfing', 'homogenizing' processes which have 'diminished' man.
The value and meaning we confer, if they are to be genuine
antidotes to nihilism, must be those which are most conspicu-
ously absent and denied under conditions of nihilism. But what
is missing in nihilism is not this rather than that value, one
rather than another meaning, but the giving of values and
meanings itself. Nihilism, after all, is 'the radical repudiation
of value [and] meaning'.(18) This is so even, or especially,
when nihilism takes the form of passive allegiance to received
valuations or purposes. The supreme value we must confer,
then, is *the value of giving-value-to*; and what confers sense
on life is *giving-sense-to* life. Giving-value-to, and giving-
sense-to, are, however, the activities of individual human
beings: indeed, they are the activities which manifest the
supreme human capacities. Hence to place supreme value and
sense on these activities is to place them upon those individuals
who manifest those capacities in their lives. These individuals
are the 'overmen'. The 'overman', that is, is the fully authentic
individual who creates values and meanings for himself, thereby
exercising those capacities which *we* must value and see significance in if nihilism is to be overcome.(19)

Marx believed that the era during which class oppression reaches its zenith is the prelude to its disappearance. This is because, during that era, consciousness of class oppression reaches a level where action becomes inevitable. The effect of that revolutionary action will be to lead men out of the dehumanized existence they have suffered in class society. Whatever the evils of capitalism, it has at least produced conditions which make it possible for men of the future to live free from purely material wants, so that they may turn to their 'human needs'. Nietzsche's position has its structural parallels with Marx's. It is the very grimness of the 'belittling' society in which we live that makes the emergence of the 'overman' a live possibility. As we saw in chapter 1, nihilism in whatever form must be gone through before the dawn of a better day. As men become increasingly mechanized, some of them will come to value all the more the human qualities that are under siege, and as the old values become and are seen to become more bankrupt than ever, there will be a demand for those who can revalue, create new values. The very technological processes which turn most men into 'suitably adapted gears' also provide the stability and well-being which free some from the everyday material concerns that leave no time for less animal pursuits. Nietzsche was very aware of the connection between stomach and mind. Finally, it is only under such conditions that that consciousness will develop which allows men to transcend the mediocre - that consciousness, that 'pathos of distance', which the 'free spirit' has of the stark contrast between himself and the 'herd'. The 'overman' 'needs the opposition of the masses, the "levelled", a feeling of distance from them; he stands on them, he lives off them'.(20) The difference between Marx and Nietzsche need hardly be laboured: the 'pathos of distance' is a matter of individual, not class, consciousness, and the achievement of humanity by some is not its achievement by all; and far from this achievement requiring an overthrow of social conditions as we know them, it is parasitic upon them.

What are we to make of Nietzsche's claims about purpose and justification? Our best policy will be to elaborate on them in the light of some predictable objections. One of these is that it is odd, to the point of paradox, to regard the value of the 'over-man' as the supreme one. For this, as we understood it, was to confer supreme value upon the activity of giving-value-to (and all that this entails in terms of 'situational' understanding, mistrust of received opinion, and so on). But this sounds paradoxical; for if the sole value were that of creating value, then the sole value would be that of creating the value of the value of creating the value of the value of . . . *ad infinitum*. Put less obscurely, the objection is this: values are to guide action, but they cannot do this if they are all of the 'reflexive', 'higher-order' type, such as 'the value of giving-value-to'. I want to evaluate two courses of action open to me: it is no help

to be referred to the value of creating values for myself, for
what I want to know is which value to accept. (A similar objection could be levelled against the idea that the sole sense to an
activity is that of giving-sense-to.)

Part of the reply to this objection is that paradox can only
arise when the value of giving-value-to is taken as the sole
one. Clearly, there is nothing paradoxical in placing value,
and very great value, upon someone being in a position to
evaluate for himself – and this is so even when I have little or
no concern with what value he then adopts. Clearly, too, I
can place great value upon the steps I now take to place myself
in a future position where I shall be able to evaluate things
for myself – even though, at present, I can have no idea how
I shall evaluate. This might be my reason for resigning from a
political or religious sect whose orthodoxy and grip over my
thinking has come to frighten me. It is not that, as yet, I have
come to reject the sect's aims and values, but I want to be in a
freer position to make up my mind about them.

But *doesn't* Nietzsche say that the value or sense of the
'overman' is the sole one? No, what he says is that the 'overman's
value is the only one that can justify life, society, or 'the
earth'. Giving-value-to is not the only valuable thing, but it is
the only thing that can lend value and sense to life. The distinction is vital, and the point a profound one. Clearly, I put various
values on various of my activities: some because they bring me
closer to my family, say, others because they prepare me to
write the great novel I have in mind, others because they make
life more cheerful for my neighbours, and so on. But I do not
regard such values as lending sense to my life, as giving value
to my existence as such. After all, I know that many people do
not share these values, but do not conclude that their lives are
senseless or valueless. Moreover, I can recall times, and perhaps
predict future times, when these activities and values will be
missing from my life: but I do not consider this to be recalling
or foretelling times when my life is without value or sense.
The reason, in both cases, perhaps is that I am not envisioning
others, or myself at other times, as being without the capacity
to confer values and significance on their activities. Had I been
envisioning that, it is less clear that I would not have been
imagining lives without value or sense. It is one thing to picture
people whose values are strikingly different from my own, but
another to picture people who are so unreflective, such passive
fellow-travellers, as to have abdicated the concern to order
their lives according to values determined by themselves. The
latter may indeed be a picture of what are only half-lives.

But how can any of this help us understand Nietzsche's claim
about the 'overman' giving sense to *society*? How can the value
conferred on the 'overman' lend value to the lives of all those
who will not even approximate to being 'overmen' themselves?
And, as Nietzsche makes clear, that is most of us. True, it
should be that 'each individual, *according to his kind*, is so

placed that he can achieve the highest which lies in his power',
but most of us belong to 'kinds' whose 'highest' is not very
high.(21) Moreover, as we have seen, the emergence of the
'overman' requires that most remain in the 'herd'; and education
for the 'overman' is not education for us all.

It is at this stage, of course, that the main objections make
their entry. Nietzsche seems to be saying that society exists
for the benefit of the few. Is this not the most intolerable
élitism? We have surely progressed from thinking that society
should be arranged for a privileged group. In particular, have
we not progressed from thinking that education should be
geared to attainment by the few?

Some of the sting of this style of objection can be drawn by
rejecting the terminology in which it is proclaimed. Expressions
like 'for the benefit of the few' or 'a privileged group' are
totally out of place. Nietzsche's 'overmen' would not form a
'group' at all, let alone one enjoying 'privileges' and 'benefits'
of any social kind – wealth, status, political power, 'perks',
special protection, or whatever. Nietzsche's 'aristocracy' is
one of the spirit, not of land or industry; not part of the
'rotted ruling classes'. Again, while Nietzsche is totally hostile
to socialism, this is because of its threat to individuality, not
because he holds a brief for the bourgeoisie. Nietzsche's many
critics of the Left would do well to mark comments like the
following: 'The workers shall one day live as the bourgeois now
do – but *above* them, distinguished through their freedom from
want, the *higher caste:* that is, poorer and simpler, but in
possession of power.'(22) Totally askew, too, is the talk of
education being 'geared to' or 'organized for' the production of
'overmen', suggestive as it is of a kind of five-year plan
involving the mobilization of society's resources for this
purpose. As I have noted several times, 'true' education is not
to be managed by state or society. What social mobilization
there may be will be in the area of *Realstudien,* with the aim of
enabling the average person to 'achieve the highest which lies
in his power'.

Most misleading of all, though, is the suggestion that achievement of society's goal, the breeding of the 'overman', will only
be 'for the sake of' the 'overman'. Nietzsche wants to insist,
on the contrary, that this will be 'for the sake of' us all. The
point emerges in this passage from *Schopenhauer as Educator:*

> How does your, the individual's life, gain its highest value,
> its deepest significance? How is it least wasted? Only surely
> through this: that you live for the benefit of the rarest and
> most valuable specimens, not of the majority. . . . And just
> this conviction should be placed and cultivated in each young
> person, so that he will see himself . . . as a testament to
> the greatest and most wonderful intentions of [Nature].(23)

The teleological point about Nature's intentions will disappear in later writings, but the idea remains that it is each of us, not only the 'rarest and most valuable specimens' themselves, whose lives gain value and significance through them.

But how could such an idea be made out? The crux of the difficulty is surely this: for something to count as society's purpose, it must be something members of that society do aim at or value - or, at any rate, *would* aim at or desire if they had not, for example, been corrupted or indoctrinated. If this is so, it seems impossible to see how the breeding of the 'over-man' could count as society's purpose, for members of society as a whole neither do, nor under thinkable conditions would, set this as their aim and value.

Nietzsche, as I understand him, would concede these constraints on what can count as society's purpose - but like many political theorists is undeterred by the difficulty the concession appears to create. It is familiar enough for a social thinker's favoured goal to be one which, apparently, is not favoured by many members of the society under consideration. Standardly, he will then employ one of two manoeuvres. Either he will insist that appearances are deceptive, and that people do in fact desire this goal; or he will argue that it is a goal which they would desire had they not been misled, corrupted, or whatever. We find the first manoeuvre employed by Hobbes. People do not seem to fancy a society dominated by a mighty sovereign, but really they must, since this is the logical consequence of things they clearly do desire - self-preservation, peace, security. The second manoeuvre is a commonplace of eighteenth- and nineteenth-century thought. For example, Rousseau's 'general will' is one that each of us would subscribe to had not a corrupt society fashioned 'particular', 'selfish' wills. And for Marx, the conservative, materialistic desires of the proletariat are 'false' and 'illusory' ones foisted upon it by an exploitative society - ones which, under other conditions, would give way to 'real', 'human' wants.

It is rarely clear, when one comes across references to 'real wants', 'true purposes', and the like, which manoeuvre the writer is employing - and this is because the distinction between the two is itself unclear. Is a person's real desire something he has, albeit confusedly and buried deep down, or is it one that he merely would have if . . . ? In fact, one often encounters a combination of the two vaguely distinguishable manoeuvres. A want may be present, but inchoate: it would only be fully present if, under better conditions, it crystallized and became explicitly avowed. (Jürgen Habermas wants to say that there are certain communicative purposes implicitly present in all speech, and which would only become explicit in 'ideal speech situations'.)(24)

Nietzsche employs both manoeuvres - or a somewhat muddied combination of them - in his reply to the objection that people at large neither do nor could value the breeding of the 'over-man' as society's purpose. All of us, he wants to say, do value the 'overman', however hidden from us this generally is; moreover, it is a value that would crystallize, and be explicitly and widely embraced, had society not conspired to make us 'decadent'. 'Decadence' is Nietzsche's term for all those conditions and attitudes which have deflected the 'basic instinct' for admiring the 'overman'. 'Every kind of decay and sickness has conspired in producing overall value-judgements . . . decadence has gained predominance in the ruling value-judgements'.(25) The idea is one we have encountered, in various forms, throughout the book. Society's dominant forms - economic, ideological, pedagogical, or whatever - have served to devalue the 'overman' by discrediting the 'special individual', by inducing fear of him or by 'mechanizing' him, and by raising the average, the everyday, to the object of admiration. Our 'educational institutions', for example, 'seek to drive the great individual into self-exile'(26) and, in the terminology of an earlier chapter, to make men 'current'. The main ideological forms - morals, and religion or its contemporary socialist and egalitarian offspring - are instruments honed to bolster up the self-esteem of the mediocre.

It is important to realize that Nietzsche's claim about what people would value, in the absence of 'decadence', is deeply counterfactual, for 'decadence' is not something to be done away with. On the contrary, 'it is absolutely necessary and to be found in every age and in every people'.(27) It is not something we can wither by rooting out its causes by social engineering or revolution. Indeed, its supposed causes - luxury, say, or crime - are really its consequences. 'Decadence' is as integral to society as the division of labour, morality, the pursuit of wealth, patriotism - as everything, in fact, which keeps society as we know it in being. It is precisely these necessary features, with their 'belittlement' of the individual in favour of the mass, which are the ground of 'decadence'. All we can hope, then, is to 'struggle with all our strength [against] the spreading of the contagion into the healthy part of the organism'.(28) Although the value of the 'overman' is one which would be generally conceded, or embraced, under 'healthy' conditions, these are not conditions which will ever obtain in societies recognizably like our own.

But Nietzsche deploys the other manoeuvre as well. He wants to say, that is, that even under conditions of 'decadence' there is a sense in which, however dumbly, we all value the 'overman'. He is saying this in the passage that follows on the heels of the one (see p. 119) where he urged the young to live 'for the benefit of the rarest and most valuable specimens':

Kultur . . . is the child of each person's self-knowledge and dissatisfaction with himself. Each person who acknowledges *Kultur* is thereby saying: 'I see something higher and more human above me than how I now am. All of you, help me to reach it! - as I wish to help each man who recognizes and

suffers the same; so that, finally, the man may emerge who
feels himself full and unbounded in knowledge and loving, in
vision and ability, and who belongs with all his being to, and
within, Nature, as judge and measure of things.'

By *'Kultur'* Nietzsche is not referring to art galleries,
museums, and the like, but to the whole transformational,
educational process whereby men have raised themselves from
animal existence - to that rope slung between the beast and the
'overman'. And he is contending that anyone who 'acknowledges'
and values *Kultur* is thereby committed to valuing the 'overman'
- that man, described in the final lines, who *inter alia* is 'judge
and measure of things'. 'Anyone', here, is each of us, for as
humans we must all value what is human, what distinguishes us
from all other existence. Hence we must all value the 'overman'.
Whoever 'acknowledges' *Kultur* is 'thereby saying' - to use
Zarathustra's terminology - 'Let the overman live!' The logic of
Nietzsche's point is similar to Hobbes's: a person is committed
to valuing that which is clearly entailed by what he definitely
values. That people do not say 'Let the overman live!' is due,
less to native lack of logic, than to the conditions of 'decadence',
just noted, which have conspired to discredit the 'special
individual'.

Nietzsche offers some speculative empirical evidence in support
of these contentions. Thus, despite the conspiracy against
valuing the 'special individual', admiration nevertheless bursts
forth when people are confronted with undeniably great 'specimens'. The admiration felt, even by his enemies, for Napoleon
'confirm[s] the belief in the autonomy of the individual', for he
represented those hopes, ordinarily dampened and suppressed,
which are 'the highest hopes of the century'.(29) It was not
Napoleon's military prowess or political acumen that aroused
admiration, but the fact that here was a 'creator', embodying
'the attempt to do new things' and 'the passion of new possibilities of the spirit and expansion of the soul'.(30) It was the
kind of admiration whose highest form would be admiration of
the 'overman'. (For, despite his greatness, Nietzsche makes it
clear that Napoleon was not the 'overman'.) Further evidence
comes from people's general dissatisfaction with their own lives,
a deep unhappiness which, according to Nietzsche, modern men
often succeed in stunning - by drink, entertainment, or
absorption in everyday trivia - but not in removing. For the
source of this malaise is 'hatred of one's own narrowness and
shrunkenness'; but this implies an envy of, and therefore an
implicit admiration or 'sympathy for the genius, who has torn
himself out of our torpor and dryness'.(31)

It is not, however, these psychological speculations, but his
a priori claims that form the heart of Nietzsche's contention. I
mean, first, the claim that it is unintelligible for men not to
'acknowledge' what is authentically human, and second, the
claim that to do so is to commit oneself to placing supreme value

on those individuals who maximally manifest what is authentically human - the 'overmen'. This second claim is like one I have urged in a number of writings, to the effect that commitment to some activity - music, say - is commitment to seeing the highest levels achieved, as against an overall improvement at the average level.(32) Someone who proclaims a commitment to music, but then proceeds to advocate policies - in connection with subsidies or musical training, say - which are designed, at the expense perhaps of concentration on genuine talent, to bring about a general and therefore slight improvement in everyday standards of musicianship, displays that his commitment was not, after all, to music, but to something else - to encouraging desirable leisure-time pursuits, perhaps, or to the social benefits of music-making.

Music, perhaps, is something to take or leave. There is no necessity in a person's placing great value upon it. But it is different, if Nietzsche's first *a priori* claim is right, with those features and activities which the 'overman' displays. These are not ones a human being can intelligibly refuse to value, since they are those which constitute his life as an authentically human one. What could we make of someone who placed no value upon creativity - in particular upon the capacities to give-value-to, and to interpret, to give-sense-to? It will follow, moreover, if Nietzsche is right to hold that it is through 'breeding' that the 'overman' is to be produced, that 'true' education is not something we can take or leave, for it alone can, in any organized fashion, foster those capacities which, as humans, we are bound to value. And to be bound to this is to be bound to the value of 'breeding' those 'specimens' who maximally manifest these capacities. (I used to speak of a commitment to education entailing one to educational excellence: but this is no longer a happy term, now that it has been captured by those who measure a university's claim to be a 'centre of excellence' in terms of A level intake, grants from industry, and its record in getting graduates ready employment.)

I do not know if my presentation, or interpretation, of Nietzsche's contention that the 'breeding of the overman' is the purpose, the justification, of society has done anything to make that contention more palatable than at first encounter. Certainly, it would be wrong to disguise Nietzsche's hostility to features of our society, which are dear to many, on the ground that these militate against the emergence of 'higher' men: his hostility towards democracy, for example. But it would be equally wrong to permit the unbridled impression that the 'centrality of education' is to mean a grand mobilization and gearing of society's resources to the task of 'truly' educating the few, at the expense of all other social goals. The 'gearing' of society to 'breeding the overman' is an essentially negative requirement: nothing must prevent individuals from attempting to 'overcome' themselves. Provided this requirement is met, the forms and

aims of political organization are not Nietzsche's concern. In
Ernst Nolte's phrase, Nietzsche's is a 'non-political radicalism'
– though his negative requirement does 'define a border line
which practical politics can approach asymptotically'.(33) We
have seen, moreover (see p. 118), that the value which lends
sense to society, that of the 'overman', is not and cannot be
the only value, the only determinant of what should be done.
Clearly, there is much that should be done in and by a society
– caring for health, for example, or for material welfare: but
it is not such things that lend sense to, and confer value
upon, human existence. Animals' lives, presumably, have no
sense: but it is hardly a matter of indifference how we treat
them. There is nothing in Nietzsche to warrant the idea that
callousness, or lack of care, is the appropriate attitude towards
those who are neither aspiring, nor educating, to live 'higher'
lives. What we do find is the insistence, more intense than in
any other writer, that society draw back from crushing these
aspirations.

8 'The higher breeding of man'

'True education', which is to give 'sense' to society, is the 'breeding of the overman', the 'higher breeding of man'.(1) In dramatic, personified terms, this is Nietzsche's view. So far I have followed his occasional practice of using such expressions as 'overman', 'higher man', or 'outstanding specimen' interchangeably. Zarathustra's insistence that it is the 'overman', not the 'higher man', whom he awaits in his mountains, makes it clear, however, that different notions are involved.(2) For all his importance, the 'overman' is barely discussed by Nietzsche. This is unsurprising, given 'there has never once been an overman',(3) and that he represents an entirely new kind of person whose total 're-evaluation' must be beyond our present capacities to describe in any detail. The analogy, once more, is with Marx, whose readers are often disappointed by the scant account of how men will be in the future, classless society. Marx's reticence is explained by the fact that these future men will be so different from we 'alienated' creatures, that a full description of them would require, impossibly, that we raise ourselves to that level of consciousness which only the transition to the classless society can effect.

The 'overman' is the ideal extension of the 'higher man' who remains 'part inhuman and part superhuman'.(4) The main difference is that what is still a matter of struggle and effort for the 'higher man' will become natural for the 'overman' of the indeterminate, or ideal future. It is a mark of 'higher men' that, within their souls, great battles are still raging – 'Rome vs. Judea', '*virtu vs.* virtue', 'egoism *vs.* morality';(5) battles that will have their successful issue in the 'overman'. It is in this light that we should understand the comments that only the 'overman' comes to a living acceptance of 'eternal recurrence', and that only he learns to 'laugh' and 'dance'. Neither the doctrine of 'eternal recurrence', nor its place in Nietzsche's thought, is at all clear: what is certain, though, is that living acceptance of the doctrine is supposed to herald the achievement of a totally 'affirmative', '*Ja-sagend*' attitude in which condemnation, criticism of the world, struggle against others and their thoughts are transcended. 'Laughing' and 'dancing' are Nietzsche's metaphors for just such an attitude. Richard Strauss, when he made the 'overman's' *Tanzlied* in his *Also Sprach Zarathustra* a jolly Viennese waltz, may have been closer to Nietzsche's conception than most Nietzsche and Strauss scholars are wont to think.(6)

Although the 'higher man' is not the final goal, it is he whom
we find the more richly described, and upon whom the educational
task must focus for the foreseeable future. Who, then, is the
'higher man', and how shall he be bred? We must already know a
certain amount about him; as much, indeed, as we so far know
about authenticity. For if I am right to portray Nietzsche's
educational concern as one for authenticity, then the 'higher
man' must be, or approximate to being, the authentic man. We
know, then, how he stands towards morality, for example, or
towards 'scholarship'. It would help us collect together and
expand upon the various themes and features connected with
authenticity if we could identify an actual person who, for
Nietzsche, counts as a 'higher man'. Hunting after such an
identification has been a favourite game among Nietzsche
commentators. Given the heuristic value of the hunt, it *ought*
not to be a game, but it is hard to take all efforts in this
direction seriously when one considers that the quarries have
ranged from Socrates to Hitler.(7) At the risk of being dubbed
just one more player of this game, let me state that there seems
to me little doubt which figure Nietzsche usually regards as
the nearest approximation to the 'higher man'. It is the figure
referred to more often in his writings than any, save Wagner;
the man of whom Napoleon exclaimed 'Voila! un homme!' It is Goethe
    Nietzsche makes it clear that Goethe is not the 'overman', not
'the great *synthetic* man', but only 'the most beautiful expression
of the type', man, as we have hitherto known it.(8) In some
early writings, during the period of his fascination with a
largely mythical Schopenhauer, Nietzsche is indeed critical of
Goethe - the man and his writings. Generally, though, the
attitude is one of unstinting admiration. Goethe is the 'finest
and brightest soul', 'superior to other Germans in all respects',
'a culture' in himself, a 'mighty, defiant, solitary rock'.(9) Let
us examine the basis for this admiration of Goethe, as Nietzsche
saw him. That qualification is, perhaps, unnecessary, for it
seems that Nietzsche's portrait was a remarkably perceptive
one.(10) It might be pedantic, too, to speak of 'the Goethean
man' rather than of Goethe himself, for contemporaries and
biographers are generally agreed that the man succeeded, to an
extraordinary degree, in living according to his conception of
how a person should be.
    'The Goethean ideal of personality', writes Erich Heller is a
'state of balance between what a man *is* and what he can *do*.'(11)
He may have had specifically in mind a passage where Goethe
describes how a person, through contemplating a fine building,
'first experiences, what a man is and what he could be'.(12)
It would be more accurate, however, to describe the dominant
theme in Goethe's writings, and life, as the avoidance of two
dangers which threaten a person's ability to live in a manner
which is 'appropriate' (*gehörig*) to him. The first is that of
having such an ossified conception of oneself, and of how things
will go, that capacities and talents are left untried and untapped.

The second is the unrestrained catapulting of oneself into this
or that project or course with only the flimsiest conception of
the person one is, and of the limitations imposed by nature or
circumstances. In *Wilhelm Meisters Lehrjahre* - that 'great
educative novel', in Lukàcs's words - Wilhelm's boyhood friend,
Werner, and Wilhelm himself, illustrate the respective dangers.
Werner has decided at an early age that he is 'cut out' to be
a man of commerce, like his father, and he grows into a narrow,
cramped person, constantly scoffing at Wilhelm's attempts to
escape his bourgeois chains. But he scoffs with some justice,
for Wilhelm's obsession with becoming a man of the theatre
emerges as a romantic one, ungrounded in a realistic estimate
of his talents and personality. The novel, indeed, is partly the
story of Wilhelm's realization of how unhinged this thespian
enthusiasm had been. (Goethe himself had been through a
similarly painful realization as a young man, when coming to
accept that his *daimon* was not to become a painter.)

Goethe's genius, of course, does not reside in simply stating
the fairly familiar ideas just mentioned, but in his development
of what they entail: and many of the significant themes in his
writings - even his scientific writings - are systematically
related to them. This is true, to begin with, of his attack on
the many fashionable and conflicting 'isms' of his day: on the
'positivism' and 'Scientism' of the Enlightenment, as much as on
the 'Romanticism', 'Transcendentalism', and 'Idealism' of the
reaction. Each in its own way, for Goethe, is guilty not only of
distorting that proper understanding of self which is a precondition for 'appropriate' creative endeavour, but of stifling
that very endeavour. Thus, the second group of 'isms' serves
both to encourage irresolvable speculations on matters that
transcend any rational understanding and any relation to actual
activity, and to demean the status of the living human being
and his actions. The world of bodies and the senses are treated
as mere shadows of some more real world, and the result, as
Hegel saw, would be a return of that 'unhappy consciousness'
which had accompanied the asceticism of medieval Christianity.
His friend Schiller, thought Goethe, would have been all the
greater had he not 'tortured himself with philosophical thoughts
which could do nothing to help him'; ones which, moreover,
placed 'the Idea above all nature'.(13) But the ideas of the
Enlightenment were no better, for these *reduced* men to nature,
by treating them as mere physical bodies, or machines, in a
larger material or mechanical whole. Moreover, the knowledge
which was the Enlightenment ideal - encyclopaedic factual
knowledge, knowledge of the laws of nature, knowledge
unmediated by human interpretation and valuation - is of a
neutral kind that offers no guidance to action, to the choice of
how to live. Goethe's obscure doctrines of 'the universal in the
particular' and of the 'symbolic' nature of the world, which
guided his own scientific researches, are to be understood as
reactions to both these sets of 'isms'. The world is a real enough

place, to be sure, but the understanding of it which is required is not of that neutral, objective kind of which 'les encyclopédistes' were enamoured. Together, the various 'isms' conspire to produce that 'misfortune' - the person dominated by ideas that 'have no influence in practical life or which even distract him from [it]'.(14) (The point need not be laboured that 'practical life' is not what 'the practical man', in today's connotation, leads.)

Goethe's distinctive notion of freedom is also related to this central theme. Like Nietzsche's, this notion is not a legal or political one. Freedom is not a matter of possessing rights, or of absence of interference from authorities. After 1789, indeed, Goethe came to see the 'liberté' of the revolutionaries as dangerous to any genuine freedom: in Hegel's words, it threatened 'the pure terror of the negative'.(15) Freedom is a property of the personality: the free man is a person of a certain kind, not someone who is free from this or that constraint. It requires, for a start, right understanding: particularly of one's own limitations, and of those imposed by historical conditions. 'No one is more a slave than when, without being so, he thinks himself free.'(16) It requires, next, powers of resistance: the power, first of all, to stand firm against the seductions of fashionable ideas that carry people off, young people especially, into directions they have not seriously paused to consider. Resistance, second, against the passions and caprices of the moment, or the month, that threaten the possibility of disciplined self-direction. The tragedy of young Werther, in one of Goethe's earliest books, is a dual one: not only is he victim to a hopeless passion for a happily married mother but he is in the grip of the idea that such desperate Romanticism is the done thing to indulge in. (To Goethe's dismay, the novel merely reinforced the fashion: he had to spend several days, incognito, persuading a young man, bowled over by the book, not to emulate Werther's example and commit suicide.) Finally, freedom is realized in disciplined creativity. 'Only law can give us freedom', says the last line of the sonnet *Natur und Kunst*; not the law of the land, of course, but self-imposed submission to order and method. Otherwise one risks wallowing in sentimental 'cow-warmth'. Discipline, though, is only a mark of freedom when it is imposed for creative ends. There is no freedom in regular habit. Werther realizes the extent to which he has become a victim when he recognizes his loss of 'that holy animating power with which I created worlds around me'.(17)

It is his concern with the dangers threatening 'appropriate' creative endeavour which explains Goethe's frequently misunderstood veneration of the 'aristocracy'. 'Aristocrat' and 'bourgeois' are his metaphors for two types of person - though he thought that, as a matter of fact, these two types tended to correlate roughly with the respective social classes. Whereas the 'aristocrat' asks 'What *are* you?', the 'bourgeois' asks 'What *have* you?', and measures himself and others by how 'useful'

they are, by what they 'produce and get'.(18) What the
'bourgeois' lacks, and the 'aristocrat' possesses is self-
reverence. In *Wilhelm Meisters Wanderjahre,* the hero leaves
his son in the school of a region whose authorities are dedicated
to educational concerns: and the aim of this school is to produce
'the highest kind of reverence, reverence of oneself . . . so
that the person attains the heights of what he is capable of'.(19)
This self-reverence, of course, is sharply distinguished from
self-satisfaction, selfishness, or boastfulness. Rather, it is
that constant concern for oneself, and the significance of one's
potential activities, which full development of one's capacities
presupposes. It is precisely this concern that Goethe thinks
threatened by the currents of the time - by the 'bourgeois'
obsession with utility and acquisition, by the 'egalité' as well
as the 'liberté' of 1789, and by those intellectual ideas, referred
to above, which debase the value of human being.

Perhaps the most salient motif in Goethe's thought and life is
that of harmony and wholeness. He rejects one dualism after
another: the naive vs. the sentimental, the mental vs. the
physical, nature vs. art, or reason vs. passion. His point is
not at all that each term in a dualism has its own proper place,
to which it must be confined: that there are moments for
rationality, others for passion, or that there are days on which
to care for mental health, others on which to cater for physical
well-being. On the contrary, such dualisms are philosophical
mistakes, which create a false, molecular picture of how men
are, and they are inimical to the 'appropriate' life. Goethe's
attack is based, in part, on his interpretation of Spinoza's
monism: the universe is essentially One, and attempts to
categorize it in the manner of the above dualisms therefore
artificial. More relevantly, he thinks such dualisms incompatible
with the 'state of balance' of which we have been speaking. This
'state of balance' is not one among several, but the central one
around which the rest cluster, and which makes dissolution of
polarities imperative. If, for example, we are to create great
things, then 'when we decide to put aside sessions for art . . .
let's not expel nature from our spirit' *(Natur und Kunst).*
Again, it is only when our passions are informed by rational
appreciation of their objects, and when rational pursuits are
fired by passions - for truth and clarity - that either emotional
or intellectual fulfilment is feasible.(20) 'Variety without
distraction', he writes, is 'the most beautiful motto' for life(21)
- the distraction, that is, which comes from hopping from one
pole of a dualism to another. A person 'only achieves the unique
and wholly unexpected when all properties are uniformly united
in him'.(22)

Consider now the fine passages, towards the end of *Twilight
of the Idols,* in which Nietzsche pays homage to Goethe:

Goethe - not a German event, but a European one: a great
attempt to overcome the 18thC. Through . . . an ascent to the

naturalness of the Renaissance, a kind of self-overcoming on
the part of this century. Within himself, he carried its
strongest instincts: sensibility, Nature-idolatry, anti-
historicism, Idealism, the Unreal and the Revolutionary
(itself merely a form of the Unreal). He accepted help from
history, science, antiquity - and Spinoza, too: but most of
all from practical activity. He placed himself within limited
horizons: he did not draw back from life, but immersed
himself within it . . . what he wanted was *totality*: he
struggled against the separation of reason, the senses,
feeling, and will . . . he disciplined himself to wholeness,he
created himself. . . . Goethe was . . . a convinced realist:
he said 'Yes' to everything that related to him. . . . [He]
conceived of a person who would be strong, highly educated,
skilful in all things physical, self-controlled, self-reverent,
who would dare allow himself the whole compass and richness
of what is natural, who would be strong enough for this
freedom: someone tolerant not out of weakness, but out of
strength.(23)

It would be difficult to better this as a summary of the elements
I have tried to identify in Goethe's thought: the hostility to
Idealism, and the dissolution of dualisms - in short, his 'realism':
a notion of freedom that is to be won and manifested by personal
endeavour, not granted by law or constitution; discipline,
harmony, control of the passions, self-reverence, and self-
creation. (The passage, incidentally, makes nonsense of
Lukács's claim that Nietzsche was the first in a line of writers,
to include Spengler and Alfred Rosenberg, who 'made of Goethe
the founder of the dominant irrationalist and reactionary
Weltanschauung'.(24))
    Taken with Nietzsche's many other admiring references to
Goethe, the passage surely confirms that it is 'the Goethean
man', or Goethe himself, who most closely approximates to the
'higher man'. From the outset, I have taken it that Nietzsche's
educational goal is authenticity; and since it is the 'higher man'
who is to be bred through education, then he must be the
authentic man. It remains, then, to relate the notion of authenticity to the type we are now regarding as the approximation to
the 'higher man' - the Goethean type. It seems to me that each
element in the Goethean 'state of balance' either pairs off with,
or is a natural extension of, some feature that has already
emerged in the development of the notion of authenticity.
Goethe's 'self-reverence', for example, pairs off with
Nietzsche's 'egoism'; the register of 'isms' attacked by Goethe
is remarkably similar to Nietzsche's blacklist; knowledge that
has 'no influence in practical life' relates to 'old maidish scholarship', as does the 'bourgeois mentality' to the 'bread-winning
mentality' - and so on.
    More generally, there are close analogies in Goethe's thinking
to those two broad components into which the concern for authen-

ticity devolved. First, there was concern for understanding oneself and one's situation, including the 'philosophical' understanding of Chapter 4. Goethe's hostility towards 'Positivism',
to an 'inner'/'outer' dichotomy, and his view of the world's
contents as 'symbols', contribute to a similar point. For both
Goethe and Nietzsche, situations are circumstances calling for
attitudes, values, and actions to be adopted: and the understanding which provides the ground for this can be supplied,
exclusively or predominantly, neither by empirical fact-finding
nor by introspection.

Less clear, perhaps, is the connection between the second
element in Goethe's 'state of balance' - the development of one's
capacities - and the 'projective' concern to make one's values
and beliefs one's own. But the connections are, in fact, intimate.
'Capacity', even 'ability', are not normally used in neutral
ways. Not everything a person is able to do would be counted
among his capacities or abilities. We do not hear, for example,
of a person's capacity for collecting tea-leaves, nor find his
knack of uttering sentences backwards listed among his abilities.
Reference to capacities typically reflects judgment on the
seriousness and value of the activities. Hence, a person's
identification of his capacities already engages his values and
beliefs. He may cease to regard some skill - doing formal, logical
proofs, say - among these capacities, not because he has lost
the knack, but because he no longer deems it sufficiently
worthwhile to develop. Moreover, since a person will have a
number of capacities, not all of which can be exercised, judgment on the relative values of these must be made. So someone
concerned to develop his capacities is doubly committed to
matters of evaluation. To be sure, he may simply go along with
some customary, official, or common assessment of what his
capacities are, and of which should be developed - but for
Nietzsche and Goethe alike, this betrayal of individuality is
almost as great as the failure to develop capacities at all.
Although 'in the character which Nature has given him in
particular, as a man of force, activity, intellect, and talent,
[he] belongs to the world', it remains that demands made of
him 'be made by each of himself . . . he should convince his
neighbour of what is good and true in him', and not let himself
be tamely convinced.(25) So the evaluative enterprise which the
development of capacities presupposes is one that each person
must take upon himself: the values which are to inform that
development must be truly his own.

The connection between capacities and authenticity works
the other way around, too. This is because, for both writers,
all creative capacities are subsumed under the general one to
create and forge values and conceptions for oneself - the
essentially human capacity. It was shrewdly said of Goethe
that he 'looked upon the world as an artist'.(26) This was
not intended to mean he was a teutonic Aubrey Beardsley,
interested only in the beauty or ugliness of things, but that he

looked on the world as an arena where men are perpetually
exercised in lending order and significance, in interpreting
symbols, in imposing values and conceptions. The arts are
only the 'most valid' testimony to human creativity: for this
resides not primarily in doing what is novel, or in outbursts
of feeling, but in ordering, simplifying, interpreting. 'So long
as he merely expresses his subjective feelings, [a person] is
not to be called [a poet]: but as soon as he knows how to
appropriate the world and express it, then he is a poet.'(27)
Art, especially poetry, is the 'most valid' testimony to
creativity only because the artist is freer than others, the
scientist for example, to break old moulds in which things are
thought, to suggest new connections and sever established ones:
freer for 'ways of worldmaking'. We have already encountered
Nietzsche's related idea of the world, or knowledge, as an
'aesthetic phenomenon'; of how it is the human lot, and glory,
to create order and harmony out of the flux of experience.
Both men are aware, of course, that most people for the most
part merely fall in with - and to a degree must fall in with - the
creations of others, those anonymous others who make up
Heidegger's *Das Man*. But the failure to struggle against total
surrender is the betrayal of the fundamental human capacity,
and hence the abdication of authenticity.

At the beginning of his travels, Wilhelm Meister naively assumes
that a fortunate natural disposition is all that is required for
talent or genius to flourish; but he is soon to realize that,
especially in one's very young days, it is vital to be put in the
way of the right experiences, to have intercourse with good
people, and to be 'so guided that, in the future, one can more
easily and more comfortably bring about what is good'.(28)
Towards the end of the book, indeed, he finds that some of
the more fruitful episodes in his development had not been
chance, but arranged in secret by the members of a pedagogic
society. It is for these reasons that Lukács can describe the
novel as the story of 'the education of man for practical understanding'.(29) For Goethe, as for Nietzsche, the development
of the admirable man is an educational matter. For both of them,
nature is a clumsy mistress, while perfectibility through social
engineering is a mere chimera.
    So what is to be the shape of the 'higher man's' education?
Tradition divides questions about education into three: into
ones about content, method, and organization. What should be
taught? How? And in what institutional or organizational setting?
Traditionally, too, the first question is logically prior, with the
answer to it largely deciding decisions on method and organization. These assumptions have rightly come under criticism.
If, for example, there is a 'hidden curriculum', then manner
and style of teaching, and the authority structure - even the
physical structure - of the school, will teach their own lessons.
We are familiar, too, with how decisions about organization - for

instance, that everyone shall be taught the same - impose
strictures on what can appropriately be taught. And if the
educational aims include 'critical awareness' or the like, these
will dictate to method as much as to content - or, better,
dissolve the distinction.

The traditional distinctions, and ordering of them, are
particularly unhelpful when the central aims surround, crudely
speaking, the development of a certain kind of person, rather
than the imparting of specific knowledge or skills. For whatever the factors may be which foster this development, we
should hardly expect them to divide cleanly into the traditional
distinctions. Nor, in so far as these distinctions do still obtain,
have we any reason in advance to suppose a particular order of
priority. (In one of Goethe's books, the pictures on the school
walls are as important as the lessons taught in the classroom.)

It is not my intention, then, to provide any curricular,
pedagogical, or institutional blueprint. Instead, I shall discuss
what I shall call four *foci*: educational emphases which are
prompted - our terrain is hardly firm enough to say 'entailed' -
by the perspectives that have emerged in this book. I dub these
foci the 'philosophical', 'linguistic', 'aesthetic', and 'genealogical'.
Let me at once state that I do not have in mind a schooling in
which an hour of Descartes is followed by an hour of English
grammar, with the afternoon dedicated to drawing or pottery.
These foci are not to be thought of as *subjects*: they are
attitudes, emphases, tactics perhaps, which are to permeate
what goes on in the school, its teaching and other activities
too. Nor are they to be thought of as clearly distinct from one
another: like the spotlights in a theatre, they will criss and
cross, sometimes merging to illuminate a single area, then part-
ing, and always in soft outlines. Moreover, I mean something
rather special by each of the dubbing terms, so it would be
rash to guess at what I have in mind.

I have little to say about the 'philosophical' focus which was not
contained in the discussion, in Chapter 4, of 'understanding as
philosophy'. The ground of that discussion was that the understanding to be developed through education be of a type that
is firmly geared to the individual's self-conscious adoption of
stances towards the significant situations which he confronts as
a human being. 'Situations', indeed, were characterized as
precisely those circumstances which call for stances, attitudes,
beliefs, and evaluations to be adopted. Together, put
dramatically, they form the 'human condition'. Sexual relations,
death, career, friendship, family - these belong to that
condition. The negative point to talking of the required understanding as 'philosophical' was to contrast it with the kinds of
knowledge provided by the 'disciplines', including professional
philosophy in some of its developments. This is not to deny the
bearing that information culled from disciplines may have; but
one does not have to be 'inside' physics or psychology to appre-

ciate the possible bearing some discovery has on a matter
about which one seeks understanding. The positive point was
that the understanding in question concerns *meanings*. This
was not to be read as saying that philosophical understanding
is to consist in what some have called 'conceptual', 'semantic',
or 'linguistic' analysis. It is the significance of death or parental
ties, not of 'death' or 'parental ties', which is important. This,
of course, is not to deny the importance there is in understanding a term's meaning; though one should beware the assumption
lurking behind much talk of 'linguistic' or 'conceptual' analysis
– namely, that what does not fall under its purview must belong
to the expert, empirical domains of the other 'disciplines'. Is
death always to be regretted? How much of a priority is it to
keep people alive? How important is it that I 'leave something
behind me'? It is reflection upon, and the answers he gives to,
questions like these that constitute a person's philosophical
understanding of death.

There is no clear limit to the kinds of investigation that might
contribute to philosophical understanding. 'Semantic analysis';
stimulation of the imagination by reading the best literature;
vicarious sharing of experiences through reading the great
diarists and chroniclers; knowledge of how things are in other
cultures; self-examination of how one came by one's pre-
reflective beliefs – each of these might be engaged. Much of
what I have in mind under the other three foci will play a part.
Especially important, I suggested in Chapter 4, was a concern
with language, in the sense of the 'stock and web' of clichés
and ready-to-hand descriptions that surround, and partially
define, the topics under consideration. In an intelligible sense,
death is not the same phenomenon in a culture where it is
spoken of in a thoroughly different way – as a welcome transition to a different life, say.

It might be illuminating to apply these remarks to a topic
which is of considerable importance both to teachers, who must
discuss it in school, and to educationists in connection with
various aspects of school policy. Sexual differences are, to
speak dramatically again, part of the human condition. Men and
women, if they are reflective, must define their stance towards
the opposite sex, and so towards their own. Rightly, in recent
years, this has been thought a topic education must concern
itself with. This does not mean that there should necessarily
be special classes on sex education; and, in general, treatment
of the topic has not developed in an encouraging way. In many
circles the main issue is taken to be whether various differences
between the sexes, on which differential treatment and attitudes
are based, are 'natural' or 'social' and 'cultural'. The guiding
assumption, which gives life to the issue, is that the 'natural'
should be left alone, since either it cannot, or can only with
great difficulty and risk, be changed: while differentials based
on the 'merely social' both can, and should, be eliminated. We
find, as a result, passionate efforts devoted to showing that,

for example, the greater scientific and technical bent of boys is – or is not – 'natural', one's attitude towards the relative paucity of female technicians or scientists allegedly depending on the outcome.

This perfervid passion is displayed in the outpouring of innumerable tomes by psychologists, biologists, social anthropologists, and others, each trying to establish empirically whether sex differences of interests, attitudes, and the like, are 'natural' or not. Differential reactions by boys and girls to laboratory tests are copiously documented; data about what men and women do in distant or ancient tribes pile up. It is the expert – the scientist, the researcher – who will tell us how things are, and so guide our policy and attitudes.

Yet there is hardly a pause to consider either the cogency of the distinctions – 'natural' vs. 'social', and related ones – which permeate the discussion; or the truth of the assumptions – for example, the relative malleability of the 'social' – which inform the investigations; or the bearing of both the distinctions and the assumptions on the questions which prompted the debate in the first place. In fact, the 'natural' vs. 'social' distinction is thoroughly opaque, while the assumption that what has a merely 'social' basis is easy, and so fit, to alter, is as a generalization absurd. Bodily hair among females is 'natural', if anything is, yet many get rid of it without trouble, while speaking English is the result of social training without thereby – at least for English people – being either possible or desirable to eliminate. It is unclear, moreover, that *any* of the data furnished by psychology or social anthropology have a strong bearing on questions about promiscuity, choice of career, adultery, and others where the differences between the sexes may be of relevance. If men are 'by nature' more promiscuous or more scientific than women, this is not so in any sense that ought to bear on whether I advise my son to settle down with a wife, or encourage my daughter to follow up her interest in engineering.

Common talk assigns to men in our society a distinctive number of responsibilities, permissions, and prohibitions: they are 'to look after women', 'allowed to swear', 'supposed to remain calm', and so on. And it places men in a web of clichés: men are 'aggressive', 'proud', 'rational', but also 'squeamish', or 'just like babies'. The important question is not whether these assignments and clichés are grounded in 'nature' or 'culture', but, in the first place, whether they are at all true. Do they belong, perhaps, merely to 'talk'? And second, does one *want* them to be true of oneself? Is it important, for a sense of identity or community, to go along with the behaviour and exhibit the attitudes that are supposed to distinguish one's sex? Is it important for the harmony of my home life that I display, even act out, feelings and attitudes markedly distinct from my wife's or sexual partner's? Do I perhaps value some of the things I do, and some of the ways I think, precisely because these contrast with my wife's activities and thoughts? These questions, and they are the ones most immediately bearing on how I shall run my life, are scarcely touched by the investigation of the expert and his 'discipline'. But it is in how one handles and answers such questions that a person's understanding - his philosophical understanding - of the significance of sex differences is manifested.

The preceding remarks have touched upon language, and indeed the 'linguistic focus', to which I now turn, is not to be sharply distinguished from the 'philosophical' one. But there are matters I have in mind under the heading of the 'linguistic focus' which have not yet emerged. Put crudely, the focus will be upon language as a defensive weapon. We can do no better than follow Nietzsche here. He was in no doubt where the central educational task lay:

> as long as [schools] do not accept as a holy duty the most immediate practical training [*Zucht*] in speech and writing, as long as they skirt around the mother-tongue as if it were a necessary evil or a dead body, I do not count those institutions as truly educational.(30)

Instead of the schools promoting 'linguistic self-discipline', Nietzsche saw them either treating language as an object for historical study and grammatical dissection, or as encouraging - too soon, and with too little constraint - the young person's 'self-expression' in the form of 'personal essays'; or, as it might be put today, 'creative writing'. For Nietzsche, there is no exaggerating the importance of linguistic mastery: a person's attitude towards it is the 'touchstone' of his attitude towards culture as a whole.(31)

But why is it so important? A persistent twin complaint of Nietzsche's is against 'big words' and ignorance of language's 'nuances'. 'Christianity, Revolution . . . Equal Rights . . . Justice: all these big words have value only for fighting, as battle-standards: not as realities, but as show-piece words [*Prunkworte*].'(32) And one is always in 'bad company' with people who have 'no sense for nuances': the young in particular despise nuances - a mastery of which, however, 'constitutes the best gain in life'.(33) The complaints are twinned, since it is the hammer-blows of 'big words' that deafen the ear for the perception of nuances. 'Axe-blows' might be better since, as the above passage suggests, the typical role of 'big words' is not to refer or inform, but to win people over and silence those who hesitate. It is not simply that words like 'equality' ring out loud without clear meaning; nor simply that, in consequence, the subtle but important differences between it and words like 'justice' or 'fairness' are levelled. It is that what people mean by them depends on the strategic positions they are trying to gain. I have argued elsewhere, for instance, that the slogan 'equality of opportunity' has been rendered useless for purposes of serious discussion, since the warring parties invest

it with whatever meanings suit their ends.(34) Assessment of
one's beliefs and values can begin only when one refuses to be
stampeded by these 'big words' and slogans; when one is able
to take a defensive and distant look at words and the differences
between them. (Some readers will be reminded of J.L. Austin's
remark that aesthetics will stay in the doldrums unless we forget
about 'beautiful' and 'ugly' and look at 'dainty' and 'dumpy'.)(35)
    Another defence that 'linguistic self-discipline' will provide
is against the so-called 'fallacy of essentialism' – the idea that
all things to which a word applies must have something importantly in common in virtue of which we apply it to them.(36)
We have already quoted Nietzsche's remark (p. 95) that nothing
with a history can be defined: for where there is history, there
is change, so that a word comes to be applied to things having
nothing essentially in common with its original referents. (He
was thinking of the word 'punishment'.) It is his view, indeed,
that in a sense *all* words are metaphors, since they serve to
combine, in their fields of reference, radically dissimilar items.(37)
Like Wittgenstein, he attributes various philosophical errors to
the 'essentialist' fallacy: for example, the idea that, despite
the obvious behavioural differences, some identical, therefore
'inner' mental event must be occurring each time we speak of
someone willing something. But there are perversions of an
everyday sort which the fallacy threatens to nurture. In connection with the word 'revenge' (*Rache*), he points out that words
are 'pockets' into which people are constantly putting this
feature or taking that one out.(38) The point is not that
'revenge' is straightforwardly ambiguous: that would merely
multiply essences. The connections between the spontaneous,
unreflecting revenge of the 'blond beast' and society's 'revenge
on maldoers' or God's vengeance on sinners are sufficiently
strong for the use of the same word to be intelligible – but the
differences are vital. We must not, for example, suppose that
what is permissible, even admirable, in the quick, and quickly
forgotten, acts of vengeance done by the 'blond beast' thereby
condones the deliberate Christian revenge so goringly praised
by Tertullian or St Thomas Aquinas. Once again, the general
point is that serious reflection on one's beliefs and values can
only begin when one ceases to assume that the words or concepts arising in this reflection express essences, that there
need be any interesting uniformity across time or space, in
what is being said, denied, valued, or condemned with their
help.
    Nietzsche twice states that a main aim of 'linguistic self-
discipline' must be to induce 'physical nausea' at the language
of 'journalists' and other public mouthpieces.(39) Today, no
doubt, he would include 'tele-journalists', pundits and other
figures whom technology has provided with a voice. Nausea at
what? First at the way in which words (and pictures) are used
to level events and people: reports and photographs of atrocities
are juxtaposed with ones of pancake-races; and while the latter

are described in hysterically hyperbolic terms - 'superstars',
I hear, are giving way to 'megastars' - the former are treated
with anodyne banalities. Nausea, next, at the crude polarities
that journalese and punditry foist upon us: the mood induced
by talk of 'moderates' vs. 'extremists', of 'the general public'
vs. 'the small minority', is reinforced by the premium placed by
the media upon controversy. Speakers or columnists must be
'controversial', and paired off with equally controversial
colleagues across the table or the newsheet. Serious examination
of a question, and a slow groping towards an answer is deemed
to make dull reading or viewing. Nausea, next, at the journalist's or the public figure's 'We' or 'Us' - 'In this country,
we . . .', 'All of us find it . . .' - against which is pitted an
equally mythical 'They' or 'Them', who precisely because they
stand outside of 'Us' are deviants or cranks whose ideas need
not receive serious consideration. Nausea, finally, against the
air of universal, infallible, packaged knowledge that apparently
omnicompetent reviewers or commentators must assume: for
if qualifications or caveats were ever present, the editor's red
pencil has struck them through long before anything reaches
our eyes or ears. This last point is related to Nietzsche's
important observation (see p. 35) that, due to the specialization
and compartmentalization of knowledge, to the 'disciplines', and
to the 'professionalization' of philosophy, there remains no one
but the journalist or pundit to speak on those matters which do
not fit neatly into a given specialism - unless facile, skin-deep
displays of omniscience have become a new specialism.

  Finally, the 'linguistic focus' will be upon the use of, sensitivity
towards, and shyness of, metaphor. By 'metaphor', I do not
mean primarily individual words or phrases used in non-literal
ways, but those large, organizing segments of discourse in
which things are spoken about in terms literally appropriate to
something else. Such metaphors are among the most powerful
determinants of how we conceive things; in many cases, indeed,
they are not to be abstracted from, without altering, our conceptions. In 1981, the Director of the Institute of Education,
at London University, sensibly organized a series of discussions
on the metaphors which have had great influence in educational
thought - the child as a plant to be reared, say, or as a con-
tainer to be filled. Such influence may have been for good or
bad, but it is surely imperative to be sensitive to these metaphors and to appreciate the limits of their application. As
Nietzsche warned, 'with metaphors and similies [Bilder und
Gleichnissen] one can convince, but not prove . . . one should
be shy of [them] . . . mistrust is the touchstone of the gold
of assurance'.(40) A good example, taken from Chapter 3, are
the organizing metaphors surrounding work and leisure. One
does a full day's work: one is in or out of work; the job may
be bigger than the man; something is a large task. Leisure time,
on the other hand, is to be filled; 'I'm doing nothing these
days', says the out-of-work actor; holiday weekends are breaks

between work. The metaphor is of work as a plenitude, something of size and substance; that of leisure is of an emptiness, a vacuum. Since men, if not nature, abhor vacuums, the metaphors reinforce the idea of life as first and foremost the life of work, while activities outside of it, however much sweat they incur, belong to the frivolous and not to the main business of life. Metaphors like these are particularly insidious, since they are so interwoven into our speech that their flavour of metaphor is lost upon speakers and hearers.(41) A teacher, it seems to me, can have few more important tasks than to alert the young to, and loosen the grip of, the many metaphors we live by.

Many educationists purport to be deeply concerned with language in schooling. Often this seems to mean little more than concern with spelling and with what, often wrongly, is regarded as grammar. In none of the documents I have encountered dealing with language and schooling, such as the Bullock Report, are the factors mentioned over the last few pages treated.

Schiller's letters *On the Aesthetic Education of Man* are not about the teaching of drawing or dance, though art and beauty do come to play central roles in the education of which he is speaking. Schiller's use of 'aesthetic', like mine when I speak of the 'aesthetic focus', is wider and older than the present-day one. (The *OED* and Fowler are surely wrong, however, to suggest that it was only in 1830, due to an earlier 'misapplication' of the term by Baumgarten, that 'aesthetic' came to have, in English, a special connection with art, beauty, and taste.) 'Aesthetic', traditionally, was used in contrast to 'logical' and 'moral' - to refer to the sensual, affective, perceptual aspects of men. Schiller's 'aesthetic education' is one in which these are emphasized, and given their place in the education of 'the whole man'.

According to Schiller, a person can fail to be a full human being either because he is deficient in the two main human drives, or because these are hopelessly out of harmony with one another. These are the *'sinnlich'* or *'Stofftrieb'* - the material drive - and the *'Formtrieb'* - the drive for form. The former is that which, through *'Empfindung'* (sensation, perception, the direction of feelings towards things), puts us, so to speak, in contact with reality: it 'gives reality to the natural tendency which [someone] bears within him'.(42) The *'Formtrieb'*, on the other hand, 'must impart form to material . . . submit the reality outside of us to the law of necessity'.(43) The presence of both drives is required for personhood or self-consciousness. Perception and sensation alone would not allow us to distinguish our own states - and hence ourselves - from objective states; while thought, without the help of perception and sensation, could not rise to a conception of outside reality, nor therefore to that of a self which is contrasted with it. The point is related to the familiar Kantian one about the mutual interdependence of 'concepts' and 'intuitions'. Or, as Schiller puts it: 'Only in so

far as he is autonomous is there reality outside [the person] and
is he a [genuine] perceiver; and there is reality in him, he is a
thinking power, only in so far as he is a perceiver.'(44) Although
both drives are required, they can be more or less atrophied and
one may come to dominate the other. As Schiller develops the
point, a connection emerges with the two main components in
our notion of authenticity. The man dominated by the 'Stofftrieb'
is like one whose circumstances and experiences do not crystallize
into *situations*, as I use that term. Recognition of a situation
requires a clear sense of self; of oneself as the agent which the
situation (by definition) calls to adopt an attitude or stance.
The 'Stofftrieb' threatens to make a man too absorbed in his
feelings and experiences, so that he cannot take stock, stand
back, and properly assess his situation. As Schiller puts it, his
'situation [Zustand] is annulled'.(45) The man dominated by the
'Formtrieb', on the other hand, in his zeal to lend form and
impose his will, is insufficiently receptive to experience. In his
case, too, 'situations are annulled', not because he is too
engrossed in the immediacy of experience and feeling, but
because he is too detached from them for his projects to be
grounded in reality. If the first man can become the 'Polonian'
figure of Chapter 1 - too bogged down in a conception of himself
and his circumstances to remain open to possibilities of reassessment and revaluation - then the second can become the 'Dadaist'
of the same chapter, ever ready to thrust himself into the novel,
but without appreciation of himself, his limits, and his conditions.

How does Schiller think the two drives are to be harmonized?
In what activities, he asks, will someone remain at once receptive,
appreciative of his situation, yet open to novel possibilities, his
urge to create undimmed? The initially surprising answer is -
in *play*. Hence the famous remark: 'a person plays only when he
is a person in the full significance of the word; and he is only
fully a person when he plays'.(46) Schiller's 'play', unsurprisingly, is of an elevated kind. Indeed, since play unites 'life' and
'form', and since beauty is 'living form', then it is in artistic
endeavour that play is most fully engaged. But how is 'play'
supposed to harmonize the two drives? In elevated 'play' -
especially art - the 'player' must be receptive, his feelings and
perceptual powers engaged; and he must have a clear view of
the situation in which he is placed - the resources available to
him, his own limitations, and the tradition of which he is a part;
but, further, he is *to do* something with these feelings, these
resources, this tradition: he is to create something, or to
improvise or to interpret. The musician, say, must not be so
immersed in a tradition or a conception of how things should be
that he can produce nothing significant; but nor in such a
creative white-heat that he cannot appreciate the scope of his
talent, or the limits that resources and tradition impose. As
Thomas Mann, in his great novel on art and freedom, put it:
the composer must overcome that 'cow-warmth' sentimentality
whose product is banality and subject himself to a 'self-imposed

compulsion to order, hence [be] free'.(47)

What would be the role of 'play' in 'true education'? Schiller himself sometimes gives the impression that it is in 'play', as the purest unison of the two drives, that the educational enterprise is properly realized. But this can hardly be right, for it is surely possible, indeed familiar, for a person to display a high degree of integration within, say, an artistic sphere, but for this to be hived-off from the rest of his life. The composer in Thomas Mann's novel is a wreck outside of music, having gone to the length of purposely contracting syphilis for the sake of his art. Whatever its 'intrinsic' value, 'play' might have two further places in education. First, it is often argued that the qualities and attitudes fostered in play will, properly directed, as a matter of psychology, spill over into other compartments of life. Piaget, for instance, thought that the self-submission to rules during play was a useful, perhaps essential, preparation for the moral point of view which, it is likewise alleged, involves self-submission to rules. Karl Groos was so convinced of the 'pay-off' value of play that he intriguingly suggested 'animals do not play because they are young; they are young because they must play'.(48) Evolution, that is, favours slowly maturing creatures, since only they have the time to engage in those forms of play which will later translate into life-saving, life-enhancing serious activities. I do not know how natural or regular such transference from play to other areas is, but the idea sounds no less plausible than many that are written into conventional pedagogic wisdom: the idea that doing mathematics promotes analytic skills in all walks of life for example, or that reading great novels promotes sensibility in actual human relations. If transference is a total phantom, then it is not only the educational value of play which is threatened.

More interesting, perhaps, would be the attempt to extend the notion of 'play' beyond Schiller's already wide sense, and to conceive analogically of a host of activities and areas of a person's life in terms of play. One aspect of this would be to pit one metaphor - that of 'play' - against another - that of 'initiation into disciplines' - when discussing the acquisition of knowledge. Instead of learning being an initiation into a discipline, with its connotations of military induction, it would be initiation into a game or art. Ironically, of course, those who speak of initiation into disciplines themselves employ the metaphor of games. But as we saw in Chapter 4, the metaphor was invoked in order to stress the rule-governed nature of the disciplines, as these writers view them. The 'play' metaphor would certainly retain the element of self-discipline that elevated 'play' involves, but it would direct attention elsewhere too: to the affective involvement of the 'players', the learners; or to the scope for interpretation that the understanding they seek must allow; or to the essentially creative nature of knowledge.(49) It was with these considerations in mind, perhaps, that Hesse made the members of his mythical intellectual community in *The*

Glass Bead Game the players of a game, albeit a game 'played'
with hypotheses, theories, and bodies of knowledge as counters.
The 'aesthetic focus', then, will highlight those features in all
areas - learning, relations with others, and so on - that bear
significant analogy to the features of elevated 'play'; for it is
in such play, perhaps, that one finds a microcosm of authenticity.
Nietzsche must have had this in mind when he said the 'overman' is distinguished in the way he *dances*. (If there is sense to
what I have been saying, the present cut-backs in musical
education in state schools must be a thoroughly retrograde step.)

The notion of genealogy has surfaced at several places in this
book. In Chapter 1 it was distinguished from criticism as
classically conceived, but recognized as a type of enquiry
into one's values and beliefs that is essential to the enterprise
of making these one's own. In Chapter 5, we met with Nietzsche's
genealogy of truth and knowledge; his account of how claims to
truth come, in general, to be accepted, and of how a certain
conception of truth, the 'realist', has come to dominate. In the
following chapter, we saw genealogy in action, in the form of
Nietzsche's critique of morality, of which it is a vital component.
    Genealogy, as an educational focus, is not a *subject*. It is a
readiness to examine beliefs and values in certain ways; a
tactic, as Foucault called it. Because it is not a subject, we
saw that it must not be confused with any branch of a discipline,
in particular with the sociology of knowledge. The point bears
expansion. Genealogy is both more and less than sociology of
knowledge. The genealogical gaze is not confined to those
origins, supports, and functions of beliefs which, in any interesting sense, can be described as social. Personal motives,
tastes, inclinations, and chance events and encounters in life,
may all have played their role in bringing about the adoption or
abandonment of a belief or commitment. It might be, too, that
there are factors which are human universals, and not sociological variants, which are at work in genealogical processes.
Freud's *Eros*, or Nietzsche's 'will to power', are not themselves
social products, even though they would manifest themselves
differently according to varying social conditions. It is less
than the sociology of knowledge, at least when the latter is
identified in terms of some of the doctrines of its main practitioners and founding-fathers. In particular, genealogy does
not start with the assumption that, in general, beliefs and
values must be ideological - instruments forged and wielded by
broadly identifiable social groups for the furtherance of group,
typically economic, interests. An important point of Foucault's
is that 'discourses', as he calls them - whole styles of speaking,
testing for truth, demarcations of sense and nonsense, or of
the weighty and the trivial - can take on a life of their own,
unhinged from whatever group interests, if any, originally set
them in motion. They become 'unowned'. But, however unhinged
or unowned, they can exert a 'hegemony' over the individual's

thinking. Discourses, unlike ideologies on the usual understanding, need not 'refer . . . to something of the order of a
subject . . . [nor] stand in a secondary position relative to
something which functions as [the] infrastructure, [their]
material, economic determinant, etc.'(50). There need be no
answer to the question 'Which group's interests are being
served by such-and-such a set of beliefs?' Nietzsche, we saw,
thought that morality serves some people rather than others;
but neither the former nor the latter forms a group in any
sociological sense. We are dealing, rather, with different types
of person.

The genealogical focus has its value in the power it offers an
individual to gain a better understanding of himself and his
situation, and to make his beliefs and values his own. It does so
in two ways: by liberating and by furnishing a critical base. One
form of liberation, we have already encountered: if I find that
I came to a belief for reasons having nothing to do with its
truth - that I would have come to it, under the circumstances,
irrespective of the evidence for or against it - then I am
immediately released from any allegiance to it. The discovery of
a *pudenda origo* for a belief or value is not, as Nietzsche
stresses, equivalent to its falsification: but it must 'prepare a
critical mood and attitude towards it.'(51) Another form of liberation through genealogical reflection is this: one is freed from
the force of arguments in favour of some policy or attitude by
coming to see that the supposed desirability of the latter is
being written into the very premises which are employed to
support it. It is not simply that writers are prone to accept
premises because these entail nice results; rather, the niceness
of the results gets built into the very truth-conditions, and so
the sense, of the premises. This practice is so widespread that
many writers, apparently without embarrassment, make it quite
explicit that they are engaging in this inversion of the proper
order of argumentation. For example, to hark back to an
earlier discussion, one author writes in her book on sex and
schools:

It is more socially optimistic and *therefore sensible* to assume
that all characteristics of masculinity and femininity are
cultural. . . . This is because biological arguments are usually
invoked to prevent social change, social policies, and
equality.(52)

The 'nurture' hypothesis, then, is more sensible because it has
the consequence the author deems desirable; in which case,
unfortunately, it can no longer be used as a reason for bringing
about those consequences. Another nice example comes from the
section of the *Land* Hesse constitution that deals with education:

The teaching of history must be directed towards the true,
unfalsified presentation of the past. . . . In doing so, the

great benefactors of mankind, the development of the state,
economy, civilization and culture, but not generals, wars,
and battles, are to be placed in the foreground. Conceptions
are not to be tolerated which endanger the basic principles of
the democratic state.(53)

So, democracy is to be defended by teaching 'true, unfalsified'
history, and part of what makes it true and unfalsified,
apparently, is that it does not endanger democracy.

Genealogy can do more than liberate from the grip of beliefs
or arguments: it can modulate into criticism. This can happen
in at least two ways. First, it may be that a person's belief not
only has been sustained by factors which, once recognized,
release him from allegiance to it, but the belief in question
could not otherwise be sustained. If, for example, egalitarianism
is necessarily grounded in envy, if the idea of a non-envious
egalitarian is incoherent, then to the degree that envy is
always to be decried, so is egalitarianism.(54) The other way
is harder to describe, and leads us into that area, remarkably
uncharted by philosophers, where interests, powers, beliefs,
values, and purposes interlock. In Chapter 5, we found
Nietzsche advocating a notion of truth according to which the
truth of theories cannot be assessed except relative to the
purpose to be served by theories in the relevant domain. A
theory of grammaticality, for example, is not to be assessed
independently of the purposes - appraisal of speakers, and the
like - which require such theories in the first place. Now it
surely happens that unsavoury purposes and interests can
intrude. It may become clear, for example, that a certain theory
of grammaticality holds sway because of the way it answers to
the purposes of those with a particular ideological axe to grind
- people, say, who are determined in advance to establish that
no group of speakers may be held to speak worse than any
other. One is tempted to reply: 'But it is not this which makes
the theory false. What makes it false is that it does the job,
which theories in this area are supposed to do, badly.' But this
is to overlook the fact that, typically, the purposes which
theories should serve are rarely crystal-clear or settled in
advance of the actual construction of theories. Sometimes it is
precisely the recognition that the purposes served by a given
theory are unsavoury which enables us to come closer to a
conception of what purposes theories in the area should serve.
A theory of grammaticality should enable us to appraise ways of
speaking - but in what manner, exactly? Well, *not* in the manner
we are forced to by *this* theory or that one over there. The
process is a dynamic one: we do not first have clear criteria -
in terms of purposes - for the truth of theories; criteria to
which questions of genealogy are irrelevant. Rather it is reflection upon the genealogy of theories - the powers, interests, and
functions they serve, for example - which enables these criteria
to crystallize; and it is only then that we can, so to speak,

round upon some of these theories and by the lights of the criteria which have crystallized, reject them.

One more word, finally, on genealogy and liberation. Genealogical reflection assumes its true importance within an approach to truth and knowledge which relativizes these notions to the purposes and aims of enquiry. And, as we saw at the end of Chapter 5, there is a sense in which this approach places the individual in a freer relation to claims to knowledge. For it is in the individual's scope to challenge and reformulate the guiding purposes, and hence the current claims to truth and knowledge. If, as Foucault puts it, the instruments of knowledge are not for putting us into contact with reality, but for *cutting*, then like the engraver's art, like any art, the will to knowledge will contain its own mixture of freedom and discipline.

No one, I hope, will regard the remarks in this chapter as providing anything like an educational blueprint. They are hints, merely, on the nature of the foci into which everything belonging to the educational endeavour - the subjects taught, the topics discussed, the disciplinary rules in force, and so on - should be placed. The foci, it is clear, criss and cross, and intensify one another. Whether the discussion is about work and leisure, sexual differences, the nature of morality or of insanity, it can be placed in each focus. A genealogical perspective on how dogmas are sustained; a sensitivity to the metaphors and clichés which envelop a topic; the attempt to assess its significance for one's own life; a 'playful' readiness to at once submit to the discipline of the discussion but to hold oneself free to reassess and revalue: all of these are to be 'bred' in an education that revolves around the notion of authenticity.

Notes

References to Nietzsche in these notes standardly consist of:
(a) an abbreviation of a work's title (the key is found in the Bibliography on page 157);
(b) a volume and page number of Schlechta's edition of 'Friedrich Nietzsche: Werke';
(c) one or more numbers in parentheses referring to the chapter, part and/or section of the work cited.
So, for example, the following reference: FW II 197 (235) is to a passage occurring in section 235 of 'Die Fröhliche Wissenschaft (The Gay Science)', and to be found on page 197 in volume II of the Schlechta edition.

The exception to this style of reference is in the case of important unpublished notes, sketches, and fragments which Nietzsche wrote in the 1880s, many of which Schlechta has gathered under the heading 'Aus dem Nachlass der Achtzigerjahre', but left unnumbered. The same notes, etc. may be found in 'The Will to Power', edited and translated by Walter Kaufmann, but in a totally different order from Schlechta's. In the case of references to these notes etc., I give both the Schlechta reference and one to the corresponding section in Kaufmann. For example, N III 679. WP 7 refers to the 'Nachlass', page 679 in volume III of the Schlechta edition, and to section number 7 of 'The Will to Power'. (NB. Translations from the 'Nachlass' in the present book are my own, not Kaufmann's.)

PREFACE
1 Martin Havenstein, Nietzsche, als Erzieher, in M. Oehler, (ed.), 'Den Manen Friedrich Nietzsches', Munich, 1921, p. 93.
2 Bernard Williams, Nietzsche's centaur, 'London Review of Books', 3, 10, 1981, p. 17.
3 Michel Foucault, Prison talk, in C. Gordon (ed.), 'Power/Knowledge: Selected Interviews and Other Writings 1972-77', Harvester, 1980, pp. 53-4.
4 Havenstein, op. cit., p. 93.

1 AUTHENTICITY
1 See, for example, Zarathustra's Prologue, Z II 277ff.
2 N III 679. WP 7.
3 N III 557. WP 2.
4 FW II 127 (125); N III 634. WP (Preface 2).
5 N III 558. WP 23.
6 N III 518. WP 33; N III 546. WP 64.
7 N III 419. WP 61.
8 FW II 165 (283).
9 N III 557. WP 23.
10 GM II 900 (3, 28).
11 FW II 157 (252).
12 N III 913. WP 767. The appropriateness of the label for the kind of value expressed here is clearer in the case of the German word 'Eigentlichkeit' which, in the philosophical literature at least, is standardly translated as 'authenticity'. The word comes from the adjective 'eigen', one of whose main meanings is own, but which can also mean 'individual' or 'peculiar to'.
13 E.M. Forster, 'The Longest Journey', Penguin, 1964, p. 164.

14 N III 722. WP 912.
15 Ibid.
16 Herman Hesse, 'Demian', Gesammelte Werke V, Suhrkamp, 1970, p. 8.
17 Two well-known examples are Aldous Huxley, 'The Doors of Perception:
   Heaven and Hell', Chatto & Windus, 1972, and Carlos Castaneda, 'The
   Teachings of Don Juan', Penguin, 1970.
18 FW II 211 (346).
19 Jean-Paul Sartre, 'Being and Nothingness', translated by H. Barnes,
   Methuen, 1957, p. 65.
20 Ibid.
21 Rainer Maria Rilke, 'Ewald Tragy, Werke', III, Insel, 1980, p. 47-8.
22 Sartre, op. cit., p. 70.
23 Sartre, op. cit., p. 38.
24 Rilke, 'Malte Laurids Brigge, Werke', III, p. 111.
25 SE I 288 (1).
26 FW II 159 (270).
27 SE I 289 (1).
28 N III 612. WP 786; N III 915. WP 483.
29 FW II 223 (355).
30 SE I 290 (1).
31 FW II 197 (235).
32 EH II 1144 and 1152-3.
33 FW II 139 (152).
34 GM II 789 (1, 13).
35 Martin Heidegger, 'Sein und Zeit', Niedermeyer, 1979, p. 42. ('Being and
   Time', translated by J. Macquarrie and E. Robinson, Blackwell, 1980. This
   translation conveniently repeats the pagination of the German original.)
36 Heidegger, op. cit., p. 298.
37 Ibid.
38 Lionel Trilling, 'Sincerity and Authenticity', Oxford University Press,
   1972, p. 121.
39 For an interesting emphasis on this aspect of Nietzsche in relation to Nazi
   ideology, see Alfred Baeumler, Nietzsche und der Nationalsozialismus,
   'Studien zur Deutschen Geistesgeschichte', Berlin, 1937.
40 N III 555. WP 15.
41 Trilling, op. cit., p. 119.
42 Z II 525 (4, 13.8).
43 R.S. Peters, Ambiguities in liberal education and the problem of content,
   in 'Education and the Education of Teachers', Routledge & Kegan Paul,
   1977, p. 62.
44 R.F. Dearden, Autonomy and education, in Dearden, Hirst, and Peters
   (eds), 'Education and the Development of Reason', Routledge & Kegan Paul,
   1972, p. 453.
45 Peters, op. cit., p. 63.
46 Ibid.
47 Dearden, op. cit., p. 457f.
48 Peters, op. cit., p. 63.
49 Dearden, op. cit., pp. 456 and 457.
50 See Michael Bonnett, Authenticity and education, 'Journal of the Philosophy
   of Education', 12, 1978.
51 Hesse, 'Klingsors letzter Sommer', Werke V, p. 51.
52 SE I 297 (1).
53 See Chapter 5, pp. 84f; Chapter 6, pp. 97f; and Chapter 8, pp. 143f.
54 N III 480. WP 254.
55 See Jürgen Habermas, 'Erkenntnis und Interesse', Suhrkamp, 1979
   ('Knowledge and Human Interests', translated by J. Shapiro, Beacon Press,
   1971).
56 Foucault, Two lectures, 'Power/Knowledge', op. cit., p. 85.
57 I insert this qualification, since it is in fact far from clear that Peters,
   Dearden, and others are entitled to appropriate the concept of autonomy
   in the way they have. They would argue that the association of autonomy

with rationality is warranted, in the philosophical tradition, by Kant's account of the autonomous will as the rational will. But Kant's account rested upon two distinctive theses to which, as far as I know, these authors are not wed. The two theses are that the autonomous self is a noumenal one to be distinguished from the empirical self of desire, inclination, and the like; and that the laws which an autonomous person legislates for himself are those binding upon all rational beings as such – hence laws of reason. If these theses are rejected, the justification for an account of autonomy in terms of rationality becomes obscure.

For an account of autonomy which escapes this criticism, see J.P. White, 'The Aims of Education Restated', Routledge & Kegan Paul, 1982. esp. Chapter 3.

2   'BREADWINNERS' AND 'OLD MAIDS'

1 III 1029.
2 EH II 1116 (3, 2.3).
3 The attempt was unsuccessful. Indeed, it was the hymn of praise to Wagner in 'The Birth of Tragedy' which helped to ensure its poor reception among critics. 'He is not ungifted', wrote one, 'but is made obstinate through his addiction to Wagner.'
4 Quoted in H. von Treitschke, 'History of Germany in the 19th Century', translated by E. and C. Paul, University of Chicago Press, 1975, p. 34.
5 Quoted in H.J. Frank, 'Geschichte des Deutschunterrichts', Hanser, 1973, pp. 244-5.
6 F. Paulsen, quoted in F. Blättner, 'Das Gymnasium', Quelle & Meyer, 1960, p. 217.
7 See H.J. Frank, op. cit., p. 512.
8 Quoted in Sir Karl Popper, 'The Open Society and its Enemies II', Routledge & Kegan Paul, 1963, pp. 34-5.
9 Treitschke, op. cit., p. 65.
10 Blättner, op. cit., p. 201.
11 Küchly, quoted in Blättner, op. cit., p. 202.
12 NNH I 278 (10).
13 ZB III 231 (4).
14 ZB III 233 (4).
15 Ibid.
16 JGB II 666 (206).
17 N III 528. WP 933.
18 See, for example, R.S. Peters, Ambiguities in liberal education and the problem of content, op. cit., and A. O'Hear, 'Education, Society, and Human Nature', Routledge & Kegan Paul, 1981, esp. Chapter 2.
19 José Ortega y Gasset, 'The Revolt of the Masses', Unwin Books, 1972, Chapter 9.
20 ZB III 191 (1).
21 R.K. Elliott, Education and Human Being, in S.C. Brown (ed.), 'Philosophers Discuss Education', Macmillan, 1975, pp. 65-6.
22 ZB III 191 (1).
23 Ibid.

3   NATURE AND TECHNICISM

1 I borrow the term 'technicism' from Ortega y Gasset, op. cit., who meant roughly what I shall mean by it.
2 NNH I 277 and 279 (10).
3 ZB III 230f (4).
4 SE I 345f (7).
5 SE I 324 (5).
6 Ortega, op. cit. p. 62.
7 N III 532. WP 117.
8 Though see R.S. Peters, The paradoxes in Rousseau's 'Emile', 'Essays on Educators', Allen & Unwin, 1981, on how the boy's education was thoroughly rigged and controlled by his tutor.

9 I am unable, unfortunately, to locate the source of these remarks.
10 ZB III 207, 204 (2), and 258 (5). Attention to remarks like these demonstrate the untenability of one author's claim that teaching, for Nietzsche, must be thoroughly pupil-oriented and extremely anti-dogmatic. H. Gordon, Nietzsche's Zarathustra as Educator, 'Journal of the Philosophy of Education', 14, 2, 1980.
11 SE I 290 (1).
12 I do not want to rule out the possibility that, in *some*, way, intensional attitudes can be accommodated within a naturalistic, e.g. physicalistic, conception of human nature. What is certain, though, is that this accommodation would have to be of such a complex and roundabout kind for it to be totally misleading to announce that a relation like being interested in simply *is* a physical relation. If it were, then my interest in X would also be an interest in Y, when X = Y; but there is clearly a sense in which my interest in Britain's wartime Prime Minister is not an interest in Jenny Churchill's Harrovian son.
13 GM II 854 (3, 9).
14 ZB III 232 (4).
15 Martin Heidegger, Die Frage nach der Technik, 'Vorträge und Aufsätze', Neske, 1978 (The Question Concerning Technology, in 'Martin Heidegger: Basic Writings', edited by D.F. Knell, Routledge & Kegan Paul, 1978).
16 Quoted in Trilling, 'Sincerity and Authenticity', op. cit., pp. 129-30.
17 Ibid., p. 129.
18 Antoine de Saint-Exupéry, 'Flight to Arras', Penguin, 1961, p. 158.
19 GM II 888 (3, 23).
20 Heidegger, Die Frage nach der Technik, op. cit., pp. 31-2.
21 SE I 336 (6).
22 For a wealth of telling examples in this connection, see Dwight Bolinger, 'Language: The Loaded Weapon', Longman, 1980.
23 On the grip that metaphors can get, see G. Lakoff and M. Johnson, 'Metaphors We Live By', University of Chicago Press, 1980.
24 Ernst Jünger, 'Strahlungen', Stuttgart, 1949, p. 101.
25 See R.F. Dearden, Balance and Coherence: some curricular principles in recent reports, 'Cambridge Journal of Education', Easter 1981.
26 Ibid., p. 116.
27 Ibid.
28 Mary Warnock, 'Schools of Thought', Faber, 1977, p. 145.
29 It is misleading to regard 'the will to power' as a universal motive, or even perhaps 'explanatory' factor. Nietzsche is insistent, at any rate, that it is not to be thought of as an inner force which brings about behaviour. The idea, rather, seems to be that it is fruitful to look at all behaviour from a perspective, as he calls it, which focuses on the ways behaviour tends to bring about an increase in the agents' power.
30 See Chapter 7, pp. 114f.
31 Warnock, op. cit.
32 One of the reasons the younger Nietzsche admired Schopenhauer is that the latter had given up University teaching. He fails to mention that Schopenhauer was a man of some means. See especially Chapter 8 of SE.
33 Warnock, op. cit., p. 151.

4 LIFE AND LIBERAL EDUCATION
1 NNH I 240 (5).
2 J.F. Herbart, 'Science of Education', translated by H. and E. Felkin, Sonnenschein, 1897, p. 81.
3 EH II 1113 (3, 2.1).
4 WWK III 333.
5 SE I 288 (1).
6 NNH I 284 (10).
7 Ambiguities in liberal education and the problem of content, op. cit., p. 55.
8 Democratic values and educational aims, 'Essays on Educators', op. cit., p. 34.

9 Ambiguities in liberal education . . . , op. cit. p. 60.
10 Søren Kierkegaard, 'Journals 1834-54', translated by A. Drue, Fontana, 1960, p. 44.
11 NNH I 209 ('Vorwort').
12 ZB III 25 (5).
13 ZB III 255 (5).
14 See Donald Davidson, Mental events, 'Essays on Actions and Events', Oxford University Press, 1980.
15 Warnock, op. cit., p. 123.
16 GM II 798 (1, 17 note).
17 WWK III 343.
18 SE I 293 (2).
19 JGB II 676 (211).
20 SE I 304 (3); N III 554. WP 27.
21 WWK III 343.
22 See Chapter 8, pp. 136f.
23 Peters, Ambiguities in liberal education . . . , op. cit., p. 61. Nor does it justify D. Daiches's welcome - at a recent seminar on research in the Humanities - of 'the recognition by some philosophers that they must master some other discipline or body of facts in dealing with issues such as euthanasia, minority rights, etc.', 'Times Higher Education Supplement', 19.3.82. p. 11. Obviously there are facts relevant to such issues, but I do not know what disciplines one must master in order to appreciate them, or to what 'body' of facts they are supposed to belong.
24 Elliott, Education and Human Being, op. cit., p. 60.
25 The philosopher who has, perhaps, brought out this point best is Hans-Georg Gadamer, a pupil of Heidegger's. See, for example, his collection of essays, 'Philosophical Hermeneutics', translated by D. Linge, University of California Press, 1977.
26 NNH I 241 (5).
27 André Gide, 'The Immoralist', translated by D. Bussy, Penguin, 1960, pp. 50-1.
28 NNH I 242-3 (5).
29 Richard Pring, 'Knowledge and Schooling', Open Books, 1976, pp. 25 and 21. See also P.H. Hirst, 'Knowledge and the Curriculum', Routledge & Kegan Paul, 1974.
30 See, for example, Hilary Putnam, Is Logic empirical?, 'Mathematics, Matter, and Method', Cambridge University Press, 1975.
    Anthony O'Hear has suggested to me a number of examples of what, he urges, are not just local procedures within disciplines: 'Look for counter-examples' in the empirical sciences, and 'Look for an interpretation which makes sense of the text' in the hermeneutical sciences, for instance. I suppose these are not just local procedures, but I cannot agree with O'Hear that they are rules. Some physicists, surely, steam ahead with an attractive-looking theory, purposely ignoring the apparent counterexamples which, sometimes justifiably, they hope will later come out in the wash. In the hermeneutical field - to take an example close to home - there are several writers on Nietzsche who start from the position that any attempt to reconcile his various contradictions is bound to be distorting. See, for example, some of the Gallic contributions to the bizarre volume, 'The New Nietzsche: Contemporary Styles of Interpretation', edited by D.B. Allison, Delta, 1979.
31 Elliott, op. cit., pp. 65-6.
32 NNH I 242 (5).
33 See Chapter 1, pp. 23f, and Chapter 8, pp. 142f.
34 Friedrich Schiller, 'Über die ästhetische Erziehung des Menschen', Reclam, 1979, p. 35. ('On the Aesthetic Education of Man', translated by E.M. Wilkinson and L.A. Willoughby, Oxford University Press, 1968).
35 R.S. Peters, 'Ethics and Education', Allen & Unwin, 1970, pp. 32-3.
36 SE I 350 (7).
37 Ted Honderich sees this as a main source of people's resistance to deter-ministic theories. One Determinism, in Honderich (ed.) 'Essays on Freedom

of Action', Routledge & Kegan Paul, 1973.
38 See, for example, the reference to Zola's 'delight in stinking', G III 437 (9, 1).
39 NNH I 253f (7).
40 George Eliot, 'Middlemarch', Penguin, 1968, pp. 229 and 233.
    Given their affinity on this point, one hopes Nietzsche might have regretted
    his reference to 'little female moralists à la Eliot'. G III 993 (9, 5).
41 JGB II 671 (208).

5 NIETZSCHE'S PHILOSOPHY OF TRUTH
1 WL III 311 (1).
2 N III 431. WP 506; N III 862. WP 522; FW II 221 (354).
3 WL III 411 (1).
4 WL III 313 (1).
5 N III 804. WP 479.
6 N III 673. WP 477.
7 FW II 220 (354).
8 N III 903. WP 481.
9 N III 751. WP 480.
10 N III 895. WP 617.
11 JGB II 584 (20).
12 JGB II 576 (11).
13 N III 863. WP 473.
14 This point is well made by Donald Davidson, The very idea of a conceptual
    scheme, 'Proceedings of the American Philosophical Association', 17, 1973-4.
    See also Richard Rorty, 'Philosophy and the Mirror of Nature', Blackwell,
    1980, esp. Chapter 6.
15 N III 627. WP 485.
16 N III 534. WP 569.
17 JGB II 567. (1).
18 JGB II 569 (4).
19 N III 556. WP 507.
20 N III 443. WP 497.
21 N III 539. WP 516.
22 WL III 311 (1).
23 WL III 314 (1).
24 JGB II 576 (11).
25 N III 486. WP 555.
26 Jürgen Habermas, Zu Nietzsches Erkenntnistheorie, in 'Kultur und Kritik',
    Suhrkamp, 1977, p. 260.
27 These and other arguments in favour of a 'realist' analysis of truth are
    discussed in Hilary Putnam, 'Meaning and the Moral Sciences', Routledge &
    Kegan Paul, 1978, Lectures 2-3.
28 JGB II 578 (14).
29 N III 909. WP 574.
30 Mary Warnock, Nietzsche's conception of truth, in M. Pasley (ed.),
    'Nietzsche: Imagery and Thought', Methuen, 1978.
31 N III 884, WP 530.
32 JGB II 600 (34).
33 G II 960 (3, 5).
34 N III 627. WP 485.
35 N III 501. WP 550.
36 GM II 789 (1, 13).
37 GM II 790-1 (1, 13).
38 N III 883. WP 579.
39 FW II 208 (344).
40 JGB II 676-7 (211); N III 919. WP 534.
41 N III 543. WP 517.
42 FW II 222 (355).
43 See, for example, N 868. WP 594.
44 FW II 212 (347).
45 N III 863. WP 482.

46 N III 726. WP 584.
47 N III 751. WP 480.
48 N III 844. WP 493.
49 SE I 303 (3). Kleist's letter is discussed by Sir Karl Popper, 'The Open Society and its Enemies II', op. cit., pp. 381f.
50 G II 960-1 (3, 6).
51 N III 440. WP 610; N III 862, WP 522.
52 FW II 36 (2).
53 Ludwig Wittgenstein, 'Philosophical Investigations', Blackwell, 1967, p. 124.
54 J. Cameron, review of R. Hayman's 'Nietzsche', New York Review of Books, 9.10.1980, p. 26.
55 JGB II 576 (11).
56 FW II 250 (374).
57 See, for example, H. Putnam, Is Logic empirical?, op. cit.
58 N III 892. WP 592.
59 N III 550. WP 585.
60 N III 479. WP 789.
61 GT I 40 (5).
62 N III 497. WP 616.
63 N III 430. WP 862.
64 JGB II 586 (22). For a recent version of the analogy between knowledge and a perpetually shifting form of art, see H.-G. Gadamer, 'Wahrheit und Methode', Mohr, 1960, and 'Philosophical Hermeneutics', op. cit. His views are discussed in Rorty, op. cit., pp. 357ff.
65 Sir Arthur Eddington, 'The Nature of the Physical World', Cambridge University Press, 1928.
66 W. Labov, The logic of nonstandard English, in N. Keddie (ed.), 'Tinker, Tailor . . . The Myth of Cultural Deprivation', Penguin, 1973. For a more detailed criticism of Labov, see David E. Cooper, Linguistics and Cultural Deprivation, 'Journal of the Philosophy of Education', 1978.
67 For some superb investigations into the interrelations between concepts, ideology, powers, and interests, see the many works of Michel Foucault – for example 'The History of Sexuality', translated by R. Hurley, Penguin, 1981, or 'Discipline and Punish', translated by A. Sheridan, Penguin, 1979.
68 Davidson, Mental events, op. cit.
69 F.T. Marinetti et al., 'The Futurist Manifesto', quoted in A. Littleton, 'Italian Fascisms from Pareto to Gentile', London 1973, p. 211.
70 See Walter Kaufmann's introduction to his translation of this book, 'The Gay Science', Random House, 1974.
71 FW II 273.
72 EH II 1127 (3, 5).

6 GENEALOGY, VALUES, AND THE TEACHING OF MORALITY

1 J.G. Fichte, 'Reden an die deutsche Nation', Sämmtliche Werke VII, Berlin, 1846 ('Addresses to the German Nation', translated by R.F. Jones & G.H. Turnbull, Chicago, 1922); John Dewey, Moral principles in education, 'Selected Educational Writings', edited by F.W. Garforth, Heinemann, 1966, p. 198.
2 Warnock, 'Schools of Thought', op. cit., p. 143.
3 See especially, P. Gordon & J.P. White, 'Philosophers as Educational Reformers', Routledge & Kegan Paul, 1979.
4 For an example of this influence in the philosophy of moral education, see D.J. O'Connor, 'An Introduction to the Philosophy of Education', Routledge & Kegan Paul, 1957.
5 This is a line taken by John Wilson in several writings, for example Moral education and the curriculum, in M. Taylor (ed.), 'Progress and Problems in Moral Education', National Foundation for Educational Research, 1975.
6 For the reactions of two philosophers to these events, see Jürgen Habermas, 'Protestbewegung und Hochschulreform', Suhrkamp, 1969, and John Searle, 'The Campus War', Penguin, 1972.
7 See A. O'Hear, 'Education, Society, and Human Nature', op. cit., Chapter 5.

8 See, for example, G.J. Warnock, 'The Object of Morality', Methuen, 1971.
9 ZB III 193 (1).
10 MAM I 771 (2, 91).
11 N III 592. WP 361.
12 N III 469. WP 980.
13 N III 835. WP 320.
14 GM II 778 (1, 6). In similar vein, Freud writes that the replacement of the power of the individual through that of the community is the decisive cultural step, 'Das Unbehagen in der Kultur', Fischer, 1980, p. 90. ('Civilization and its Discontents', translated by J. Riviere, Hogarth Press, 1963).
15 N III 860. WP 404.
16 N III 907. WP 287.
17 N III 592. WP 361.
18 G II 865 (5, 4).
19 N III 688. WP 305.
20 N III 858. WP 596.
21 Thomas Mann, Nietzsche's philosophy in the light of contemporary events, in R. Solomon (ed.) 'Nietzsche', Anchor, 1973, p. 368.
22 JGB II 658 (201).
23 GM 789f (1, 13).
24 MAM I 504 (1, 96).
25 JGB II 597 (32).
26 GM II 785f (1, 11).
27 G II 980 (6, 3).
28 GM II 820 (2, 13).
29 GM II 832 (2, 21).
30 N III 902. WP 261.
31 N III 905. WP 283.
32 N III 867. WP 266.
33 GM II 813f (2, 10).
34 N III 480. WP 284.
35 N III 534. WP 370.
36 N III 788. WP 293.
37 GM II 826f (2, 17). A point, of course, later developed by Freud, op. cit.
38 FW II 196 (335).
39 N III 593. WP 382.
40 See Raymond Geuss, 'The Idea of a Critical Theory: Habermas and the Frankfurt School', Cambridge University 1981, pp. 43f.
41 N III 806. WP 397.
42 N III 866. WP 266.
43 G II 967 (4, 4).
44 Dewey, Moral principles in education, op. cit., pp. 198 and 201.
45 G II 969 (2, 6).
46 Z II 521 (4, 12).
47 See Gilbert Harman, 'The Nature of Morality', Oxford University Press, 1977.
48 N III 671. WP 332.
49 G II 969 (4, 6).
50 N III 907. WP 269.
51 G II 979 (6, 1).
52 This paragraph was written in response to a point made to me by Ray Elliott, who thinks I make rather a meal of the prescriptivist issue. In Nietzsche's critique of universal prescriptions, Elliott thinks, the whole critical weight is against universality. This, I have argued, is wrong, Nietzsche has an independent interest in denying that his own valuations are prescriptive; to treat them as such would be to assimilate them to kinds of judgment very different from those Nietzsche regards himself as making.
   Heidegger, in 'Sein und Zeit', op. cit., stresses that authenticity is not a moral value - or indeed a value at all. One of his reasons, I think, is the Nietzschean one that no one who really understands the nature of authentic life could fail to want to live it, if he is capable of it - so that exhorting

him to would be otiose or useless. See also, Michael Bonnett, Authenticity and education, op. cit.
53 N III 619. WP 292.
54 JGB II 685 (221).
55 Dewey, op. cit., pp. 203-4.
56 Stefan Zweig, 'Ungeduld des Herzens', Fischer, 1976, p. 16.
57 JGB II 689f (225).
58 N III 788. WP 373. Compare Heidegger: 'Solicitude [Fürsorge] . . . has two extreme possibilities. It can, as it were, take away the Other's care [Sorge] . . . and leap in for him. . . . In such solicitude, the Other can become dependent and dominated. . . . Against this, there is the possibility of a solicitude . . . [which] does not take away care, but first returns it authentically as such . . . it helps the Other become transparent to himself in his care, to become 'free' for it'. ('Sein und Zeit', op. cit., p. 122).
59 N III 788. WP 373.
60 GM II 771 (1, 1).
61 N III 789. WP 373.
62 N III 472. WP 365.
63 George Meredith, 'The Egoist', Oxford University Press, p. 100.
64 JGB II 608 (44).
65 MAM I 620 (1, 283).
66 JGB II 604 (40).

7 THE JUSTIFICATION OF SOCIETY
1 See, for example, H. Gordon, Nietzsche's Zarathustra as educator, op. cit.
2 FW II 214 (348). The final phrase is taken from Goethe.
3 See Walter Kaufmann's useful discussion in his 'Nietzsche: Philosopher, Psychologist, Antichrist', Princeton University Press, 1974, Chapter 10.
4 N III 781. WP 47.
5 N III 668. WP 936.
6 Dewey, 'Democracy and Education', Free Press, 1946, p. 86.
7 Fichte, 'Reden an die deutsche Nation', op. cit., p. 273-4.
8 Schiller, 'Über die ästhetische Erziehung des Menschen', op. cit., p. 27.
9 JGB II 661 (213).
10 M I 1133 (3, 179).
11 SE I 349 (7).
12 MAM I 678 (1, 467).
13 JGB II 661 (213).
14 GS III 285.
15 N III 628-9. WP 866.
16 Albert Camus, 'The Rebel', Penguin, 1962, p. 70.
17 Z II 280 (Prologue, 3).
18 N III 881. WP 1.
19 For an interesting account of the relation between the overman, values, and authenticity, see Heidegger, 'Nietzsche II', Neske 1961, esp. pp. 291ff.
20 N III 629. WP 866.
21 N III 558. WP 763.
22 N III 843. WP 764.
23 SE I 328 (6).
24 J. Habermas and N. Luhman, 'Theorie der Gesellschaft oder Sozialtechnologie', Suhrkamp, 1971. See also R. Geuss, op. cit.
25 N III 661. WP 39.
26 ZB III 228 (3).
27 N III 820. WP 41.
28 Ibid.
29 N III 420. WP 1026; N III 553. WP 27.
30 N III 833. WP 829.
31 SE I 329 (6).
32 See, for example, 'Illusions of Equality', Routledge & Kegan Paul, 1980, and Delusions of modesty, 'Journal of the Philosophy of Education', 1982.
33 Nolte, 'Three Faces of Fascism', translated by L. Vennewitz, Mentor,

1969, pp. 170-1.

8 'THE HIGHER BREEDING OF MAN'

1 EH II 1111 (4, 1.4).
   It should be clear from earlier discussions that by 'breeding', Nietzsche
   is not referring to a programme of eugenics - though he did expect cultural
   advance to come from greater racial mixing. There are no passages where
   the eugenic interpretation is required, and many where it would be impossible,
   as when he writes 'There is need of a doctrine strong enough to have the
   effect of "breeding"' (N III 430. WP 862). The German words 'Zucht' and
   'Züchtung' can be more comfortably used than the English 'breeding' to
   refer to education, and this is what Nietzsche usually means by them. A
   number of factors may explain his fondness for these terms; first the
   doctrine of the inheritance of acquired characteristics, with its consequence
   that education (= breeding) is 'a means of a tremendous storing-up of the
   strength of mankind, so that generations may build upon the work of their
   forefathers' (N III 810. WP 398). Second, he probably wanted to exploit
   the rather tough connotation of 'breeding', for as we have seen, a
   Nietzschean education is a demanding enterprise, under the direction of
   hard task-masters, See Kaufmann's useful discussion of breeding in his
   'Nietzsche', op. cit., pp. 304ff.
2 Z II 518 (4, 11).
3 Z II 351 (2, 4).
4 N III 520. WP 1027. Usually Nietzsche's references to 'higher men' are
   complimentary, but an exception is a section in Part 4 of Z, 'Die Begrüssung'
   ('The Welcome'), where Zarathustra has some harsh things to say to them.
   But the more normal attitude returns two sections later. Incidentally, I
   have followed Kaufmann in translating 'Übermensch' by 'overman' rather than
   'superman'. Apart from being more accurate, it discourages associations
   with Clark Kent and/or blond SS giants.
5 GM II 795 (2, 16).
6 This dance, writes Norman Del Mar, 'revealed the less discriminating side of
   (Strauss's) genius. . . . There are few things more strange than . . . its
   first appearance in "Also Sprach Zarathustra"', Richard Strauss, vol. I,
   London, 1962, p. 142.
7 For the Socrates candidature, see Kaufmann, 'Nietzsche', op. cit., and
   for the Hitler candidature, see Alfred Baeumler, who proclaims 'when we
   cry out to [German] youth "Heil Hitler!", we are at the same time greeting
   Friedrich Nietzsche with this cry' ('Nietzsche und der Nationalsozialismus',
   op. cit., p. 294).
8 N III 532. WP 883.
9 GM II 840 (3, 2); MAM I 800 (2, 170); MAM I 928 (2, 125); N III 462. WP 791.
10 See Erich Heller, 'The Disinherited Mind', Bowes & Bowes, 1975, esp.
   Chapter 3.
11 Heller, op. cit., p. 105. J.P. Stern, in correspondence, has pointed out
   that my attempt, over the next few pages, to fix upon some fundamental
   themes in Goethe is an extremely selective one. My defence is that I am
   less concerned to define 'the' essential Goethe than to draw out those
   aspects of his work and life which clearly impressed Nietzsche, and which
   interestingly relate to the discussions of the present book.
12 Goethe, 'Wilhelm Meisters Lehrjahre', Deutscher Taschenbuch, 1979, p. 579.
13 J.P. Eckermann, 'Gespräche mit Goethe', Vollmer, p. 73.
14 Goethe, 'Wilhelm Meisters Lehrjahre', op. cit., p. 373.
15 G.W.F. Hegel, 'Phänomenologie des Geistes', Suhrkamp, 1977, p. 439.
16 Goethe, 'Die Wahlverwandschaften', Reclam, 1979, p. 164.
17 Goethe, 'Die Leiden des jungen Werthers', Reclam, 1979, p. 100.
18 Goethe, 'Wilhelm Meisters Lehrjahre', op. cit., p. 313.
19 Goethe, 'Wilhelm Meisters Wanderjahre', Reclam 1979, pp. 143-4.
20 Compare R.S. Peters's discussion of the education of the emotions in
   'Ethics and Education', op. cit.
21 Goethe, 'Die Wahlverwandschaften', op. cit., p. 176.
22 Quoted in K. Viëtor, 'Goethe: The Thinker', Harvard University Press,

1950, p. 143.
23 G II 1024f (8, 49).
24 Georg Lukács, 'Goethe and his Age', translated by R. Anchor, Merlin 1968, p. 16.
25 Goethe, quoted in Viëtor op. cit., p. 152.
26 See G.H. Lewes, 'The Life and Works of Goethe', Dent, 1908.
27 Eckermann, op. cit., p. 177.
28 Goethe, 'Wilhelm Meisters Lehrjahre', op. cit., p. 129. Eckermann reports Goethe as saying of a young self-taught painter: 'One can see the young man has talent; but the fact that he has learned by himself is not something to praise him for, but to scold him for. A talent is not born in order to be left to oneself, but to be applied to art and good masters, which will make something out of it' (op. cit. p. 191).
29 Lukács, op. cit., p. 59.
30 ZB III 204 (2).
31 ZB III 199 (2).
32 N III 668. WP 80.
33 EH II 1150 (4, 10); JGB II 596 (31).
34 Cooper, 'Illusions of Equality', op. cit., Chapter 3.
35 Austin, 'How To Do Things With Words', Oxford University Press, 1975.
36 But *is* essentialism a fallacy? In recent years there has been a strong revival of the old idea that many terms, e.g. 'tiger' or 'tin', are Natural Kind terms, referring to all those entities sharing a common essence. (See, for example, Hilary Putnam, The meaning of meaning, in 'Mind, Language, and Reality', Cambridge University Press 1975). But the bearing of this claim on the point being made in the text is remote. First, the terms Nietzsche is most concerned to talk about - revenge, punishment, good, justice, etc. - are not, presumably, Natural Kind terms. Second, the point made by Nietzsche (and Wittgenstein) - that there need not be something in common to things *in virtue* of which we apply the same word to them - is not the one denied by Putnam et al., who insist in fact that essences (microphysical structures, say) are typically remote from criteria for every-day application.
37 WL III 314f (1). See also, J.P. Stern, Nietzsche and the idea of metaphor, in M. Pasley (ed.), 'Nietzsche: Imagery and Thought', op. cit.
38 MAM I 893 (2, 2.23).
39 ZB III 199 & 206 (2).
40 MAM I 933 (2, 2.145).
41 For this reason, there are those who would - wrongly, I believe - deny that we are still dealing with metaphors. See my Metaphor, 'Proceedings of the XIIIth International Congress of Linguists', 1982.
42 Schiller, 'Über die ästhetische Erziehung des Menschens', op. cit., p. 45.
43 Ibid.
44 Schiller, op. cit., p. 54.
45 Ibid.
46 Schiller, op. cit., p. 63.
47 Thomas Mann, 'Doctor Faustus', translated by H.T. Lowe-Porter, Penguin, 1968, p. 188.
48 Quoted in R. Caillois, 'Les Jeux des Hommes', Gallimard, 1958, p. 314.
49 A point made by H-G. Gadamer, op. cit.
50 Foucault, Truth and Power, in Gordon (ed.), 'Power/Knowledge', op. cit., p. 118.
51 N III 480. WP 254.
52 Sara Delamont, 'Sex Roles and the School', Methuen, 1980, p. 7.
53 'Frankfurter Allgemeiner', 23.1.1982.
54 See my Equality and Envy, 'Journal of the Philosophy of Education', 1982.

Nietzsche bibliography

The edition of Nietzsche's writings I have used, and to which all references in the Notes are made, is *Friedrich Nietzsche: Werke*, edited by Karl Schlechta (published by Ullstein in paperback in 1979, and earlier in hardback by Carl Hanser in 1969 (6th impression)). This edition contains all Nietzsche's published writings and a large selection of his unpublished ones. It has, in addition, a very useful index.

The individual works to which reference is made in my book are listed below, with a key to the abbreviations of titles used in the Notes. In parentheses, I mention good and easily available translations, where these exist. When no translation is mentioned, one can nevertheless be found in the sadly unreliable 'The Complete Works of Friedrich Nietzsche', edited by Oscar Levy (Macmillan 1909–11; Russell & Russell, 1964).

A	*Der Antichrist* (*The Antichrist*, translated by W. Kaufmann, in *The Portable Nietzsche*, Viking, 1960).
EH	*Ecce Homo* (translated by W. Kaufman, in *Basic Writings of Nietzsche*, Modern Library, 1968).
FW	*Die Fröhliche Wissenschaft* (*The Gay Science*, translated by W. Kaufmann, Random House, 1974).
G	*Götzen-Dämmerung* (*Twilight of the Idols*, translated by W. Kaufmann, in *The Portable Nietzsche*, op. cit.).
GM	*Zur Genealogie der Moral* (*On the Genealogy of Morals*, translated by W. Kaufmann, in *Basic Writings of Nietzsche*, op. cit.).
GS	*'Der griechische Staat'* (*'The Greek State'*).
GT	*Die Geburt der Tragödie* (*The Birth of Tragedy*, translated by W. Kaufmann, in *Basic Writings of Nietzsche*, op. cit.).
JGB	*Jenseits von Gut und Böse* (*Beyond Good and Evil*, translated by W. Kaufmann, in *Basic Writings of Nietzsche*, op. cit.).
M	*Morgenröte* (*Daybreak*, translated by R. Hollingdale, Cambridge University Press, 1982).
MAM	*Menschliches, Allzumenschliches* (*Human, All-too-human*).
N	*Aus dem Nachlass der Achtzigerjahre* (*from the literary remains of the '80's*). (The same notes, sketches, etc. were published, in a different order, by Nietzsche's sister under the title *Der Wille zur Macht*, and are translated in that order by W. Kaufmann and R. Hollingdale as
(WP)	*The Will to Power*, Vintage 1968.)
NNH	*Vom Nutzen und Nachteil der Historie für das Leben* (*The Use and Abuse of History*, translated by A. Collins, Bobbs-Merrill, 1979)*
SE	*Schopenhauer als Erzieher* (*Schopenhauer as Educator*, translated by J. Hillesheim and M. Simpson, Gateway 1965).*
WL	*'Über Wahrheit und Lüge im aussermoralischen Sinn'* ('On truth and falsehood (lying) in an extra-moral sense').
WWK	*'Wissenschaft und Weisheit im Kampfe'* ('Science and wisdom in conflict').
Z	*Also Sprach Zarathustra* (*Thus Spake Zarathustra*, translated by W. Kaufmann, in *The Portable Nietzsche*, op. cit.).
ZB	*'Über die Zukunft unserer Bildungs-Anstalten'* ('On the future of our educational institutions').

*NNH and SE are the second and third of Nietzsche's four *Unzeitgemässe Betrachtungen* (*Untimely Meditations*).

Index